How to Hire & Retain Your Household Help — A Household HR™ Handbook

By Guy Maddalone, the nation's household help expert

Published by
Guy Maddalone
GTM Household Employment Experts™
7 Halfmoon Executive Park Drive
Clifton Park, NY 12065

How to Hire & Retain Your Household Help: A Household HR™ Handbook
Copyright © 2004 by Guy Maddalone
First Edition

How to Hire & Retain Your Household Help: A Household HR™ Handbook by Guy Maddalone is available through many bookstores and online. To contact GTM Household Employment Experts directly, call (888) 432-7972 or visit www.GTM.com.

Library of Congress Control Number: 2004110940

ISBN 0-9754018-0-7

Printed and Bound by Sheridan Books, Ann Arbor, Michigan

Paperback   10 9 8 7 6 5 4 3 2 1

"I applaud Guy's efforts to educate household employers about labor and tax laws. Making employers aware of all rules, policies and practices plays an important role in ensuring the household employment industry establishes itself as a professional structure whose activity is lawful and just."

—Rep. John E. Sweeney, member of US Congress (NY-20)

"I believe that one of the most important ways to enact societal change is through education. The Domestic Worker Law that I passed in 2003 was aimed in part at educating workers and employers of their rights and responsibilities. The information in Guy's book is crucial to educating people who employ domestic workers and ensuring that they know and understand the relevant laws and regulations."

—Gale A. Brewer, New York City council member (D-Manhattan)

"Guy Maddalone has done it again. After many hours of hard work, he has created an important tool for household employers. Families should review the contents of this book before hiring an employee. They will find a wealth of information to help make the working relationship in their home a success."

—Annie Davis, president, Alliance of Professional Nannies Association, and president, Annie's Nannies, Seattle, WA

"After nearly a decade in the field of private service, I am thrilled to finally find the missing link in the employment process. Guy Maddalone's book elevates the employment relationships of the staffed homes of the world—from the servile nature of centuries past—into a functional likeness of today's corporate culture. Many, many thanks!"

—Natalie Asper Carnes, founder, International Association of Household Professionals, Bloomfield Hills, MI

"I commend Guy in his effort to educate and support our industry by writing and publishing this very valuable handbook. Employers and agencies will appreciate having this resource to turn to whenever questions arise."

—Pat Cascio, president, International Nanny Association, and president, Morningside Nannies, LP, Houston, TX

"As an agency owner for more than 13 years, I have added How to Hire and Retain Your Household Help *to my list of essential guidance books for families. There is so little consistent information available today that provides good, sound advice in this arena. Thank you, Guy, for educating and informing household employers on effective household management!"*

—Julie Biondi, founder, Choice Care Nannies & Baby Nurses, Westfield, NJ

"Often we only see one side of the story—our own. Guy Maddalone pulls from a variety of viewpoints bringing about a well-rounded glimpse of the domestic employment relationship. Often domestic relationships fail because of unreal expectations or a difference in value systems. Guy reveals the experiences from all involved and provides families with invaluable information."

—Leann Brambach, owner, Home Details, Inc., Seattle, WA

"Having been a nanny agency owner for the past 13 years, I understand that for most families obtaining and applying for tax and labor law information can be cumbersome and confusing. With this easy-to-follow instructional handbook, Guy Maddalone streamlines an otherwise complicated process for the domestic employer. I applaud his contribution, and I look forward to continuing to recommend the services of GTM knowing my clients will be in very good hands."

—Daryl Camarillo, president, Stanford Park Nannies, Menlo Park, CA

"For the past ten years, Guy has been a leader in helping families, nannies and placement agencies. The winners are the children! His ethical business practices underlie all that he oversees. We in the industry are proud to have GTM as our right-hand resource."

—Barbara Chandra, co-owner, Boston Nanny Centre, Inc., Boston, MA

"The household employment industry has needed such a book as this for a long time. And I can't think of a better person to have written it. Guy Maddalone is a visionary in the industry and a man of integrity who is very well respected by partners, clients and competitors alike. Guy has greatly contributed to the professionalism and growth of the industry. Thank you, Guy, for bringing these human resource issues to the attention of all and for always being a business partner that we can trust and count on."

—Denise Collins, CEO, In-House Staffing at Aunt Ann's, San Francisco, CA

"Guy Maddalone has an unsurpassed commitment to the in-home employment industry. His many years of experience assisting thousands of families, coupled with his personal experience as the eldest of 13 and father of two, enabled him to have an unparalleled perspective and influence on the professional employment needs of today's American families."

—Betty Davis, president, In Search of Nanny, Inc., Beverly, MA

"There is arguably no person in the industry better equipped to write this book. As an agency owner, I have followed Guy Maddalone's success (and referred clients to his company) for nearly a decade. As an author, he has the rare combined insight of being a household employer himself and owning a business, which services clientele nationally. His commitment to trade-related organizations (and the sound influence he infuses to the many boards he serves on) immeasurably benefits the industry as a whole. In a sense, Guy has dragged this industry—sometimes kicking and screaming—to a new level of professionalism and recognition. This book is a must read."

—Emily Dills, president, The Seattle Nanny Network, Inc., Kirkland, WA

"Working with GTM as a partner has brought so much satisfaction to a number of our client families. We are continually given positive feedback about the high level of service and cutting-edge knowledge of household payroll and taxes. GTM has a marvelous way of answering tough questions and demystifying the complications of taxes and issues of employer vs. employee responsibilities. It is such a relief to refer anxious parents to our prized experts, the kind people at GTM. I hope that they will be around for a long time."

—Marsha Epstein, president, American Nanny Company, Boston, MA

"The legal complexities of human resources can be daunting to a non-professional hiring in-home child or house care. This book by Guy Maddalone should ease the burden considerably, as it ties together in a logical and understandable way of the employment process. It is a much needed resource."
—Alan Friedman, owner, A Choice Nanny, New York, NY

"I have worked with Guy Maddalone for many years and found him to be an expert in providing clear, concise, up-to-date and valuable information to household employers and their staff. His new book will be a valuable resource to increase the knowledge and raise the standards for all household employers and our industry."
—Anne Guerin, president, Staffing Solutions @ Mothers' Aides, Fairfax, VA

"This book is a valuable resource for every household employer. It covers a wide variety of subjects and makes understanding the complexities of household employment seem easy. I am proud to be a part of this effort and highly recommend this book for anyone considering employing any household employee."
—Bob King, Esq., Legally Nanny, Irvine CA

"Guy Maddalone has been an innovator in this profession for many years. His book is the first I have seen that tells potential nanny (and other domestic staff) employers what they need to be told, what they really know but do not want to admit or recognize. Readers would do well to pay careful attention to its advice. That will result in better hires, longer stays and more pleasant relationships for themselves and their children."
—Bob Mark, president, America's Nannies, Paramus, NJ

"With the knowledge and reputation of Guy Maddalone and GTM, this book will be a wonderful aid for families and nannies. It will expertly answer almost any question and addresses the concerns of employers and employees. It will be a valuable tool and a welcome addition to my agency."
—Andrea McDaniel, owner, The Nanny Agency, Inc., Dallas/Fort Worth Metroplex, TX

"Over the last 30 years that I have been doing human resources, I have found that many household employers are confused about hiring practices. Most employers want to do the right thing, but don't know what to do or how to go about it."

"I think it's a must read for not only household employers but also domestic employees. It really takes the confusion out of the process. I particularly like the approach of giving the facts and then complimenting them with real life stories and comments by folks who are actually involved."
—Jack McGaughnea, president, Northeast HR for Hire, Schenectady, NY

"Guy Maddalone is using his business expertise to create a new tool for families and agencies to provide guidance and clarity to the often confusing area of household employment. This new handbook will help agencies to continue to educate parents on issues of hiring, employing and hopefully keeping their household employees. This is a new milestone in 'professionalizing' our industry."
—Judi Merlin, owner, A Friend of the Family, Athens, GA

"I have known Guy Maddalone professionally for more than a decade and have always admired his dedication and integrity to his business. This book is a must read for anyone hiring a household employee. It is clear, concise and full of invaluable information and applicable tools. It is a well-needed book in this industry."
—Janet Nodine, owner, Heaven Sent Nannies, Derry, NH

"Guy Maddalone has been a pioneer in the household human resource industry and has established the nanny industry with professional standards practiced from successful small businesses to Fortune 500 companies. In his book, Guy has defined confusing legal domestic employment tax issues in a simplified manner without sacrificing any details. How to Hire and Retain Your Household Help—A Household HR™ Handbook *is an immensely helpful guide for parents, nannies and nanny placement agencies."*
—Gena James Pitts, owner/director, Childcare Resources, Alpharetta, GA

"In a comprehensive guide, Guy Maddalone has compiled all the information a household employer needs to properly manage anyone working in the home. He covers the range of domestic help from hiring one nanny to employing a full staff. With practical information and accurate facts, How to Hire and Retain Your Household Help—A Household HR™ Handbook *will be a valuable resource and handy tool for all household employers and employees."*
—Wendy Sachs, president, The Philadelphia Nanny Network, Inc., Philadelphia, PA

"Most of our clients are extremely busy and are relieved to hear that there is a payroll tax service to help process legally mandated household employee payroll obligations. When we meet with our clients and give them a GTM brochure, a smile and look of relief returns to their face. GTM provides a 'real value' that eliminates a time-consuming activity a parent doesn't have to worry about when hiring and employing a nanny. GTM has been a consistent and exceptionally helpful resource for our clients."
—Lorna and Courtney Spencer, owners, A Choice Nanny, Columbia, MD

"I'm delighted that Guy Maddalone and GTM have created a much-needed manual on household employment issues. It will bring focus and understanding of these most important issues to both employers and service staff. As Starkey International has long stood for the importance of education in the household, my sincere congratulations to GTM for positioning itself at the forefront of giving sound and pertinent advice on how to comply with labor laws and how to better manage household service employee(s). Mr. Maddalone's handbook should be an essential resource for all successful household employers."
—Mary Louise Starkey, CEO, Starkey International, Denver, CO

"Caring for children is the most important profession there is. A handbook for household employers will be a tremendous help in ensuring adequate compensation for these valuable employees. I applaud Guy Maddalone for seeing and responding to this need."
—Sue Vigil, owner, A Choice Nanny, Florham and Wyckoff, NJ

DEDICATION

To my supportive and loving wife, Diane, who keeps it all together as we strive to achieve an effective work/life balance. And, to household employers, who seek to achieve the same by *hiring and retaining* the best household help possible.

DISCLAIMER

The author hopes that you find the information provided herein helpful. However, the information should not be misinterpreted as a replacement for competent legal or accounting advice. **Accordingly, use of this information is at your own risk.** In particular, while the information herein is believed accurate, the applicable laws and regulations are complex and change from state to state. Therefore, the author cannot be held responsible for any errors or omissions in the text, or misunderstandings on the part of the reader. We strongly recommend that you consult an experienced employment law attorney or accountant to address any questions or issues that you may have. Furthermore, any references to outside sources provided herein do not indicate an endorsement of the services or products provided by those sources.

Table of Contents

Introduction

Effective household employment contributes to the smooth and sound operation of your most important organization—your home. With someone working for you, that job is someone's livelihood. In many ways, household employment should be treated as a business. Neither your household nor your employee's career should be taken lightly; hence, guidance on how to best manage the employment relationship is offered in this handbook.

A household employer could be anyone—from busy, dual-income working parents to large estate owners to foreign diplomats residing in the United States. This handbook will help you professionally manage your household employee—whether he or she be your personal assistant, housekeeper, nanny, gardener, eldercare worker or other staff member— just as you would professionally manage and/or treat employees at your place of business. As you read through this book, you'll realize that effective household management relies on clear communication and treating your household employees as professionals.

I first became involved in household employment soon after my grandfather became ill. My mother, Joyce, a registered nurse, and I began a home health care and hospital staffing agency. While running this agency, I met many people who juggled caring for their own families while attending to the needs of their ailing parents. Truly, these people are sandwiched between generations, with each demanding extensive care, time and energy. In order to help them further, I knew I needed to add childcare to the agency mix. Thus began GTM—first as a nanny placement agency, then extending to payroll and tax services and finally evolving to the household employment experts. Today, GTM Household Employment Experts™ is known throughout the United States as the leader in the industry and has built an impeccable reputation and complete client confidence by consistently providing accurate, timely and extremely valuable services in a way that consistently yeilds, a 99 percent client satisfaction rating.

As a young entrepreneur starting a family, I once again looked to a household employee to care for my son, Michael. As I am one of 13 children, family has been and always will be extremely important to me. So, when it came time to raise my own children, naturally, I wanted the very best for them. Home is where they are secure and comfortable and where they are not forced to adapt to our work schedules (i.e., awoken and sped off to the day-care center in the morning, napping at the direction of a day care worker, and disrupted, bundled up and brought home in the evening). For my wife, Diane, and me, there was just one choice—employing a nanny to work in our home. That was the start of my own family working with household employees. Today, we employ both a nanny and a housekeeper.

As I learned from being an employer, an operator of a third-party staffing company and as an observer of the industry, it's not enough to simply hire an employee. Your relationship with your household help goes far beyond the hiring point. To ensure a safe and happy home, you must ensure a safe and happy workplace. *How to Hire and Retain Your Household Help, A Household HR™ Handbook* is the human resources guide for the household employer: it directs the employer on important issues involved in managing a staffed household. By following and implementing the rules, policies and practices detailed in this guide, a household employer ensures his or her activity is lawful and just, and the employer sets the stage for a satisfying work relationship.

Based on media reports, it is clear that many people choose to ignore labor laws and tax requirements. Disregard for labor and tax laws jeopardizes a household employer's personal finances—and, possibly, his or her professional career. Ten years later, we remember Zoe Baird's short-lived nomination for US attorney general. Baird had in the past knowingly paid two illegal aliens "under the table" for household childcare work. Bringing the issue of legal household management to national attention in the early 1990s, Baird stepped down from consideration in the Clinton Administration cabinet after the national media dubbed her deliberate disregard for US law "nannygate".

Although her name is tagged with nannygate, Baird is not alone. After Baird's consideration for a cabinet post, the George W. Bush Administration faced problems when it was revealed that Linda Chavez, Bush's nominee for labor secretary, had in the past hired an illegal immigrant who lived in Chavez's home and performed work for her. While serving as governor for the state of California, Pete Wilson was accused of failing to pay social security taxes for wages paid to an undocumented foreign maid that he and his then wife employed in the late 1970s. (Although the law did not at that time require the Wilsons to document the maid's eligibility to work in the United States, employment tax laws mandated that taxes be paid on her earnings, as they do today.) Others affected by nannygate and attracting media attention to a household employer's tax responsibilities include: federal judge Kimba Wood; prominent attorney Charles Ruff; Clinton Commerce Secretary Ron Brown; Clinton Surgeon General Joycelyn Elders; and, Supreme Court Justice Stephen Breyer. Many more people are doing the same things. The practice of insufficient human resources management—out of ignorance, scrimping on budgets or disregard for the law—is common to many household employment situations. Good human resources practice, as you'll see in this handbook, can be quite involved. However, you need to be committed to it. GTM Household Employment Experts™ makes it easier with this handbook, its household HR consulting, employee benefits, and payroll and tax services.

Education is vital for all involved in the household employment industry—not only to ensure that they know the legal requirements and their rights but also to highlight issues that may arise within household employment. Although the status of the household employee is changing—and has made great progress during the last decade in gaining public recognition as a genuine and valid profession—much more needs to be done. There remain misperceptions, misunderstandings and downright avoidance to accepting household employment as a legitimate (and long-term) profession.

Today, the household employment industry is working to establish a professional structure around a very informal and often customized situation. And, this situation is very often viewed differently by employers and employees. Often, employers view hiring staff for their home and personal lives as an emotional responsibility, whereas employees know it to be a logical responsibility, as it is their occupation, their profession, and their career.

Americans' attitude toward household employment is changing—and it will continue to change as more and more people consider hiring household help as a way to balance their personal and professional lives.

This handbook will help you be a successful household employer. It offers easy-to-access guidelines, examples, practices, procedures, laws and regulations. I know you'll use it throughout your household employment experience—whether you are reading it through for the first time or referencing specific sections as household employment issues arise. The handbook covers hiring household help, using a referral agency, the work agreement, personnel practices for the home, wages and hours, employee benefits, payroll and tax management, health and safety rules and tips, illegal discrimination in the home, termination, resignation, and saying goodbye to in-home staff.

It's all here for you—with invaluable insight from GTM partners, clients and employees to help you do it right, because this is one of the most important employer-employee relationships you will ever have.

—*Guy Maddalone*

Acknowledgements

THANKS TO:

. . . my wonderful and supporting wife, Diane, and to our three terrific children, Michael, Elise, and Jeffrey who provide me great joy as I watch them give Nanny Ester, Missy and Venus a run for their money.

. . . my mother, Joyce, for our first entrepreneurial experience in home care and to Henry, my father, who taught me work commitment, responsibility and determination.

. . . my management team: Todd Maddalone, Jeannine Dubiac and Rob Ward and all the GTM experts who give it their all in order to make a difference in our clients lives.

. . . my good friends: Steve, Paul, John, Frank, Mike, Jerry, Bruce, Deborah and others for all the years of support and encouragement.

. . . Wayne, Dave, the accountants, attorneys and advisors, who help us stay profitable.

. . . Bob Mark and no-nonsense seminars that inspired GTM's educational arm.

. . . Thea, Greg, Dale, Mike and Amit for helping us with our organization and communication.

. . . PT, Craig, Rusty, Chris, Mike, Steve, Jaime, Paul and Patty for the monthly peer exchange.

. . . Frank, Brian, Dave, Jamie, Dave and Todd for believing in my leadership skills and selecting me as your YEO chapter president.

. . . the Growth Guy, Verne Harnish, and my MIT Birthing of Giants classmates, who challenged me to write this book.

. . . all agency, accountant, financial and legal referral partners who have sent their clients to GTM over the years.

. . . Colleen, Rob, Shelley and Gloria at GE for your belief in GTM's work/family benefit program.

. . . my brothers, Todd, Matthew, Michael and James, who strive to make GTM into a company we are all proud to share with others.

. . . household employers, Jim Chaney, Stephanie Oana, Denise Shade and Zuzka Polishook, who gave their time and shared their stories so others may learn from their experiences.

. . . household employment agency owners and managers Leann Brambach, Pat Cascio, Kim Cino, Denise Collins, Janet Cook, Annie Davies, Sylvia Greenbaum, Cliff Greenhouse, Hilary Lockhart, Judi Merlin, Ilo Milton, Arline Rubel, Mary Starkey, Lin Taylor-Pleiman and Susan Tokayer, who gave their time and shared advice and experience so others could learn from them.

. . . household employees John Robertson and Bruce Reynolds, both of the International Butlers Guild, Trish Stevens, Liz and other household employees, who gave their time and shared advice and experience so others could learn from them.

. . . The GTM marketing team including Marketing Director Rob Ward, Gemma Lavender who worked diligently to keep this project on track as well as Debbie Sgroi, who worked tirelessly interviewing and researching information for this book.

. . . employment attorney Robert E King, Esq., of Legally Nanny, who contributed to the federal and California legal aspects detailed within this book.

. . . employment attorneys Heather Diddell, Esq., & Ellen Bach, Esq., of Whiteman, Osterman & Hannah, who contributed to the federal, immigration and New York legal aspects detailed within this book.

. . . Wendy Sachs, Greg Moran, Wayne Davis, Esq., HR Consultant Jack McGaughnea and my wife, Diane, for reviewing this book and offering honest and straightforward feedback.

. . . the thousands of household employers who allow GTM to serve their needs daily.

. . . anyone I may have unintentionally omitted.

Chapter 1

Hiring Household Help

Household employment is increasing for Americans who continually strive for a manageable balance between life and work. For many, the solution to managing pressures and obligations in personal and professional worlds is hiring staff to work in the home. Whether an employer hires a household manager to maintain an estate, an eldercare provider to tend to a disabled parent or a nanny to care for young children, he or she is working to ensure that their home is happy, secure and comfortable.

Maintaining a committed and content household help keeps employers and their families pleased. To achieve a safe, convenient home life, an employer needs to create a happy workplace. A happy employee equals a happy employer, which ultimately yields a happy family.

DO IT RIGHT. THIS IS THE MOST IMPORTANT HIRING DECISION AN EMPLOYER COULD EVER MAKE

Employing household help is not just any personnel decision. By hiring household help, an individual is entrusting what he or she holds most precious—his or her child in the case of a nanny hire, his or her parent in the case of eldercare hire, and his or her home, family and privacy in the case of any household employee hire.

THE CITIZEN AND NON-CITIZEN EMPLOYEE

Household employers should hire only those people who are legally authorized to work in the United States. These people include US citizens, legal residents, immigrants and authorized aliens. Many household employers in the United States hire non-citizens, largely for financial reasons, and many hire people not legally authorized to work within the country. According to a 2002 article published in the *New Statesman*, during the last decade, it is estimated that 30,000+ domestic workers entered the United States on special visas, mostly sponsored by foreign diplomats and international civil servants stationed in the United States who prefer to engage household help from their homeland. This is just a sliver of what is estimated to be the migrant population working in the United States in domestic positions. According to Cornell University's Lance Compa, senior lecturer and author of an extensive labor report,

Case Study

Jim Chaney
Household Employer
Vice President, Human Resources
Georgia-Pacific Building Products
Atlanta, GA
GTM payroll and tax services client

The trials and tribulations of raising a child were not new to Jim Chaney, father of two older children and, who, just months ago, began a second family with his wife, Carla Chaney, upon the birth of their son, Brandon. The trials and tribulations of human resources (HR) were not new to either Jim or Carla Chaney, as both are HR executives with Georgia-Pacific (GP) in Atlanta, GA. When the Chaneys decided to hire a live-out nanny, they went to an Atlanta agency for help.

"This is not like any other employment," said Jim Chaney, HR vice president for GP's building products division. "It is much more meaningful. I hire people [at GP] with whom I don't spend nearly as much time talking with as I did with our nanny. I had to think, 'Do I really, really want this person in my house alone with my baby?' This is the most important hire you'll ever make. Make sure you do it well."

The Chaneys both work demanding and time-consuming jobs. (Carla Chaney is HR director for GP's consumer products division.) While GP offers a company day-care center that Jim Chaney said is "attractive and wonderful" and had a space available, the Chaneys decided to hire a live-out nanny for Brandon's first year of life. They believed that the nanny solution would save their son from disrupted sleep and schedules, protect him from germs and sickness and ensure that their son had someone to immediately respond to his cries.

The Chaneys required childcare from 7:00 a.m. to 6:30 p.m., flexibility to travel with them and the ability to stay later into the evening when provided with enough notice. "It was hard to find someone to commit to that," Jim Chaney noted. Luckily, the couple found a nanny, who had two school-age children of her own, to fill the job in under five weeks' time.

"You can press right through," Jim Chaney said. "It was three weeks to contract with the agency and go through the applicants. The agency checked references and did background checks. Then, interviewing took about two weeks. I use agencies all the time [for Georgia-Pacific]. That's what I pay them for. You can do it [all] yourself, but you're going to spend a lot of time. It can be overwhelming."

(continued)

Despite a wealth of experience in HR and previous experience hiring household employees for eldercare, Jim Chaney admitted that he was surprised by several household employment issues that arose during the hiring process. Some such issues follow.

1. Costs. "Quite frankly, it's pretty shocking when first finding out the prices of nanny services," he said, adding that there are "hidden and below-surface" costs that may present a challenge. "The margins of whether a person can afford a nanny become somewhat of an issue, but the trade-offs are well worth it."
2. Gross vs. net. "You need to understand when negotiating with nannies that they clearly understand what their pay will be," he emphasized. "If a nanny says she needs to be paid $500, you need to be clear if that $500 is $500 less taxes [net]. So, the amount she takes home and the amount stated on her check may not say $500. Or, if she says $500, that $500 will be the full amount she takes home. That was a big thing . . ."
3. Auto insurance. According to Jim Chaney, he required his nanny to be a licensed driver with a safe driving record. The nanny uses the Chaneys' car when she is on duty, and the Chaneys ensure that she is covered under their auto insurance.
4. Holidays. "Typically, a nanny expects holidays off," Jim said, which he admitted was a surprise. The eldercare workers with whom he worked in the past were ingrained to 24-hour care, holiday or not.

Much of this was worked out through the agency and the nanny prior to hire. Following a format offered by the agency, the Chaneys and their nanny poured over a work agreement for more than an hour to clarify expectations. "To [the nanny's] credit, she asked for the work agreement," Jim Chaney said, "and we went over it together."

"It's wonderful having a nanny," he added. "She's got a lot of freedom, and we've built a lot of trust."

One of the biggest challenges facing the new household employer is creating the job description and becoming a manager of an employee while ensuring that all is within budget. The household employer must simultaneously

- manage hiring, agreements, job requirements and salary negotiations;
- communicate effectively; and
- assess who is the best choice to become the next household employee.

To access a handy tool to negotiate and communicate gross to net salary, visit GTM's online salary calculator at www.gtm.com/resourcecenter.—*Guy*

there are some 800,000 migrant domestic workers. (Compa defines a migrant as someone born in a foreign country and working in the United States.) The Federal government recognizes this as a labor problem, and the United States Congress has legislation pending that seeks to further regulate compliance with labor and tax laws. (see Bush article below)

Employers hiring non-citizens must comply with filings and procedures stipulated under United States immigration law. Compliance is particularly important in light of the United State's homeland security programs. All employers in the United States must complete a Form I-9 for every employee hired (See Appendix 1, Employment Eligibility Verification). Form I-9 attempts to ensure that only people legally eligible to work in the United States are hired. Therefore, employers use Form I-9 to verify the identity and eligibility of employees.

Bush immigration reform could bolster labor law enforcement for household employment industry

On Jan. 7, 2004, President George W. Bush proposed immigration worker reform that could go a long way to help enforce labor laws for the American household employment industry. According to President Bush, America needs an immigration system that serves the American economy and reflects the American dream. Therefore, he said, this reform would make America's immigration laws more rational, consistent and humane, without jeopardizing the livelihoods of American citizens. The proposed reform would match foreign workers with willing American employers when no Americans can be found to fill the job. New foreign workers would be offered legal status as temporary workers, and this temporary worker status would extend to the millions of undocumented workers now employed in the United States. President Bush's plans provide a chance for a large proportion of the estimated 8 million undocumented workers in the United States to move toward legal status. Such legal status would be offered for a term of three years and be renewable. However, eventually the workers would return to their home countries.

Today, employers must first make every reasonable effort to find an American worker, and employers cannot hire undocumented aliens or temporary workers whose legal status has expired. All temporary workers hired must be reported to the government. Consequently, the reform calls for increased enforcement against employers who hire illegal workers.

This federal immigration worker reform will help ensure that employers obey the law by paying payroll and employment taxes and paying at least the minimum wage for the area in which the employer is located. The reform could impose a greater degree of documentation for household workers, which could mean increased risks for household employers who are not paying taxes on immigrant household workers.

The impact of these proposed reforms could be enormous on the household employment industry, increasing the number of workers available and hereby increase the number of employers paying payroll taxes and, thus, augmenting the amount of taxes collected by state and federal governments.

Case Study

Liz
Nanny
Stamford, CT

Liz, a professional nanny for 16 years, came to Connecticut for work by way of Saudi Arabia, Germany, England and Scotland.

Born and raised in Ayr, Scotland, Liz said she heeded her mother's advice to be a nanny because of her love of children and because it is a good career choice in the UK. First she worked for a single father in Scotland, and then moved on to work for military families in Germany and England. Next she served as nanny for the Saudi royal family, and finally she journeyed to the United States—first to New Orleans and then settling in Stamford, CT.

"To be a nanny, you have to be very adaptable," said Liz, who did not want her full name disclosed. "You have to be flexible to family dynamics, the way the family operates. You bring a lot of yourself to the job—your knowledge and experience."

According to Liz, she prefers to work as part of a team with the parents. "You're ultimately responsible for that child and what takes place on a daily basis," she said. "Nannies and families can outgrow each other and, over time, families can take nannies for granted—especially in the United States, where nannies need to be recognized as professionals. In the UK, being a nanny is a career choice."

The disparity between how America and the United Kingdom view household staff propelled Liz to become a political activist. With her knowledge and experience, Liz is working with her congressional office and the US Department of Labor (DOL) to gain federal acknowledgment of nannies and other household workers as skilled professionals. To win recognition of the problem and support for a resolution, she has spent much of her own time and money, often burning the midnight oil, to: travel to Washington, DC, for meetings; make important telephone calls every day; and, to send faxes to more than 100 political offices. She said that the DOL has opened the door to defining nannies and household workers as skilled professionals.

One of the problems in the United States, said Liz, is that many people seek household employment while still deciding which profession they really want to pursue. This results in the attitude that being a nanny is not a true profession but a stepping stone to something else.

(*continued*)

"We take our jobs very, very seriously," said Liz. "That child is a very high priority. Our lives intervene quite a lot . . . It's a role a lot more intimate than other employment relationships."

According to Liz, a nanny needs the respect and trust of the family to do the job. She recommends that families pay fairly and above board so both the family and nanny are protected, and that they offer benefits. "A happy nanny is a good nanny," said Liz, "so treat her well."

It is important for household employers to determine how employees view their positions. Perceptions and actuality can often be very different. A realization by the employer about how employees feel within the household organization and how employees feel about their jobs could cause an employer to adopt different management and employment practices.—*Guy*

EMPLOYEE VS. INDEPENDENT CONTRACTOR

Household employers need to recognize the difference between an employee and an independent contractor, as the employer's tax requirements are contingent on whether the professional is working for the employer or working for himself or herself.

Under the US Fair Labor Standards Act (FLSA), household employers need to determine whether they have control or direction over the worker. In deciding, employers must consider the following:

- Who has the right to control the work being performed? The more control an employer has, the more apt the worker is to be considered an employee.
- Does the worker face an economic risk in doing the job? If so, he or she would more likely be identified as an independent contractor.
- Whose equipment and facilities is the worker using to perform the job? If the worker attends to job requirements on-site at the employer's home or facility and uses the employer's equipment and tools to do so, then she or he is probably deemed an employee.
- Are specific, specialized skills required for the worker to perform the job? The more specialized, the more probable it is that the worker is an independent contractor.

- Are the worker's contributions integral to the business? Will the business suffer if the worker was not contributing to its operations and success? If so, employee status is likely.
- Is the working relationship permanent? A permanent working relationship is likely an employee-employer relationship.

(For detailed information on FLSA, go to www.dol.gov.)

Employers hiring independent contractors are not required to withhold income tax or make employer contributions to the worker's Social Security fund. If an employer pays an independent contractor $600 or more per year (as of 2004), then he or she must report it to the IRS using Form 1099-MISC. Upon hiring the contractor, an employer should request the contractor complete a Form W-9, which provides his or her Social Security Number or Employer Identification Number.

The vast majority of household workers are employees, not independent contractors. However, some temporary babysitters who work for many friends and neighbors on an irregular, sporadic schedule are considered independent contractors. For assistance in determining status, the U.S. Internal Revenue Service (IRS) offers Form SS-8 (Determination of Worker Status for Purposes of Federal Employment Taxes and Income Tax Withholding), which can be downloaded from www.gtm.com/resourcecenter or www.irs.gov, see Appendix 2, Form SS-8.

The IRS established 20 factors to use when determining the status of an em-

---

Ask Guy

Q. What is the difference between an au pair and a nanny?

A. An au pair is a foreign national living in the United States as part of the host family and receives a small stipend in exchange for babysitting and help with housework. Legally authorized to live and work (only as an au pair with the host family) in the United States for up to one year in order to experience American life, an au pair may or may not have previous childcare experience. An au pair is usually provided with a weekly stipend that is calculated as the federal minimum wage less an allowance for room and board. Details are included in the 1997 Minimum Wage Law.

In contrast, a nanny works in the household, where she or he may live-in or live-out, to undertake all tasks related to the care of children. Duties are generally restricted to childcare and the domestic tasks related to childcare, such as preparing a child's meals and doing a child's laundry. Although a nanny may or may not have had formal training, she or he often has a good deal of actual experience and oftentimes has been educated in child development. A nanny's workweek usually ranges from 40 to 60 hours, and a nanny typically works unsupervised.

ployee or independent contractor. Much of the IRS factors follow the FLSA considerations, and both can be used to determine a worker's status. Based on the IRS, an employee relationship exists when a worker:

1. must comply with the employer's instructions about when, where and how to do the job;
2. receives training from or at the direction of the employer;
3. lacks a significant investment in facilities used to perform services;
4. receives payments for business and/or traveling expenses;
5. does not offer services to the general public;
6. receives payment of regular amounts at set intervals;
7. cannot make a profit or suffer a loss from services;
8. can be terminated by the employer;
9. can quit work at any time without incurring liability;
10. has a continuing working relationship with the employer;
11. provides services that are integrated into the business;
12. must provide services personally;
13. hires, supervises and pays assistants on an employer's behalf or pays assistants for the worker;
14. must work in a sequence set by the employer;
15. must submit regular reports to the employer;
16. relies on the employer to furnish tools and materials;
17. works for only one employer at a time;
18. follows set work hours;
19. works full time for the employer; and,
20. does work on the employer's premises or on a route or at a location designated by the employer.

(For more information, go to www.irs.gov.)

THE HIRING PROCESS

Developing the job description

First and foremost, a thorough, comprehensive and well-developed job description will help any employer immensely in the hiring process. Really think about what the job will entail; cover all aspects of household duties, tasks, responsibilities, work hours and requirements—and put it into words for everyone to understand. The best job description will clearly set out what the position needs to accomplish, what tasks and duties are needed and what skills, abilities and talents are best used to adequately complete the job. This job description not only helps start the job search, it also helps tremendously in developing the work agreement with the hired employee. (See Appendix 3, Work Agreement Sample.)

Advertising a job position

With a comprehensive job description prepared (see previous section), a job advertisement can be written and placed in various media or provided to an agency. Be as specific as possible in the job ad. List requirements such as previous experience, education, a current/valid driver's license, fluency in English (or other languages) and work schedule.

Interviewing

It is good practice to open the interview by reviewing the job requirements (provide a written copy to the applicant) and confirming at the start of the discussion that the applicant can meet them. Prepare a list of questions (see Appendix 4, Interview Questions.) before the meeting, such as what prior experience do you have, what kind of household have you worked in, when are you available to start work, etc. The prepared list helps to keep the interview on track and help ensure that all questions are asked and all topics are discussed. This is also helpful when multiple candidates are interviewed, allowing the employer to make comparisons and considerations by examining different answers to the same questions, and aiding in the employer's decision making.

Employers interview to learn about the candidate, so allow the candidate to do the majority of the talking. Employers need not dominate the discussion. They can, however, direct it by asking open-ended questions, requiring the candidate to do more than nod his or her head yes or no. This will generate more knowledge about the candidate and force the interviewee to respond more fully. Open-ended questions most likely begin with the following words: how, why, when, who, what and where. For instance, when interviewing a candidate for a gardener position, ask, "What is it about gardening that you like?" instead of "Do you like gardening?" The same phrasing can be used when interviewing another candidate: ask a nanny candi-

"The key to finding the right nanny for a family is honesty: honesty in job description, honesty in duties and responsibilities, hours, expectations, living arrangements (if a live-in job), etc. Parents that sugar coat the difficulties of the job are simply going to find themselves hiring the wrong nanny for the job. The net result is that the family will end up in a revolving door situation. If more families would recognize this simple fact, there would be a lot less problems making proper matches."

Bob Mark
President
America's Nannies
Paramus, NJ

> "We wanted the kids to be on their own schedule, not on our (work) schedule."
>
> Denise Shade
> Household employer (nanny)
> Mother of two
> Key Bank Senior Vice President, Foreign Exchange

date, "Why do you want to work with children?" not "Do you like children?"

Another useful interviewing technique is to begin with softer questions, allowing the interviewer to gain a rapport with the candidate. Elicit conversation to keep him or her talking openly once more difficult or uncomfortable questions or topics are broached.

Many interviewers rate a candidate on his or her job ability, experience, job knowledge, presentation, communication skills, interaction with others and attitude, as well as how he or she will fit in with the already established household. All of this should be considered before offering the candidate a position.

It is easy to be swept up in an interviewee's excitement or focus on a common interest and neglect an important consideration. With just a little preparation before the interview, and review of an application for employment (see Appendix 5, Application for Employment) an employer helps ensure that he or she gathers all the necessary information from the individual candidates.

Interview questions: Legal vs. illegal

US law—in particular, the FLSA (see p. 57 for information on FLSA)—protects against employment discrimination by prohibiting employers from asking the applicant certain questions. On the next page Table 1.1 lists some examples of questions that are legal and illegal to ask an applicant.

A household employer should be prepared to answer questions, too. This exchange enables the candidate to have a clear understanding of the position and workplace and sets the groundwork for the work agreement to be developed.

> "A good household employee has dignity, nobility, great discretion and not an ounce of judgment. Judgment is often the death curse for a domestic employment relationship."
>
> Leann Brambach
> Owner/operator
> Home Details, Inc.
> Seattle, WA
> GTM partner agency

Investigating Backgrounds and checking references

As with any job application, checking references and background is one of the best ways to learn about a candidate. By speaking with references, employers can learn crucial information about the candidate's abilities, personality, strengths and weaknesses.

Reference checking is particularly important in household employment, said Pat Cascio, owner and president of Houston-based Morningside Nannies, LP. "Nannies are people with

Table 1.1: Legal vs. illegal applicant questions

Legal	*Illegal*
Your (applicant's) full name?	Your (applicant's) maiden name?
Have you ever been convicted of a crime?	Have you ever been arrested?
Is there a felony charge pending against you?	Have you ever been arrested?
Are you 18 years or older?	What is your age?
How long have you been a resident of this state?	What is your date of birth? Where were you born?
Are you a US citizen?	In what country are you a citizen?
Name and address of person to be notified in case of emergency?	Name and address of nearest relative in case of emergency?

Source: U.S. Department of Labor

special talents and personalities that you can't really test for, so this is where references come into play," she said.

A good practice is for an employer to obtain a signed release from the candidate to check employment and personal references from the applicant (see Appendix 5, Application for Employment). Provide a copy of the reference release to the candidate. (The original should be filed with the applicant's completed job application and should remain in the employee personnel file if he or she is hired.) Employers need to be cautious not to violate an applicant's right to privacy when performing background checks. Many employers check financial backgrounds to help judge a candidate's responsibility, maturity and honesty. If an employer uses credit reporting as part of the background investigation, then he or she must provide an applicant with a copy and summary of his or her credit report if the applicant is rejected for employment, per the US Fair Credit Report Act.

Leann Brambach, owner and operator of Home Details, Inc., (HDI) a Seattle firm that places various types of household employees (nannies, household managers, doulas, chefs, etc.), said that, although her firm checks references, clients are strongly encouraged to perform their own reference checks. "Sometimes, a mom talking to another mom will provide more information," said Brambach.

Cascio noted that the Zoe Baird nannygate incident instigated standard background checks on prospective household employees. "In the 1980s, background checks were rarely done," said Cascio. Since then, she noted, the household employment world has changed significantly. She added that she only interviews potential nannies who have legally lived in the United States for at least three years. Why? "It's just too hard to check credentials in some foreign countries," Cascio said, adding that available foreign information is often suspect because many records are not updated.

Spending approximately an average of two hours with each prospect prior to accepting her or him as a nanny candidate, Cascio's agency cautiously checks backgrounds and US-only references, questions the nanny on why she or he wants to be in the profession and studies a nanny's social interaction. Cascio also recommends clients do the same.

"Now, you can't be too careful," she said, noting that today parents' fear extends beyond the US Immigration Service to include kidnapping and child abuse. "You have to become a detective yourself."

Background checks can unveil startling information important to any employer

In late 2003, the media reported a tragic story: a California nanny was arrested for vehicular manslaughter in a hit-and-run accident that killed two children. The woman, who worked as a nanny, drove onto a sidewalk and killed a ten-year-old boy and his seven-year-old sister. Upon investigation, the alleged killer had neither a current, valid driver's license or insurance. Plus, Department of Motor Vehicle records showed the woman's driver's license was suspended twice for an excessive blood-alcohol level and suspended numerous times for negligent operation and insurance problems. Additionally, the woman had been arrested in the past for public drunkenness.

The woman was hired by the family as a nanny from an ad on the Internet, and the family failed to do any background checks. A check of her driving record would have immediately dismissed her from consideration as a nanny or for any other household position.

When speaking with references, some good questions employers need to ask include:

- Would you hire her or him again and why/why not?
- What do you believe are her or his strengths and weaknesses?
- Why did she or he leave your employment?
- What were the dates of employment?
- Was the employee punctual?
- Were all aspects of the job completed?

Suggested background checks include the following:

- driving record (Department of Motor Vehicles)
- Social Security
- credit history
- criminal conviction (county, state and federal)
- drug testing
- personality testing
- sex offender/child abuse registry
- professional licensing
- higher education verification
- trust line (for California)
- fingerprinting
- character references
- employment references

At-will employment

All household employees are employed at-will. This employment is at the discretion of the employer and the employee. Employment may terminate with or without notice or cause. Employees are also free to end employment at any time, for any reason, with or without notice.

Making an offer

An offer should always be made verbally and in writing. When offering employment to an applicant, take care to avoid any appearance of a promise of long-term employment. Send a job offer letter that states the position, whether it is full-time or parttime, the start date, the schedule, the starting salary and any available benefits. Remember to state if he or she is an at-will employee. (See Appendix 6 for an example of an offer letter for household employment.) Ask that the letter be signed, dated and returned to the employer for the offer to be accepted. It is OK for the employer to request that the letter be signed and completed by a certain date. That way, the employer may contact other candidates until the job is filled.

Stephanie Oana, a lawyer in Oakland, CA, and GTM payroll and tax service client, employs a nanny to care for her two young children. According to Oana, she writes extensive offer letters that include all of the terms of employment. The offer letters, she noted, serve as the work agreement. "The candidates really prefer it, because with it they know what the employer wants," she stated.

Oana said she prefers using the offer letter because in the business world a countersigned offer letter often acts as the work agreement. Oana includes all pertinent and relevant information in the offer letter, including benefits, vacation, insurance, use of car, use of telephone, hours, when overtime applies, etc.

Rejecting a candidate

While not mandated by law, it is common human resource (HR) practice to inform rejected candidates that another person has been hired. Many rejection letters (See Appendix 7, Rejection letter to candidate) simply state that another candidate deemed more appropriate for the job has been hired. The letter should be filed with the application and other information regarding that particular candidate.

Rejecting candidates is often an awkward and unpleasant task. The benefit of working with an agency is that the agency handles candidate rejection, not the household employer. (See Chapter 2: Using an Agency to Hire Household Help.)

HIRING LAWS

Employers must be aware of several federal, state and local laws when hiring an employee. Key federal laws that all employers must follow are discussed after the case study.

Ask Guy

Q. How do I hire or sponsor someone who isn't legally authorized to work in the United States?

A. The US Department of Labor Employment & Training Administration (DOLETA) website (www.dol.gov) provides information on hiring foreign workers, as well as access to the necessary forms. According to DOLETA, hiring foreign workers for employment in the United States normally requires approval from several governmental agencies. A labor certification filed with the Department of Labor via Form ETA 750 (labor certification request) is often the first step. DOL works with local State Workforce Agencies (SWA) to process Form ETA 750. Then, an employer must petition the Bureau of Citizenship and Immigration Services (BCIS) for a visa by submitting Form I-140 (Immigrant Petition for Alien Worker). With a visa number issued by the State Department, the foreign worker gains US entry. Also, an applicant must prove that she or he is admissible to the United States under the INA (Immigration and Nationality Act).

According to DOLETA, qualifying criteria for hiring a foreign worker include the following:

- The foreign worker must be hired as a full-time employee.

- The employer must have a bona fide job opening.

- Job requirements cannot be tailored to the foreign worker's qualifications but must follow what is customarily required for the job within the United States.

- The employer must pay at least the prevailing wage for the job in the location of the anticipated job.

Case Study

Stephanie Oana
Household employer
Lawyer
Oakland, CA
GTM Payroll and Tax Service Client

After Stephanie Oana watched friends maneuver through their own nanny searches, she and her husband, Joe Osha, elected to use an agency. She said doing so saved her time and helped ensure she was hiring for the role she wanted. With both parents busily juggling demanding schedules, frequent business travel and unpredictable work hours, they have over several years hired three nannies: one, a live-out, in New York City and two live-in nannies in the San Francisco Bay area.

Oana, a lawyer, said she worked with a number of agencies simultaneously each time she searched for a nanny. "You have to be very clear with the agency about what you want," she said. "Agencies are very helpful with identifying and screening applicants, but the matchmaking is up to the employer and the candidate."

"Families need to think clearly and be upfront and fair to the people interviewing," said Oana, "and give a realistic view of the situation." Oana addressed her unpredictable work schedule during the interview process to ensure the nanny would be flexible. "It is a lot easier to balance a schedule with weird hours with a live-in nanny," Oana added. "It can be very hard to balance certain responsibilities if a nanny has her own children or obligations she needs to get home to."

According to Oana, as the job evolves, communication is very important. "I talk every day with my nanny about the kids," she said. "At least every couple of months, we speak about the job and issues."

Oana cited an incident in which a nanny wanted a raise. Because open communication was fostered, Oana and the nanny were able to talk about the circumstances and strike a balance. "It was a very beneficial conversation," noted Oana.

The Oanas sought in-home childcare because they believe very young children need a lot of individual attention. "My kids have gotten the kind of attention they would receive from a stay-at-home parent," Oana stated. "I was not interested in being a stay-at-home parent, but I could hire a nanny to provide high-quality, in-home care."

> Detailing the full working arrangement in a household employee's job offer letter proves to be a good way to make sure the candidate understands the job requirements prior to accepting the position. Employers who do this are crossing their T's and dotting their I's prior to employment commencing, and, as a result, helping to prevent future communication problems from arising.—*Guy*

ADA

When hiring employees, employers with 15 or more employees must comply with the American with Disabilities Act (ADA) and Title VII, which prohibits discrimination. (See p00 for ADA information.)

EEOC/AA

Federal and state Equal Employment Opportunity Commission (EEOC) regulations protect people from discrimination regardless of race, color, gender, age, national origin, religion, disability, sexual orientation, marital status, citizenship status or veteran status. Affirmative Action (AA) is how an organization or an employer addresses protected classes, such as minorities, women, people with disabilities and veterans, from problem areas, which may include under-representation in the workforce or some action(s) that may adversely affect that group (or employee). Employers need to be sure that their commitment to EEOC/AA is included in hiring, training, compensation, benefits, retention and promotions.

Ask Guy

Q. How can I legally ask an employee candidate if she or he smokes?

A. An employer can ask a candidate whether he or she smokes while working on the job. It is important to keep it in context of the job to be performed.

INA

The Immigration and Nationality Act (INA) requires employers to verify the employment eligibility of staff hired. To verify employment eligibility, US employers must complete and retain a Form I-9 (Employment Eligibility Verification) for all employees, including US citizens and non-citizens. With Form I-9, the employer verifies the employee's employment eligibility within the United States, identifies the documents presented by the employee and records the information. Once the employer has given the employee this form, the employee must present it and the necessary documentation within three business days after the employment start date. (An employer may legally terminate employment if the employee does not produce documentation within three business days—as long as this practice is uniformly applied to all employees—or if the employee does not produce a receipt of the documents within 90 days.) Form I-9 lists the documentation that can be used to establish the employee's identity and work eligibility (i.e., US passport, driver's license with a photograph, US ID card, US Social Security Number card, unexpired employment authorization card, etc.).

Employers must keep the completed Form I-9 on file separate from the employee personnel file for three years after the employee's date of hire or for one year after the employee is terminated or employment is ended (whichever is later). While the US Bureau of Immigration and Customs Enforcement does not require Form I-9 to be filed, the employer must make it available for inspection by authorized government officials.

The US Justice Department offers a downloadable *Handbook For Employers* on completing Form I-9 (publication M-274). In addition, Form I-9 may be downloaded. Both are available from www.gtm.com/resourcecenter or www.uscis.gov.

Employee Polygraph Protection Act

The Employee Polygraph Protection Act bars private employers from using any type of lie detector test either for pre-employment screening or testing of current employees.

WHERE YOU LIVE DETERMINES THE LAW

Every household employer is subject to federal law, state law and local laws. Jurisdiction is generally based on the physical location of the household. Examples from New York, Massachusetts and California follow.

NYC Local Law No. 33: A first in the nation

One of the first of its kind in the nation, the City of New York Local Law No. 33 for the Year 2003 mandates that every licensed employment agency under the jurisdiction of the commissioner and engaged in the job placement of household employees shall provide to each applicant for household employment, and to his or her prospective employer, a written statement indicating the rights afforded to household and domestic employees under the law, as well as employer obligations under the law. "The law" is that of New York City, New York State *and* the United States of America. The statement must include (at least) a general description of mandated employee rights and employer obligations regarding minimum wage, overtime and hours of work, record keeping, workers' compensation, Social Security payments and unemployment and disability insurance coverages.

The New York City Council enacted Local Law No. 33 to protect the rights of the city's hundreds of thousands of domestic workers by mandating licensed employment agencies provide to each prospective household employee a written statement, in a form approved by the commissioner, that fully and accurately describes the nature and terms of employment, including the name and address of the person to whom the applicant is to apply for such employment, the name and address of the person authorizing the hiring for such position, wages, hours of work, the kind of services to be performed and agency fee. Every employment agency must keep on file in its principal place of business for a period of three years a duplicate copy of the written statement of job conditions.

GTM Household Employment Experts™ testified and provided the council with information on tax laws to be considered in household employment, as well as what is considered reasonable within the industry. Several agencies were involved during the City Council's decision to enact this law, including My Child's Best Friend, A Choice Nanny, Pavillion Agency, Robin Kellner Agency, the Professional Nanny Institute and Best Domestic.

At present, this is the only such local law in the nation, but it may be replicated in other localities.

"I have Local Law 33 on my side," said Janet Cook, owner and director of My Child's Best Friend. "Local Law 33 is a foundation for a work agreement. With a work agreement, half the battle to employ a nanny is done, because parents talk and think about what they need and want."

Massachusetts labor law

The state of Massachusetts' Department of Labor requires all placement agencies to inform clients about labor laws that apply to them. Each agency has to provide a copy of the Department of Labor's leaflet, which discusses Massachusetts Minimum Fair Wage Law (including information on who is covered, payment of wages, overtime, child labor, service, deductions, meal breaks, minimum daily hours and so forth), to every family and every employee who applies to the agency.

California Fair Employment & Housing Act

The California Fair Employment & Housing Act (CA FEHA) requires that any person employing five or more employees not to discriminate on the basis of sex, race, age, national origin or physical disability in employment or housing.

Case Study

John Robertson
International Household Trainer, Coach, Consultant
John G. Robertson, Inc.
London, England

A leading trainer and coach for all aspects of the personal service industry—in particular, household services—John Robertson said that after working in the personal service industry and in the corporate world he much prefers personal service.

Robertson began his career in his early 20s as a household manager/butler in North America and then spent many years in the Fortune 500 business world. Today, Robertson operates his own international training company for employees and employers in the personal service industry and teaches at the International Guild of Professional Butlers' International Butler Academy in the Netherlands. Traveling throughout the world, he works one-on-one with household employers and employees, as well as with private associations and service-centric businesses such as luxury hotels and golf clubs.

In addition, private service employers contract with Robertson to assist them in hiring service employees. Robertson conducts telephone interviews to narrow the field of candidates. One of the first questions he asks candidates is what good service means to them, explaining that by identifying the experience that made someone feel like $1 million, he can readily equate that episode with what the employee will be doing daily for his or her employer.

"The most important thing to understand in household employment is where you are and what you are doing," he said. "High energy, motivated people do well . . . Being in service does not mean being servile . . . The job is not to set the table; it's to support a lifestyle, to provide service . . . I can teach pigeons to set a table!"

Every household employee must know his or her employer's mission of the home, said Robertson. The key focus of the home may be on the family, children's education, recreation, charitable fundraising or political endeavors. Everything the employee does furthers that mission, he said.

"It is a true honor to be allowed to work with someone in his or her home," said Robertson. "There is a tremendous deposition of trust and responsibility—even if the job is dusting baseboards with a toothbrush."

(*continued*)

Laughing, Robertson said he "was born a butler. I thought it was the neatest job . . . It is a job for someone who takes control, organizes and strives for perfection . . . It must be perfect; that's what we do."

According to Robertson, general awareness of the private service market has grown, particularly within the United States. Stressing that personal service employees must be in the field for the right reasons, Robertson noted that, while the industry offers no job security and no unions, there is a job for everyone—those who want to work weekends, those who do not, etc.—and that if someone loves what he or she does for a living, then the money will follow and overall employee benefits and perks can be tremendous.

When interviewing, a household employer should try to determine the candidate's attitude toward personal service and the potential effect it may have on the household. Ask yourself: Is this applicant's outlook appropriate in order to meet the household's service goals?—*Guy*

HIRING CHECKLIST

✓ Know and abide by federal, state and local employment and labor laws.
✓ Be thorough and clear in writing job descriptions and work agreements/contracts.
✓ Be professional. Household employees are pursuing their careers in "real jobs".
✓ Interview, check references, send offer letters and provide new hires with an employee handbook.

For up-to-date information, go to www.gtm.com/resourcecenter

Notes

Chapter 2

Using an Agency to Hire Household Help

Hiring household employees is not easy. There's much to know and much to do. Retaining a good agency is convenient, efficient and a helpful resource in finding an employee. After all, household employers hire staff to make life more convenient, easier and fun—enabling the employer to direct his or her energies toward enjoying his or her family or home. An agency will take applications, screen candidates, help match candidates with employers, conduct interviews and offer advice on household employment, job descriptions, work agreements and employment practices. Ultimately, the household employer saves time and energy by using an agency to sort and match candidates for the specific needs of the home and job description.

In the household employment industry today, there are more than 600 agencies in the United States. The quality of agencies can be as different as night and day; from the experience of the principals involved, the candidate selection and the processes in place to save the client time in order to ensure the best opportunity to hire an employee. A consumer needs to know what to look for when selecting an agent. The following information helps identify what to look for in an agency and what to consider when working with an agency.

WHY USE AN AGENCY?

Benefits of an agency

There are many benefits to using an agency to hire household help. First, household employment placement is what these agencies do; they reinforce these careers as professions and take great care in their placements, often spending extensive time and energy interviewing household employers and candidates for household help. Finding a good household employee can take a lot of time. So using an agency can save a tremendous amount of work for the household employer. Agency staff have extensive hiring experience and meet with many candidates and households. Therefore, they usually have great success in weeding out "bad apples" or anyone not right for a position. Agencies also have rigorous screening methods that ensure that the candidates they select—and eventually place—are reputable, professional, experienced and qualified.

Figure 2.1
Most Valued Agency Characteristic When Finding, Hiring a Nanny
Source: GTM 2003 Nanny Employer Survey.

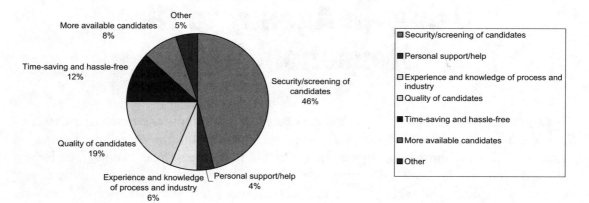

HOW TO FIND A REPUTABLE AGENCY

The best way to find a reputable agency is to talk to other people who have already hired a household employee through an agency. Personal recommendations give an honest story and will provide much-needed details.

Also, employers may investigate agencies online and in the Yellow Pages. See if the agency is a member of an industry association. For example, a nanny placement agency may be a member of the National Alliance of Professional Nanny Agencies (www.theapna.org) or the International Nanny Association (www.nanny.org). Also, when contacting an agency, always ask if it is licensed, insured and bonded.

QUESTIONS TO ASK AN AGENCY

When working with an agency, an employer needs to know:

- what the agency offers—full-time, part-time, live-in or live-out workers—and what the agency's placement practices are (i.e., the agency provides the employer with a minimum of three candidates, and the agency will replace a worker if for some reason a placement does not work out during a set probation period);
- the agency's fees and what they cover (i.e., does an agency fee cover a candidate's background checks, or is that a separate responsibility for the household employer?);

- what kind of support the agency provides after a candidate has been hired;
- the "extras" and their costs;
- if the agency requires payment only when a nanny is placed, or if there are "up front" fees that the household employer must pay;
- is there a payment schedule;
- the guarantee policy and what must occur to ensure that it is in effect (i.e., the employer and employee must fully complete and sign the work agreement and submit it to the agency within three weeks after hire);
- the refund policy;
- whether the agency has candidates to fill the position now;
- the standard time frame to fill a position;
- how the agency recruits household workers and the experience and skills the agency requires from them;
- how the agency screens applicants (i.e., are all applicants interviewed in person? If so, how many staff in the agency interview the applicant?);
- if the household employer interviews candidates are travel expenses paid for by the agency, the candidate or the household employer;
- the number of references required for an applicant (i.e., what questions does the agency ask? Can the household employer see the written references? May the household employer contact the applicant's references?);
- other than background checks does, the agency conducts other screening such as personality profile, drug testing or a medical exam;
- how information about the household is gathered (i.e., does the agency visit the home or check references of the family? Is a written application part of the placement process?);
- the kind of training the agency offers candidates (i.e., does the agency hold CPR classes for nannies or time management training for personnel assistants?);
- the average candidate's profile (i.e., age, education, salary range); and,
- how long the agency has been in business, and, during that time, how many placements the agency made, where they were and generally how long they lasted.

> "Good home care can have a beneficial effect on the children's development and on the family's home life. In-home childcare [for instance] should not be perceived as a threat. It should be a welcome joy to a family."
>
> Ilo Milton
> President
> FamilyWise, Inc.
> Bedford, NY
> GTM Partner Agency

Case Study

Denise Collins
CEO
In-House Staffing at Aunt Ann's Agency
Daly City, CA
GTM Partner Agency

In-house Staffing at Aunt Ann's Agency, Inc., in operation for 45 years, refers an equal number of nannies and other household help to clients in the San Francisco Bay area. According to the agency CEO Denise Collins, clients are highly educated, highly salaried people who often have been raised with staff and are now hiring staff themselves. These employers offer benefit packages to their household help and recognize them as professionals.

"This has been our core clientele, and they take care of their household help very well," said Collins. "In the 1980s, we began to see two-income families looking to hire help, and we experienced huge growth in housekeeping placements and, then, childcare. It is a quality-of-life decision, and along with that came a higher set of expectations that this person would be included in the family. New employers need to put in place all the tools to make the working relationship successful. They have to learn how to hire a person who will come into their home to work. The accountability of the working relationship is the family's, the employer's, not the agency's."

For these first-time employers, Collins said the agency needs to educate them on everything to do with employing household help. "Even people who handle HR issues at work need to be educated because of differences in the workweek, payroll, taxes and laws," she noted. "Plus, they must file different forms."

To help, the agency holds public education sessions on employing childcare and eldercare professionals in the home. "It's a buyer beware market," said Collins, who noted that some unethical agencies are a big issue in California. "There's no certification or regulation. It's pretty predatory, and the population most affected are the seniors."

An effective household employer conducts effective human resource management. This begins with deciding whether or not to outsource the recruiting and screening to an agency. The role of an agency is to make it a much easier, more convenient process while presenting the best candidates that match an employer's philosophy and position requirements. A good agency adds value by how well it advises an employer on the position, management techniques and tools that help the employer be successful.—*Guy*

Case Study

Cliff Greenhouse
President
Pavillion Agency
New York City, NY
GTM Partner Agency

Continuing a business begun by his father 40 years ago, Cliff Greenhouse works in tandem with his brother, Keith, at the agency.

With the mid-1980's growth in dual-income families, Greenhouse instituted a nanny placement program that matches well-educated, experienced nannies with affluent families. In addition, he created The Nanny Authority, a sister company based in New Jersey that places high-quality nannies with dual-career families. According to Greenhouse, his agency's success lies in its meticulous and thorough screening and matching services.

The agency not only works to fill clients' requirements, said Greenhouse, but to establish long-term relationships. "The agency guides their clients—we seldom need to give advice or educate them on their role as an employer," he added. The vast majority of his clients grew up with nannies and housekeepers. "So, basically what I do is identify their needs and find them people that will satisfy their requirements while fitting in to the 'personality' of their home."

The one issue Greenhouse does see throughout the industry is communication. "Staff not knowing the proper way to communicate, especially when they are unhappy and when employers are not being polite enough," he said.

According to Greenhouse, his clients are comforted knowing that the agency has interviewed and spoken with household employees at length before placement. "That's what makes us who we are," he noted. "It works for us, and we are very proud of what we have here.

"We have experience and can handle the needs of very demanding families," Greenhouse added. "Our household help are highly intelligent and accomplished people . . . but why we are so successful is that we are very professional in an industry that is not very professional. The people I place view this as a career and comparable to any other industry. They are serious, proud of what they do and extremely professional themselves."

> When consulting an agency, a household employer should understand the role the agent can play—from setting an applicant's expectations to developing the job description, defining and communicating the home's culture and what the employer's expectations are long before the employer ever meets the applicant.—*Guy*

TOP CONCERNS

Top concerns to discuss with an agency on what the household employer wants in an employee include the following:

- relevant experience
- relevant qualifications
- personality type preferences
- references
- salary
- benefits (paid vacations, health insurance, car use, holidays, retirement plans, etc.)
- hours/schedule
- philosophy on service (i.e., a nanny's philosophy on child rearing)
- languages
- appearance and conduct
- responsibility
- communication skills
- team player
- reliability
- commitment

WHAT TO TELL AN AGENCY

Ask Guy

Q. What is nanny sharing and how does it work?

A. Nanny sharing, also known as shared care, is a solution for many employers on a limited budget. Agencies can help an employer (or employers) formulate a nanny share position.

Actually, nanny sharing offers two solutions:

1. a nanny can be shared by families who need a limited number of hours of childcare on a regular basis, enabling a nanny to work at employer A for part of the workday or workweek and then at employer B for the other part of the workday or workweek; or,

2. a nanny may provide childcare at one home/workplace for children from different families. For instance, two neighboring families may opt to nanny share and employ a nanny to watch both families' children simultaneously in one of the family's homes.

For nanny sharing to work successfully, the employers/families need to be fairly close in proximity and agree on job expectations and childcare philosophy.

Honesty is the very best policy. The agency needs a clear and an accurate representation of the family, household, job requirements, etc., to be able to place the best household employee for the position. Employers will need to apply their honesty in "packaging" themselves, their employment practices, the household's culture and what they need and are seeking in the household employee. When speaking to an agency, employers need to specify details regarding the following:

- hiring time frame
- the work schedule
- all individuals' needs within the household, including other household help
- their expectations of the agency

- their expectations of the household employee
- compensation and benefits packages
- any and all special requirements, such as extensive travel with the family, holiday needs, on-call hours, and so on.

Remember, open communication is the best policy when acquiring agency assistance. Anything but the truth will potentially delay the hire, misconstrue employment objectives and create uncertainty, misunderstanding, and, worse yet, hard feelings, mistrust and anger.

USING AN AGENCY CHECKLIST

✓ Find out as much as possible about the agency, including its placement procedures.

✓ Prepare a list of questions for the agency, including practices, fees, post-placement support and background screening.

✓ Ask whether the agency belongs to any industry associations; if so, ask which ones.

✓ Go to an agency with a clear idea on the household employee required, and know what responsibilities, experience and personality traits the household employee should have to best perform within the household.

For more information, go to www.gtm.com/resourcecenter

Notes

Chapter 3

The Work Agreement

Work agreements are essential with household employment, since household positions are so customized to the specific home in question. From the start, the work agreement establishes a clear understanding between the employer and employee regarding the employee's duties, responsibilities and all that is expected from both the employer and employee. The most effective work agreement is in writing and covers all aspects of working in the household—including the employee's work schedule, required daily duties, compensation, benefits, termination and confidentiality clause.

Lack of a work agreement can contribute to dissatisfaction in the workplace and a high employee turnover rate. Therefore, work agreements can be considered an important step in building a long-lasting relationship in which all parties clearly understand their responsibilities and expectations.

A CRITICAL STEP IN BUILDING A SUCCESSFUL RELATIONSHIP

Figure 3.1
"The Household HR Steps"

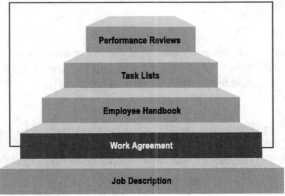

Performance Reviews

Task Lists

Employee Handbook

Work Agreement

Job Description

Performance Reviews	A means to communicate employer feedback to employees regarding how well they are meeting the objectives of the household demonstrated by task list activities and satisfaction of the employees constituents, such as dependents, other staff and household manager and homeowner.
Task Lists	The "to do" lists to meet the job descriptions objectives. Could be daily, weekly, special projects, seasonal activities, etc., and if a task has to be done with percision it may call for a specific procedure.
Employee Handbook	Comprehensive set of policies addressing expectations for employment responsibilities and conduct. Including use of property, time off, resignation, paydays, performance reviews, etc.
Work Agreement	Detailed outline of the employment engagement with specific compensation, benefits, terms, etc. Establishes a clear understanding between the employer and employee regarding the employee's duties, responsibilities and all that is expected from both the employer and employee.
Job Description	A precisely written description of the responsibilities/requirements that specify employer objectives.

Case Study

Lin Taylor-Pleiman
Owner/Operator
American Domestic Agency, Inc.
Whiteford and Greenville, DE
GTM Partner Agency

The agency offers domestic-related employment placements in Maryland, Delaware and Pennsylvania. The agency opened in 2002 after the owners spent ten months exhaustively researching household employment legal issues, contracts, insurance and other critical matters.

Noting the delicacy of the household employment industry, Lin Taylor-Pleiman said a signed work agreement is proof that "the parties sat down, talked and worked out issues so the employee and the employer are fully aware of each other's expectations."

(*continued*)

The agency is so adamant about the written agreement that it requires clients to submit a copy of the agreement within seven days of an employee's start date. If a client fails to do so, the agency will not honor its replacement guarantee if the placement fails.

"We've learned it's a must," said Taylor-Pleiman. "It addresses a multitude of areas, even what happens when there's a snow day. Both parties must know the expectations of the other party in order to have a good relationship, in which the employee can focus on her duties and not worry about being treated unfairly."

Taylor-Pleiman speaks from experience. Her agency was begun after her daughter left a very dissatisfying experience as a nanny.

"There are standard areas that need to be addressed, regardless of position," she noted. "The importance of communication is paramount. With this work agreement, most of the time problems can be rectified . . . Most employers want the employees to be an extension of the family, and, for the most part, want a good, close relationship."

Stating that the work agreement is an advantage to both the employer and employee, Taylor-Pleiman said she believes the work agreement helps household employees gain recognition as professionals. "Employees are demanding taxes be paid and that they be legitimized. The work agreement is an instrumental step in that."

As a household employer, clear expectations are paramount. This is why the work agreement is so critical to the beginning of the employer-employee relationship, even for a relationship on the best of terms. Work agreements spell out the employment conditions, general tasks and responsibilities of the employer and employee within that household. With it, both the employer and employee are reducing the likelihood that problems will occur.—*Guy*

JOB DESCRIPTION

A work agreement and job description go hand in hand. Often, they contain the same material, but a household employer needs to develop both, as a job description is written *before* an employee is hired, and a work agreement is written *after* the employee is hired and is developed *with* the employee before his or her first day on the job.

Prior to all else, thoroughly think through what the position needs to accomplish, which tasks and duties are required to achieve the positions goals and what skills, abilities and talents the employee must have to satisfactorily perform all that is required. Only then can a comprehensive job description be developed. Consider, for example, the following:

- Will the household employee need a car and a valid driver's license? (Will the nanny be required to drive the child to a play date or school? Will the cook need to drive to the grocery store for necessary ingredients? Will the gardener need to drive to a nursery or an equipment store?)
- Will a nanny or household manager be required to take the child to the park or playground on a schedule or from time to time?
- Will a nanny caring for two children be expected to prepare and feed the children breakfast and lunch?
- Will the nanny be required to clean lunch dishes after the children have eaten?
- Will all household employees be expected to answer the telephone and take messages?
- Will all household help be expected to sign for deliveries and packages?
- Will an employee need protective clothing or equipment? (Will the gardener need protective goggles when operating equipment? Will the driver need cover-ups and gloves for car maintenance tasks? Will the eldercare employee need face masks, gowns and protective gloves?)

"I strongly recommend work agreements between household employers and domestic employees. A work agreement outlines your nanny's terms of employment and specifies how you expect her to care for your child. Although not legally required, an agreement is enforceable and greatly reduces potential disputes. Overall, an agreement is an integral part of any working relationship and provides important protections to both the employee and the employer."

Bob King, Esq.
Founder and CEO,
 Legally Nanny
Irvine, CA
GTM Partner

There's a lot to think about and much to decide. If an employer is seeking a nanny, then he or she will want the nanny to focus fully on caring for the children, not to necessarily perform housekeeping chores. It may be that the employer will need both a nanny and a housekeeper. It varies greatly with each household's needs and the household employer's situation.

Job descriptions should list all of the necessary qualifications (skills, education, certification or license), essential job functions and functions that are desired but not mandatory. Comprehensive job descriptions begin the employment on solid ground. With the job description in hand, the hiring process can begin.

Leann Brambach, owner/operator of Home Details, Inc., in Seattle, WA, can log as much as 150 hours on some accounts when placing a household employee, and she spends hours with clients, meeting in their homes. "Every job is customized, so you can't have a cookie cutter job description or profile," she said. "I spend a lot of time getting to know the family and know what they want. I walk them through the whole specifications of the job. This research ensures the right person for the job is placed."

Brambach leans heavily on the job description and work agreement. Regarding nannies, Brambach, who started her career working as a full-time nanny, said "Generally, people don't realize how tough of a job it really is—how much work and responsibility it is. It is a real job requiring super-power intuition and the ability to make executive decisions on behalf of someone else, sometimes without guidance or with little feedback."

(See Appendix 8, for sample job description)

WORK AGREEMENT

Why the Work Agreement Is Important

There are many reasons why household employers enter into a work agreement (see Appendix 3, for sample work agreement) with their new household employee(s). The most popular reason is to help ensure clear and concise communication around terms and conditions of employment. As all relationships seem to have an initial honeymoon period, verbal agreements and commitments can sometimes be fuzzy and possibly forgotten and, as a result, strains the employment relationship. The work agreement outlines these commitments in a professional manner, creates the seriousness that the houshold position and employment require, and help to reduce employment disputes.

> "People do treat the work relationship in a relaxed manner, as a friend rather than employer-employee. That's when issues come up."
>
> Sylvia Greenbaum
> Co-owner
> Boston Nanny Centre, Inc.
> Boston, MA

> "Hiring a nanny for our newborn son, who lived-out and had two school-age children . . . was an initial concern . . . But, that concern did not last long. The nanny brought her children with her to a meeting at our home to complete the work agreement. Their well-mannered and obedient behavior became a huge selling point for hiring her . . . The nanny has inspired our trust and confidence. So much so, she is allowed to take our son with her to attend her children's school meetings. Plus, her children may spend an occasional afternoon or evening at our house while their mom works, particularly when we cannot provide enough advanced notice for her to obtain babysitting care for her children. I welcome them in my home."
>
> Jim Chaney
> Father of three
> Household employer
> HR vice president for building products, Georgia-Pacific

"An in-home care-giver's primary responsibility is the care and nurturing of young children, not folding the laundry or mopping the kitchen floor. Employers need to remember the nanny's priorities—first, provide a happy, safe, convenient child-care atmosphere; then, if there's time, a nanny can fold the children's clothes."

Anne Johnson
Long-term Placement
  Director
A New England Nanny
Clifton Park, NY

Why Enter Into A Work Agreement

The work agreement helps to safeguard the cost of recruiting and obtaining a household employee. Turnover costs could run thousands of dollars considering: the cost of advertising; time spent to screen, interview, and reference check; placement agency fee; training costs; and employer time lost from work or other activities.

A work agreement is legally enforceable. However an employer may not want to enforce the terms of the agreement as it would not serve the household to retain an uninterested or disgruntled employee. Yet, an employer may very well want to enforce the confidentiality clause (see Appendix 9, for Confidentiality/Non-Disclosure Agreement) to protect the family's personal affairs that an employee may have learned during the course of employment. For the household employee a legally enforced work agreement serves to protect his or her compensation, benefits, severance pay, as well as job description requirements.

How To Create a Work Agreement

Ideally consulting with an employment attorney is a best practice, in developing a work agreement. However, some placement agencies may offer template agreement, or provide samples obtained from its other clients. Employers may extrapolate ideas from template samples, and obtain input from friends or colleagues who have developed their own work agreements for their own household help.

Key Elements of a Work Agreement

The following list of key elements provide an overview of the common components that are included in most work agreements.

1. **Recitals**
    ❏ Employer is an individual and a "Household Employer", resident of _____(state), and over the age of 18.
2. **Employment**
    ❏ Employment under this agreement is to begin on _____ and continue unless sooner terminated as provided herein.

3. **Compensation (see FLSA Chp. 5)**
   - ❑ Subject to the following provisions of this agreement, the Employer agrees to pay the Employee a gross compensation hourly rate of $_____.

4. **Benefits (See Chp. 6)**
   - ❑ Employee is entitled to _____ days of paid vacation annually. The vacation must be scheduled 30 days in advance and agreed to by employer. Vacation is based upon normal payment for a 40-hour workweek.

5. **Terms and conditions of employment**
   - ❑ Employee may not drink alcohol, use illegal drugs or smoke while on duty for the employer.

6. **Termination of agreement (see Chp. 10)**
   - ❑ Employer may terminate employment by Employee for violation of paragraph D 1 (see Appendix 3, work agreement).

7. **Modifications and interpretation**
   - ❑ The job description may change by mutual consent.

8. **Applicable laws**
   - ❑ The provisions of this agreement shall be constructed in accordance with laws of the state of _____.

9. **Signature and date line**
   - ❑ Employer and employee should sign and date original and each revision of the work agreement.

10. **Work schedule (optional)**
    - ❑ Additional detail of a daily schedule broken down by day, by hour.

Case Study

Sylvia Greenbaum
Co-owner
Boston Nanny Centre, Inc.
Newton, MA
GTM Partner Agency

According to Sylvia Greenbaum, co-owner of the agency, the lack of clear job requirements is a top reason household positions do not work—particularly when a family wishes a nanny to perform other household work unrelated to childcare.

Greenbaum cited an example in which a nanny placed through the agency was charged with caring for twins. A work agreement specified that the nanny tend to the twins, and it did not require her to do any household work. The nanny worked hard caring for the twins, and the family agreed that she was doing an excellent job. Yet, after some time, the family began leaving daily notes asking the nanny to perform household chores and tasks. She became nervous and upset about the daily notes and saw no end in sight to her daily compounding responsibilities, which were not stipulated in the work agreement. The family, first-time household employers, was upset with the nanny's attitude. Tension quickly and steadily increased.

The parents then angrily confronted the nanny, who immediately resigned, believing her employers did not value or appreciate the high-quality care she provided to their children. The family's anger increased when left without a nanny, and the family threatened to withhold payment for the five days the nanny had already worked that week. (The agency reminded the family that as the employer it was legally responsible to pay the nanny for days she had worked.) Both client and nanny felt angry and mistreated. The family gained childcare coverage quickly through the agency, but the nanny left the profession, seeking another type of job.

"Clearly, it would have been better had the family and nanny discussed what household responsibilities were needed and what the nanny felt comfortable doing," said Greenbaum. "If this had been written in the agreement, the nanny and family would not have each felt taken advantage of."

According to Greenbaum, mixing household chores with childcare depends on the personalities involved. "Sometimes nannies will do other jobs (around the house) without being asked," she said. "It depends on the relationship. So many factors go into it."

(*continued*)

Greenbaum's agency provides each client with a detailed work agreement and strongly encourages clients to complete it. However, many parents are new to parenthood, as well as to the employer role, and they don't yet realize all they wish their nannies to be and do. "They think that it's not totally unreasonable to say, 'Let's see how it is going', or 'We're sure it'll work out'," noted Greenbaum. "All nannies who care for children are doing other things, like preparing food, doing the children's laundry, cleaning and organizing their toys. Yet, when children are in school or napping, some will do some shopping, run errands and put a load of the employers' laundry in the washer. Some say, 'I'll care for the child but not for the parents', or some say, 'I like to keep busy.' It is so individual. It's best if all requirements are talked about before the nanny is hired."

Greenbaum said difficulty is inherent in the nanny-employer relationship. "People do treat the work relationship in a relaxed manner," she said. "Sort of as a friend rather than employer-employee, and that's when issues come up."

Greenbaum has great empathy for families, who must learn so many different pieces that go into the employer role during a stress-filled time while trying to meet all of their professional and personal obligations. Plus, added Greenbaum, stress naturally arises when parents first leave their children with another adult.

Often referring parents to GTM for employer information and wage and tax assistance, Greenbaum noted that the hiring process is both complex and lengthy, typically taking a while to find the right person for the right job and the right family. "[Hiring a nanny] is such a personal decision," she said. "People have to feel that it's right. It can be a very long process. Sometimes there's magic, and it all comes together. It could take one day to find the right nanny, but I tell families, if possible, give it at least two months."

Given all of the processes and pieces, Greenbaum is not surprised that a first-time hire does not often go smoothly. "People are busy," she said, "and the nanny process is time consuming, so all these pieces that need to be included in the work agreement form are pushed to the back burner. It's understandable why some serious problems happen."

Household employers must take the same professional attitude toward job descriptions and work agreements in the household as do corporations. Doing so will greatly help establish the first-time employer, as well as experienced employers, as professionals and puts structure around the position.—*Guy*

THE WORK AGREEMENT CHECKLIST

An experienced employment attorney should review your work agreements. As you are preparing the agreement here are a few tips to keep in mind:

- ✓ Think clearly about what to include in the work agreement and, if using an agency, get its input.
- ✓ Be concise. There is no room for ambiguity in the phrasing of the work agreement.
- ✓ If using a standard work agreement template, customize it to suit the household's specific needs.
- ✓ Leave no stone unturned: include everything the job will involve.
- ✓ Once written, discuss the work agreement with the employee.
- ✓ Make sure the employee signs and dates the agreement and receives a copy.
- ✓ Be sure the agreement is in place prior to the employee's start date.
- ✓ Agreement should be signed and dated by both the employer and employee, as well as being witnessed.
- ✓ An agreement should be written so it is understandable by a high school graduate.
- ✓ Font size is a minimum 10 point size.
- ✓ Agreement should cover all essential facts.
- ✓ Bold face important passages.
- ✓ Specify time periods and note reasonable limitations.
- ✓ A confidentiality clause is included in the work agreement. This clause extends during and after employment with the household.
- ✓ If the employee expresses a concern, the employer should recommend that the employee may seek his or her own legal counsel.
- ✓ Provide a signed copy to the employee and file a signed copy in the employee's personnel file.
- ✓ If working with a third-party, such as a placement agency or attorney, send a signed copy to him or her for his or her records and for safe keeping.

For more information, go to www.gtm.com/resourcecenter

Notes

Chapter 4

Personnel Practices for the Home

The household employment industry is working to establish a professional structure around a very informal situation. The perception of the household occupation and the role within the home is often different for employers and employees. Many employers view hiring staff for their home as a personal responsibility, whereas household employees see it as employment. Even though the employment is not in an office or a retail setting, it is a worksite where employment laws prevail. But, of course, as an employer it also is a home and a sanctuary. It'll take some effort for a household employer to view her or his home as another's workplace.

Clear communications, respectful treatment, openness to discussion and adaptability should be what everyone within the household will work toward to maintain a satisfying workplace.

Figure 4.1
Household Employment Problems
Source: GTM 2003 Nanny Employer Survey

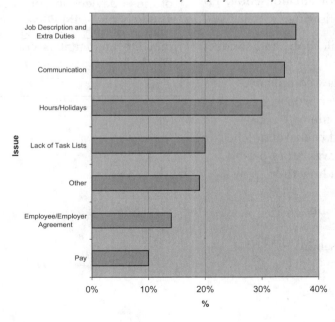

THE EMPLOYEE HANDBOOK

Like any employer, household employers must establish fair personnel practices and policies and apply them equally to all staff. Providing each employee with an employee handbook explaining the household workplace's rules, practices and policies is a necessity and presents clear advantages to the employer.

An employee handbook lets employees know what the rules and practices are within the household. While highly prevalent in the corporate workplace, employee handbooks to date are noticeably absent in the majority of households today. In tandem with the work agreement, the employee handbook cements the household's employment policies and personnel practices.

All new employees should receive a handbook immediately upon hire or on their employment start date. The employer should have the employee sign a release (see Appendix 10, for an employee handbook acknowledgment receipt) stating that he or she received the handbook. Then, the employer should file the release in the employee's personnel file. The statement shows that the employee was provided with information on important household HR issues, such as the following:

- household philosophy and conduct
- dress code
- immigration law compliance
- use of employer property
- the personnel file
- references and background checking
- introductory/evaluatory period
- labor laws and how they apply
- time off
- employee benefits
- retirement
- short-term disability
- Social Security

Ask Guy

Q. As a new parent, I am concerned with leaving my infant with my newly hired nanny. If I install a nannycam in my home, am I required to inform the nanny that she may be monitored?

A. It is fair and proper for a household employer to fully disclose to a job applicant whether he or she will monitor the household. Check your local law for the legal use of these devices in your home and/or your employee's workplace. Disclose this information during the hiring process to ensure that the applicant is comfortable with this practice.

- payroll and taxes
- timekeeping and work schedules
- salary increases, bonuses and gifts
- workplace safety
- performance reviews
- discipline
- termination, resignation and exit interview procedures

When developing a handbook, address any questions an employee has or any information an employee wants to know about his or her job and the workplace. For more insight into how to develop an employee handbook and create your own customized version go to www.gtm.com/resourcecenter.

EXPENSE REPORTS AND REIMBURSEMENT FOR WORK-RELATED EXPENSES

An employer should detail in the employee handbook the process an employee must follow for reimbursement of work-related expenses or disbursement of spending money for an upcoming event. As part of the process, it is helpful to stipulate that an expense report must be submitted each month, fiscal quarter or event, and whether the employer requires the original sales receipt or a photocopy of the sales receipt. Also, employers may include guidance on the minimum dollar amount when an original sales receipt or photocopy of the sales receipt is required (i.e., all expenses of $10 or more must be submitted with a receipt or photocopy of a receipt). For example, if a nanny spends $2 on an ice cream bar for a child at the playground, then a receipt (or photocopy of the receipt) is not mandatory; however, if a personal assistant spends $12.50 on office supplies, then a receipt (or photocopy of the receipt) must be attached to the expense report. (See Appendix 11 for a sample expense report form.)

A list of approved employer-covered expenses should be included within the employee handbook and amended as necessary. To ensure clarity, some employers also include a list of non-covered expenses. For instance, some employers may cover an employee's mileage, tolls and parking but not maintenance costs or gas (which are actually included in the mileage reimbursement rate). Or, some employers may cover the costs of work-related cell phone calls but not the cost of the cell phone or its monthly service charge. The handbook and the expense reimbursement form may include a clearly worded sentence recommending that an employee with any questions regarding reimbursement and employer-covered expenses check with the employer regarding coverage approval prior to the event or task.

Case Study

Trish Stevens
Nanny
New York City, NY

Trish Stevens said she became a nanny because she wanted to be "Mary Poppins".

"I knew I wanted to take care of children," said Stevens, who has been a nanny for 20 years and has worked in Indiana, Ohio and New York. "Each job is different . . . Today, it is more of a profession, with more people thinking of it as a real job. Now, there are personal days and paid holidays. It's more than being a babysitter and more like being a teacher."

Stevens, who now cares for three children in New York City, ensures that work agreements are in place with her employers to clearly describe the job requirements. "It's not easy finding (the right) nanny, and it's not easy to find (the right) nanny job," said Stevens.

The agreement helps, but Stevens offers some tips on how household employers should treat their employees, including the following:

- say thank you
- remember that your nanny is there for the children, not to keep house
- offer the business standard of five paid personal days and five paid sick days each year
- pay for at least half of the employee's health insurance
- if a nanny goes on vacation with the family, remember that it's the employers' vacation not the nanny's (she or he still must care for the children), and she or he still needs downtime
- if an employer cannot afford a raise or a bonus, offer some time off, if appropriate
- understand that a household employee does not have the same resources as the employer. If an employer decides to take the next few days off, an offer for the employee to "get away" or use her or his vacation days during that time is not as generous as it may appear to the employer. Unexpectedly offering the employee an opportunity to take vacation time in just a matter of days does not allow for economical travel planning and scheduling
- pay a nanny on the books, with the correct taxes withheld

(continued)

For nannies, Stevens offers these tips:

- speak English, or the language agreed upon by employer and employee
- support the parent, even if you do not agree
- be trained in CPR and first aid
- be sure to develop a work agreement with the employer

An issue Stevens said she is adamant about is paying the required taxes from her earnings. "It's one of the first questions I ask (a potential employer)," she said.

Stevens said she would like to see nannies portrayed in a positive light on the evening news and throughout the US media. For instance, the media could report that Stevens carries with her to the park an inflatable potty, along with food coloring, glue sticks, hopscotch chalk and other playthings for the children.

A household employee's perspective is interesting to hear and is really no different from the expectations of those who work for large companies. All of these tips may be achieved by taking into account the employer's goals and the employee's needs when developing personnel policies and by setting the stage for ongoing communication. In this case, an employer would most likely provide an employee handbook stating: the termination, personal time off, salary increase policies, payroll policies, and employment policies that promote acheiving household goals.—*Guy*

MEDICAL RELEASE FORMS

For childcare and eldercare workers, an employer should prepare a medication release form allowing the caregiver permission to administer medication for prescribed and over-the-counter medication. Also, caregivers need to prepare a temporary medical care release form that allows a child to be treated by a physician or healthcare organization without a parent present. The caregiver can present this medical care release form with the employer's health insurance card to obtain treatment. (See Appendix 12 for a sample of a medical care release form and Appendix 13 for a sample medication permission form.)

Case Study

Denise Shade
Household Employer
Senior Vice President
Foreign Exchange Unit, Key Bank
New York City, NY
GTM payroll and tax service client

Denise Shade, mother of two and senior vice president of Key Bank's foreign exchange unit, first sought in-home childcare so her children could be on their own schedules and not adhere to their parents' work timetables. "Primarily, the kids did not have to mold to our jobs," she said. "They could nap when they wanted and not be woken up by us to be transported someplace else. Plus, as newborns, in-home childcare limited their exposure to germs compared to a setting with many children."

Shade first hired a nanny six years ago when her daughter was born. First intending to hire a live-out nanny out of concern for their privacy, the Shades hired a live-in nanny because they wanted to hire a particular candidate who needed a live-in situation. They've had live-in nannies ever since.

"It worked out better than we expected," said Shade, who takes great care to respect the nanny's time. "We ensure that the nanny is done with work at 6 P.M. If we need childcare at night, we hire a babysitter, or, if we need to, we'll hire the nanny for the night as a babysitter if she is available."

Respect for the nanny and her or his abilities is the key to Shade's successful employee relationships—and is the foundation for close connections that continue today. Shade's first nanny was ideal for the care required for a single newborn. When Shade gave birth to her son three years later, another nanny with multi-tasking skills was hired. Unfortunately, when the Shades moved from Ohio to Connecticut, the second nanny did not relocate, preferring to stay in close proximity to her family.

Shade's current nanny has been with the family since early 2003. In all, the family has had "great" experiences with nannies, and these have countered one "poor" experience—the result of the nanny having different expectations, said Shade.

Although already having enjoyed fantastic nanny relationships, Shade said that one was a "difficult experience for everyone in the family. We learned that small issues can quickly disrupt the functioning of the entire family." Along with unrealistic expectations, the nanny was a difficult and unhappy person, Shade said. She explained that the nanny complained about the water bottles purchased just for her because they had screw tops

(continued)

and not pop-up tops; the rug for her room was not soft enough on her feet; and, she disliked the car provided for to her to drive. Because the nanny held an associate's degree in child development, she believed she was the final authority when it came to the children. She also claimed that she was the "number one nanny" the Shades could have.

What really ended the relationship, however, was the nanny's maverick manner. According to Shade, the nanny medicated her daughter three different times without informing either parent—despite the fact that the daughter's father was working from home during her illness. When confronted, the nanny claimed that during her work hours—despite a parent's presence in the home—she had the final say on childcare. Also, the nanny caused an incident at her daughter's elementary school by taking her out of school early on a snow day without informing the staff. The nanny had removed their daughter from school when she was picking up their son at the end of his standard half-day. (Her daughter's school, Shade said, locks down when a child is thought missing.)

Along with providing great respect to her nanny, Shade also strictly adheres to fair and honest financial dealings with her nanny. If anything, said Shade, she ensures that all financial circumstances are in the nanny's favor. For instance, Shade religiously monitors the nanny's time worked. If Shade is late, she pays the nanny for all extra time worked. Also, if during a pay period Shade has come home from work early or taken a vacation day, then she will pay the period's full salary wage.

"We really try not to take advantage of her," said Shade. "And, we don't dump extra tasks on her. If the chore is in our contract, she does it. If not, we don't want her to do it."

In exchange for respecting her in-home employee's time and workload and for her compensating fairly and considerately, Shade said she receives enormous loyalty. "The nanny really makes an effort to be available, because she knows we need her help," she said.

A household employer improves with each new experience. Showing consideration for an employee's feelings helps even the playing field between employee and employer and is the correct management approach when dealing with employment issues. Employees must understand that an employer needs to be a manager, which includes establishing initial goals, communicating philosophy and/or fostering household culture, as well as supervising the household employee. Plus, employees need to know up front how you will measure his or her performance. Set periodic review meetings to: evaluate those goals and the employee's performance; handle lingering communication issues; clarify household policy; and coach the employee to improve his or her skills during his or her employment.—*Guy*

MAINTAINING AN EMPLOYEE PERSONNEL FILE

Keeping an employee personnel file ensures that the employer obtains and maintains information required by law and establishes a documented work history for that particular employee.

The file contains all related information to that employee, such as the job description, job application, letter offering employment, Form W-4 (see Appendix 14, for a sample employee's withholding allowance certificate), the state withholding certificate (if applicable), a signed statement that the employee received an employee handbook, the work agreement, attendance record, (see Appendix 15, for a sample attendance record of household employee and Appendix 16, for a sample of a time-off request form) performance evaluations, benefit forms, compliments and complaints from co-workers, awards, etc. Keep personnel records confidential and locked in a safe location so no one can access them without the employer's expressed consent.

Some states require employers to allow both past and present employees access to their employment files. Employers usually can ask the employee to look through the file on the worksite, with the employer present, ensuring that nothing is altered or taken. Some states allow employers to copy parts of the file and provide them to the employee, enabling the employer to shield sensitive information from the employee. Employers should include information on employees' access to their personnel records in the employee handbook.

PERFORMANCE REVIEWS

Companies of all sizes establish periodic (written) reviews and evaluations of employees. It is a good employment practice to implement, particularly for new employees, because it allows the employer and employee to communicate what the employee has accomplished and areas that may need development. With the reviews, employees are provided an opportunity to improve, and the employer has a documented history of the employee's performance and problems.

While informal employer-employee discussions relating to job performance and goals are encouraged and expected throughout an employee's tenure, it is common practice for an employer to perform a formal written performance review (see Appendix 17, for a sample performance evaluation form) at the end of an employee's introductory period and then on a scheduled basis. Many employers choose to review employees on a yearly basis. Some prefer to evaluate employees every six months. The work agreement and the employee handbook should detail expected review times.

When reviewing an employee's work performance, employers need to remember to focus on work performance and not on the employee's personality or characteristics. Employers should:

- be as positive as possible but be very clear about situations—speaking frankly and straightforwardly
- offer a review of both strengths and weaknesses
- cite specific examples of when the employee has exceeded, met or failed in job expectations
- set reasonable goals for the employee to work toward (and meet) in developing and/or improving skills
- schedule a second review to determine the employee's progress if her or his performance is weak. This could be done in three months or six months—whichever is considered a fair amount of time for the employee to improve and demonstrate better performance
- list in the review any disciplinary actions, including termination, if the employee fails to improve his or her performance

Employees may thoroughly examine all performance reviews and may provide a written opinion to be placed in the personnel file. Some evaluation forms have a designated area for the employee's response. It is common practice for both the employer and employee to both sign the review. This documentation helps protect the employer from any false claim made by a current or former employee.

Performance reviews may or may not be accompanied by a salary increase consideration. Employers should clearly state that salary increases are awarded in light of an employee's significant performance and at the employer's discretion—and certainly not guaranteed. Salary increases are evaluated by the employee's:

- ability to perform all job tasks and functions;
- attendance and punctuality;
- willingness to work;
- ability to cooperate with other employees and household members; and,
- adherence to all household policies.

DISCIPLINE

While household employment is largely at-will employment (see chapter 10, p. 131 and Appendix 6, for a sample offer letter of household employment including at-will employ-

Case Study

William Bruce Reynolds
Owner/Consultant
Estate Consulting and Management, Inc.
Columbia County, NY

William Bruce Reynolds spends much of his time working with the staffs of private homes, resorts and restaurants teaching them how to provide the utmost in customer service. A director of the International Guild of Professional Butlers, a chef trained at the Culinary Institute of America, a Certified Executive Protection Specialist and an experienced household manager, Reynolds helps others find employment and uses the wealth of his experiences to train others to succeed in the household and service professions.

Reynolds said he believes the industry is divided into two groups:

1. those people who are trained and highly motivated; and,
2. those people who are untrained and poorly motivated.

An employer who has spent millions of dollars creating his or her dream property looks to a professional household manager to train and supervise a staff capable of delivering the highest degree of professional service. The position of household manager is quite comprehensive and requires proper training and education.

The household manager is required to create a multi-faceted program specific to the estate that he or she is managing. The plan will include, but not be limited to:

- safety and security
- property systems
- maintenance
- organization
- operations
- staff management
- managing vendors, trades and outside laborers

Reynolds reminded those working in the household profession that they do so at the whim of the individual or family. All questions should be answered beforehand, and both parties should know what is expected from the arrangement. The position will last only as long as the requirements set forth in the working agreement are carried out.

(continued)

"For household help to be treated as professional, they must always conduct themselves as professionals," noted Reynolds.

Hiring a household manager to outsource the management responsibilities of an estate is similar to a growing company's founder hiring a chief operations officer to run the firm's operations. As multimillion-dollar companies have objectives and budgets to manage, so do households. Therefore, a household manager, who is tasked with keeping a close eye on the balance sheet and the estate's expenses, requires higher skill sets than typical household employees. For a maximum return on investment, an effectively run estate—whether a small, 5,000 square foot estate or a large, 60,000 square foot estate—benefits from a well-managed program featuring detailed policy and procedure manuals for all aspects of the estate and its operations.—*Guy*

ment) in most states, an employer will generally take disciplinary actions before dismissing an employee. Such discipline can be implemented in progressively more serious actions, such as a verbal warning followed by a written warning, then counseling, probation, suspension and finally termination. By employing a progressive disciplinary practice, an employer can demonstrate that the employee knew about the problems and, for whatever reason, did not improve the situation. In the employee handbook, detail the disciplinary policy but state that employees may be fired at will. Ensure, too, that all employee actions will not be spun through the progressive process; a serious infraction of household policy and serious misdeed will result in immediate dismissal. For household employers, if an employee proves untrustworthy and instills fear that harm will be done to a household member, a co-worker or employer property, by all means, remove the employee from the workplace *immediately*. In the employee handbook, state that the employer will decide which situation warrants what type of disciplinary action. (See offer letter Appendix on p00 for a sample statement explaining at-will employment.)

FIRST DAYS

The employee needs to become acquainted with the household. According to *Mrs. Starkey's Setting Household Standards, the Key to Successful Service for Employers and Household Managers* (©1997), "the service flow of your home affects all your household employees, whether they arrive weekly to clean or daily to perform estate management activities." Whoever is employed, it is beneficial to outline the service standards that could relate to childcare, cleaning, clothing, security and so forth. According to Starkey, some questions an employer may want to address include the following:

- What is the desired result?
- How do you want the given tasks to be accomplished?
- Is there a right time of day to complete each task?
- Do you know how often the task needs to be performed each day, week or month to meet your standard?

Each employer should ask himself or herself how each standard has been accomplished in the past and whether any changes need to be established for the future. It is also wise to identify any valuable objects (such as artwork, a particular car, etc.) that an employer prefers the employee leave undisturbed.

A welcome practice is for the employer and employee to spend the first days of employment together for training. The employer can show the employee where things are, review household procedures, give his or her preferences for the household (i.e., keep all bedroom doors closed, or put all notes and messages on a dry-erase board affixed to the refrigerator), demonstrate how to operate household equipment, review work and safety procedures, etc. It also is an opportunity for both to get to know each other, to treat one another with respect and professionalism, and begin to establish trust. During the first few weeks of employment, an employer may check in by telephoning and stopping home unexpectedly to ensure that all is well.

Schedule a meeting for one week after the start date for a discussion on: how the job is going, issues that have arisen or may arise, questions that need to be answered and so forth. This will help ensure that any uncertainty is resolved and will establish the relationship with open and clear communication. An employer's efforts to be available to employees for reviews and discussions of the job, expectations, work environment, and the like, will go a long way to foster a respectful and trusting relationship.

Various training materials are available to household employees. For example, many agencies provide educational materials to parents and caregivers. Parents in a Pinch, a Massachusetts-based agency, offers its clients and nannies a CD-ROM on basic childcare training, including health, safety and developmental topics.

PERSONNEL PRACTICE CHECKLIST

✓ Note that while household employment is largely a customized situation often it is handled as an informal situation. In fact, it is a professional endeavor requiring HR and personnel practices and policies.

✓ Write and update job descriptions.

✓ Establish household policies and procedures.

✓ Develop and maintain an employee handbook detailing all policies: work schedule, performance reviews, dismissal, severance, references and so on.

✓ Provide an orientation during the first few days of employment with on-the-job training for the household employee.

For more information, go to www.gtm.com/resourcecenter

Notes

Chapter 5

Planning and Scheduling Wages and Hours

Wage and hour concerns are complicated; therefore, they create a lot of uncertainty within households that employ help.

Through the job description and work agreement, wages and hours should be clearly defined and agreed upon by both employer and employee. To even begin the interviewing process, employers should define a specific work schedule for the employee, as well as a policy for when work is required and/or performed beyond the specified regular workday. In addition, before beginning employment, wages should be negotiated and agreed upon, and pay schedules should be clearly established. But there is much more involved with wages and hours—the law. Employers must be aware of their legal requirements on federal, state and local levels in order to lawfully hire and employ a household employee.

So, why is there uncertainty? Well, there are many laws, as well as misinformation and antidotal recommendations from friends and advisors who are not experts in household employment. In wage and hour issues, the problem exists of not knowing what the requirements are—and there is much to know and manage. This chapter will discuss why employers must pay an employee according to the law and provide information on how to properly plan for and manage wages and hours. With the following information, employers will be more informed—and more comfortable—with wage and hour legal requirements.

THE FLSA

The US Fair Labor Standards Act (FLSA) establishes minimum wage, overtime pay, record keeping and child labor laws affecting full- and part-time workers. Under FLSA's individual coverage provision, domestic service workers—housekeepers, nannies, cooks, chauffeurs, etc. are covered if: their cash wages from one employer are at least $1,000 per calendar year; or, if they work a total of more than eight hours a week for one or more employers.

According to the US Department of Labor (DOL), the FLSA requires employers to pay the more than 80 million covered employees at least the minimum wage (presently [2004] set by the federal government at $5.15 per hour) and overtime pay of one and one-half times

Case Study

Annie Davis
Owner/operator
Annie's Nannies, Inc.
Seattle, WA
GTM Partner Agency

Annie's Nannies, Inc., a nanny referral agency based in Seattle, places nannies throughout Washington state. Most nannies, who are predominantly viewed as salaried employees, work 40 to 50 hours per week, said owner Annie Davis. Yet, overtime pay still applies to domestic workers, who are live-out.

One nanny who Davis placed cared for a child for four years. At the job's outset, both nanny and employers agreed on hours and salary. After four years, however, the nanny decided to end the relationship because she was working longer hours than previously agreed upon. Additionally, during the entire four years of employment the nanny was not furnished with a meal while on duty. She submitted one month's notice. The nanny and the child's father argued, and the father asked the nanny not to return to work.

The family blocked the nanny's unemployment insurance claim. The nanny, upset with being out of one month's salary and with being denied unemployment insurance, contacted her attorney, with whom she had previously worked to gain US citizenship.

The nanny took the family to court to obtain unemployment benefits. The family failed to attend the court proceedings, and the judge ruled in favor of the nanny to access unemployment. The judge, reviewing the nanny's hours worked, informed the nanny that she was entitled to overtime pay for the period she worked. The nanny then sued the family for all of the overtime pay she was entitled to during her four years of employment. According to Davis, the case was settled out of court for $15,000, and the nanny likely would have been awarded more money if her suit went through the court process.

It's an expensive lesson to learn. "My guess is most families do not abide by the overtime laws for domestic employees, and, in fact, most do not even know domestic employees are covered by law," said Davis. "As an agency, you have to educate families on everything. Families need to know their legal requirements, including tax and payroll requirements."

Prior to hiring an employee it's very important for any household employer to understand his or her obligations as an employer and which laws apply to the household. Generally, employers don't look to take advantage of their help but often feel "cheated" when matters that adversely affect their financial expectations arise—whether the matter entails tax obligations, misunderstanding gross wages vs. net wages or assuming overtime rules doesn't apply to them.—*Guy*

the employee's regular pay rate. (See Table 5.1 on p. 63 for minimum wage rates per state.) Overtime pay must be paid for work over 40 hours per week—with some exceptions. (See box below on what the FLSA does not require). Overtime wages (as required by FLSA) are due on the regular payday for the pay period covered. FLSA exempts overtime pay for live-in domestic workers. However, household employers with live-out staff must comply with the FLSA labor law.

FLSA record keeping

According to the law, employers are required to keep records on wages, hours and other items as specified by DOL record keeping regulations. Records to be kept for minimum wage and overtime pay include the following:

- personal information including employee's name, home address, occupation, sex and birth date if under age 19
- hour and day workweek begins
- total hours worked each workday and each workweek
- total daily or weekly straight time earnings
- regular hourly pay rate for any week when overtime is worked
- total overtime pay for the workweek
- deductions from or additions to wages
- total wages paid each pay period
- date of payment and pay period covered

Employers subject to FLSA's minimum wage requirements must post (and keep posted) in the workplace the federal minimum wage rate. Posters can be easily downloaded at www.dol.gov or obtained at state labor departments.

For more on FLSA, go to www.dol.gov or call the wage-hour toll-free information and helpline at 1.866.4USWAGE (1.866.487.9243).

FLSA does not require[*] *(but please be advised that some local laws may require)*

- vacation, holiday, severance or sick pay
- meal or rest periods, holidays off or vacations
- premium pay for weekend or holiday work
- pay raises or fringe benefits
- discharge notice, reason for discharge or immediate payment of final wages to terminated employees
- overtime for persons employed as companions to the elderly or infirm

Source: US Department of Labor's "Handy Reference Guide to the Fair Labor Standards Act".

In addition, many states set minimum wage and overtime pay laws. So, employers need to ensure they comply with the laws set in their locality. See p. 63 for minimum wage state rates. State labor departments can provide more information to employers on state and local requirements.

Figure 5.1
Information Source Regarding Appropriate Nanny Salary and Benefits
Source: GTM 2003 Nanny Employer Survey

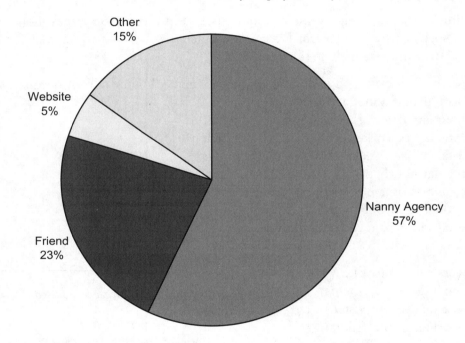

SALARIES AND MINIMUM WAGE

Salaries vary greatly in the household employment industry—just as positions and work-places differ. The household position is often customized to meet the needs of one particular household; therefore, salaries reflect that. No standard salaries exist within the household employment industry other than federal minimum wage requirements. Presently, in 2004, the minimum wage in the United States is $5.15 per hour, unless the state in which the household employee works mandates it to be higher. (The US Congress has been considering raising the minimum wage. To ensure that you know the current minimum wage rate, go to www.dol.gov.)

Case Study

Judi Merlin
President
Kim Cino
Placement Director
A Friend of the Family
Smyrna, GA
GTM Partner Agency

In its 20th year of service, the agency places childcare and eldercare workers in Atlanta, GA, sees a trend in the industry: caregivers are raising their salary requirements even after the 2001 economic downturn experienced throughout Atlanta.

"Some caregivers have not made accommodations regarding the present economic conditions and are not skilled in making cost-of-living adjustments," said Judi Merlin, president, of the agency. "The caregiver salary is [generally] in a very good range, but we see cases where the caregiver inflates his or her worth for no other reason than he or she wants to. As an agency, we spend a lot of time educating those clients and caregivers [on how] to meet in the middle."

The agency invests a lot of time educating clients on fair compensation at time of hire and as the relationship progresses. In fact, the agency's staff will check in with recent placements about every four months to ensure fair wages are being paid for the number of hours worked.

According to Kim Cino, the agency's placement director, a key aspect of the agency checking in with clients and household help several times a year is to determine if a new employer-employee contract needs to be re-drafted to reflect new circumstances and fair compensation. "We feel this will make for happier clients and nannies," she said.

Despite the trend of rising costs to employ in-home caregivers, Cino said many caregivers who have worked with families for a while—and older nannies unsure of their current market worth—are unfairly compensated. She said one reason for this is that the employers, who have worked with a particular nanny for several years, are unaware of the current market rate for childcare. A recent incident proves her point.

(continued)

A nanny took a position caring for a three-year-old child and doing light housekeeping. She worked a 52.5 hour workweek. Three years later, the mother remarried, and a father with two children was added to the household. Still working 52.5 hours per week, the nanny now had a significantly heavier workload. Although provided with a raise during her employment, the nanny was never compensated for the additional responsibilities.

The nanny spoke with her employers about a pay increase to reflect her new duties, but the employers stated they did not believe the nanny should receive a higher salary. At the nanny's second request for fair compensation for the workload, the employer and nanny agreed to keep the nanny's salary the same but to reduce her hours to 45.5 per workweek.

While the nanny is satisfied with the solution, Cino maintained that the nanny remains underpaid, largely because employers working with one employee for many years are not familiar with current compensation practices or other household employment services.

Ensuring that a household employee is fairly compensated is one of the keys to retaining a household employee. To combat the double threat of an employee feeling underpaid or being pursued by a recruiter, employers must make sure that their employees are paid for all hours worked, including overtime, and that their wages are in line with the market. A good way to assess the market value is to ask agencies and other employers, as well as to participate in annual industry salary surveys.—*Guy*

Wendy Sachs, president of The Philadelphia Nanny Network in Ardmore, PA, a GTM partner agency, said she believes that a nanny's salary and compensation package should reflect her or his background and experience. "The more experienced, educated nanny typically is paid in the higher salary range," she said. "As in any industry, an individual who brings more to the job by way of a broader and deeper experience will be compensated accordingly".

Ilo Milton, president of FamilyWise, Inc., in Bedford, NY, a GTM partner agency, said she has little to offer families that want to underpay employees. When it comes to household employee pay, Milton said she lives by the maxim "you get what you pay for. Our children are worth more," she said, "Salary is not a place to cut corners."

Janet Cook, owner of My Child's Best Friend in New York City, NY, another GTM partner agency, agreed. "An employer is paying for one-on-one time with his and/or her child,

Table 5.1: 2004 Minimum Wage Rates Per State

State	Rate [2004]	State	Rate [2004]
Federal	*$5.15*	*Federal*	*$5.15*
Alabama	$5.15	Montana	$5.15
Alaska	$7.15	Nebraska	$5.15
Arizona	$5.15	Nevada	$5.15
Arkansas	$5.15	New Hampshire	$5.15
California	$6.75	New Jersey	$5.15
Colorado	$5.15	New Mexico	$5.15
Connecticut	$7.10	New York*	$5.15
Delaware	$6.15	North Carolina	$5.15
District of Columbia	$6.15	North Dakota	$5.15
Florida	$5.15	Ohio	$4.25
Georgia	$5.15	Oklahoma	$5.15
Hawaii	$6.25	Oregon	$7.05
Idaho	$5.15	Pennsylvania	$5.15
Illinois	$5.50	Rhode Island	$6.75
Indiana	$5.15	South Carolina	$5.15
Iowa	$5.15	South Dakota	$5.15
Kansas	$2.65	Tennessee	$5.15
Kentucky	$5.15	Texas	$5.15
Louisiana	$5.15	Utah	$5.15
Maine	$6.25	Vermont	$6.75
Maryland	$5.15	Virginia	$5.15
Massachusetts	$6.75	Washington	$7.16
Michigan	$5.15	West Virginia	$5.15
Minnesota	$5.15	Wisconsin	$5.15
Mississippi	$5.15	Wyoming	$5.15
Missouri	$5.15		

* Current legislation is pending (as of April 2004) to increase the New York State minimum wage to $7.10 per hour.

Source: www.dol.gov.

with no downtime," she said. According to Cook, a client who wanted to employ a nanny for 40 hours for four workdays "flipped out" over the suggested salary range of $450 to $550 per week that nannies were being paid. "I told her, 'This is not your Mercedes Benz or Toyota Camry. You're trying to cut cost in the wrong place. You must think of it as an investment in your child's well-being'," said Cook.

THE FMLA

<table>
<tr><td colspan="1">

Ask Guy

Q. If I employ a household worker who is an immigrant—not a US citizen—must I pay US minimum wage?

A. Yes. Minimum wage, as well as federal and state labor laws, generally apply to domestic and household employees working in the United States or a US possession or territory, regardless of their citizenship or immigration status. (Please note: some household workers are exempt from certain FLSA requirements.) (See p. 57 for information on FLSA.) You should also ensure that the worker is eligible to legally work in the United States.

</td></tr>
</table>

The Family Medical Leave Act (FMLA) generally requires employers of 50 or more people to provide up to 12 weeks of unpaid, job-protected leave to eligible employees for the birth or adoption of a child or for the serious illness of a child or parent. While FMLA does not apply to the majority of household employers due to the stipulation of 50 or more employees, family medical leave, or a variation of it, is a valid consideration for employers to offer their domestic help.

Some states have family and medical leave acts, but most, like the federal law, apply to employers with at least several employees, generally not to a one-employee business. However, it is best to check on individual state and locality medical leave requirements. For instance:

- Employers in the following states and federal district are required to provide employees pregnancy, maternity or adoption leave; Iowa, Maine and the District of Columbia.
- California's Paid Family Leave (PFL) program, effective in 2004, extends benefits to cover employees who take time off from work to care for a seriously ill child, spouse or partner, or to bond with a new child. Funded through State Disability Insurance (SDI), California's PFL is available to any employee, as long as the employee contributes to the SDI program. For more on California's PFL program, go to www.dfeh.ca.gov; and,
- Hawaii's Family Leave Law, enacted two years before the FMLA, requires private sector employers with 100 or more employees to allow an employee who has not worked not fewer than six consecutive months for the employer from whom family leave benefits are sought to be allowed up to four weeks of unpaid leave per year to care for a new baby or sick family member.

Case Study

Lin Taylor-Pleiman
President/Manager
American Domestic Agency, Inc.
Whiteford, MD
GTM Partner Agency

As an owner/operator of the agency Lin Taylor-Pleiman places workers with many household employees who she said come to her agency because she requires clients to submit a signed work agreement covering all aspects of work hours and wages.

One nanny came to the agency after working without a work agreement. She had been caring for three children, one with significant behavioral and emotional problems. The nanny accepted a request to travel with the family on vacation, but when she asked her employer about payment for the vacation work, the employer angrily told her that the trip was on hold. "The family, it turns out, thought room, board and air were compensation enough," said Taylor-Pleiman.

From that point on, the relationship deteriorated. According to Taylor-Pleiman, the nanny received nastily worded notes daily and endured constant complaints and nit-picking. The family hired its former nanny to care for the children during the trip and did not pay the current nanny for the days they were away.

After six months, the nanny left the position without having a chance to say goodbye to the children, with whom she established a good relationship.

Household employers must remember that their vacation time is not their household help's vacation also. The employee traveling with the family and performing work responsibilities should be paid accordingly. Many times, employers view family vacations as a perk for the employee, whereas the employee views it as a continuation of his or her employment responsibilities, which is, of course, exactly what it is.—*Guy*

Case Study

Susan Tokayer
Owner/operator
Family Helpers
Dobbs Ferry, NY
GTM Partner Agency

Susan Tokayer, owner, of a household employment referral agency in Dobbs Ferry, NY, said she has seldom seen nannies use sick time. Despite this, Tokayer experienced one incident regarding a nanny's sick time.

A nanny was out sick nine times during the four months that she was employed. The family thought this was excessive. While a completed work agreement listed sick days "as needed", no concrete number of paid sick days were specified. Therefore, neither the nanny nor the family clearly understood what sick time compensation would be provided.

According to Tokayer, this occurrence demonstrates the need to be explicit in all areas of the work agreement. "Sometimes clients don't get detailed enough, even though we supply a work agreement," she said. "People don't see down the line that it could be a problem. Instead of writing 'sick time as needed', put four days down on the work agreement. Then, depending on circumstances, be open to compensation after those four days are used." Tokayer said household employees generally have three to six sick days (or sick/personal days) to use during an employment year.

According to Tokayer, household employers, particularly those new to household employment, want to start off the relationship congenially—so they do so delicately. "People say the work agreement seems too hard line, too firm," she said. "This relationship is unique. It's a work relationship, but it's an intimate, friendly relationship. Families don't want to come across as too intense or too formal. But, if the work agreement isn't completed thoroughly, something could be misconstrued, or there could be a problem down the line."

Tokayer said her clientele is educated, affluent and knowledgeable about the household employment industry. Outside of help with a newborn or child, clients most likely have not had household help before. Yet, Tokayer still has advice for all potential household employers—and that is, know yourself. "Be honest," she said. "Know who you are, what your family needs and present that honestly. Then, pay well . . . No matter how hard the job is, if the nanny is well compensated, she will stay forever."

(*continued*)

Although not required by law, an employee benefit of sick or personal paid time is standard in the corporate workplace and should be considered in the house. Many household employers shy away from hiring temporary help when a household employee is off work, and it is often detrimental if a household employer misses work him- or herself to cover for his or her household help. This is why household employers must and do take great pains to stress the importance of reliability to their household help.

Household employers should consider implementing a sick and personal day policy that distinguishes between sick and personal days and a plan that accrues available hours each pay period, up to a maximum allotted amount over a one-year period. It's then important to also consider allowing employees to borrow (or not borrow) against time yet to be accrued. Ultimately, a good policy benefits all, and a well-documented policy safeguards against most eventualities. A policy that allots time-off hours to those employees who did not miss a workday the previous month may not work; if an employee is contagiously ill, no one wants him or her on the worksite, exposing others to the illness. So, employers need to establish a policy that protects everyone within the household and that covers all circumstances.—*Guy*

TIME-OFF PAYMENTS

Time-off payments for sick, personal or vacation days should be agreed upon by the employer and employee prior to hiring and written in the household employment work agreement and employment handbook. Be certain to specify if time off may be taken in full and half day amounts and when a doctor's note regarding sick time will be required.

Employers are typically mandated to provide time off for voting, jury duty and military/National Guard training and/or active service.

DEBTS OWED BY EMPLOYEE TO EMPLOYER

Information about whether an employee may borrow money against future wages from the employer should be provided to the employee (and included in the employee handbook). If such activity is permissible, then the employer should detail what needs to occur to necessitate an employer loan to the employee, what process an employee needs to follow to request an employer loan and what steps will be taken to obtain payment of the loan. When considering granting a loan, the employer should take into account the length of time that is considered reasonable for the employee to repay the loan.

Employers should obtain a signed "I owe you" promissory note from the employee for any significant amount of money loaned (say, $25 or more). This note should include:

- date of loan
- loan amount
- payment method (i.e., loan payments taken directly from paychecks)
- payment schedule
- the employee's and the employer's signatures

The promissory note should be filed in the employee's personnel file, and a photocopy of the note should be provided to the employee.

GARNISHMENT

The federal Wage Garnishment Law limits the amount that may be legally garnished (withdrawn for payment to another, per legal direction, such as an ex-spouse for childcare payments) from an individual's income and protects an employee whose pay is garnished for payment of single a debt from being fired. For the most part, these amounts cannot be more than 25 percent of an employee's gross wages. Specific guidelines will be listed on formal garnishment orders.

OVERTIME

According to the US Labor Department, FLSA requires employers to pay overtime pay of one and one-half times the regular pay rate. Overtime pay must be paid for work over 40 hours per week—with some exceptions (see p. 59 on FLSA), including live-in employees.

In most circumstances, the federal Fair Labor Standards Act (FLSA) requires employers to pay covered live-out employees at least the minimum wage, as well as overtime pay at one and one-half times the regular pay rate for hours worked beyond 40 in a week. (See overtime information on wages and hours on p 57.) Live-in employees are not subject to overtime regulations however state and local laws for overtime vary and may supersede the federal FLSA.

In addition, domestic service workers employed to provide babysitting services on a casual basis, or to provide companionship services for those who cannot care for themselves because of age or infirmity, are exempt from the FLSA's minimum wage and overtime requirements, whether or not they reside in the household where they are employed. Finally, it is important to note that some states impose their own requirements, which may differ from federal law.

California Wage Order 15

Under the California IWC Wage Order 15, household employees who qualify as personal attendants, such as most nannies or eldercare providers, are exempt from the state's overtime requirements, but not the FLSA's minimum wage requirements. However, other household employees who do not qualify as personal attendants, such as most butlers, cooks, gardeners, maids, etc., are subject to the state's overtime requirements, as well as the FLSA's minimum wage requirements.

To be clear and help avoid overtime issues, an employer and employee should discuss overtime while developing the work agreement. Specify what the overtime rate is and when it will occur, as well as whether overtime will be paid on holidays (and, if so, which holidays).

For help with overtime calculations, go to GTM's overtime calculator at www.gtm.com/resourcecenter.

GTM's online resources center offers valuable employer information and tools, including a tax calculator to help employers determine an employee's overtime pay rate.

Figure 5.2
Tax Calculator—Overtime Rates

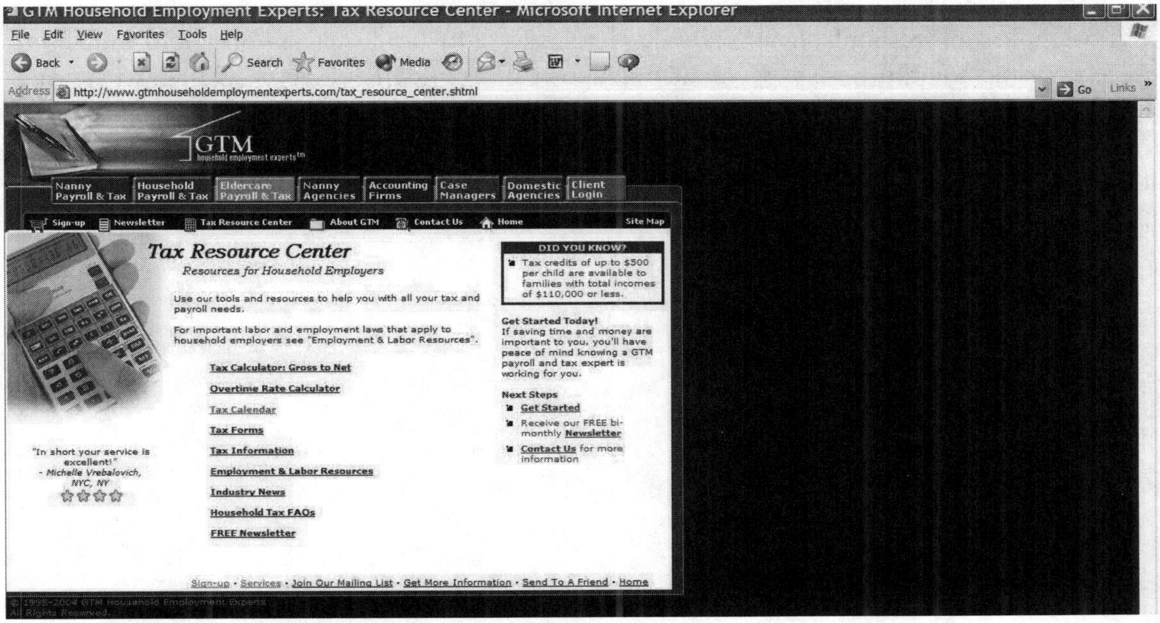

COMPENSATION DURING TRAVEL AND OFFSITE EVENTS

Before an employer hires an employee, the employee's compensation must be detailed fully, including vacation, mileage reimbursement, paid auto insurance, etc. It is important to spell out what compensation a household employee will be paid when he or she travels with the family or when he or she attends an offsite event as part of the workday.

Employees using their own cars for work tasks and work-related events should be reimbursed for mileage. The federal mileage reimbursement rate for 2004 is 37.5 cents per mile. It is useful to include a copy of an expense report, which includes a section on mileage in the employee handbook. (See Appendix 11 for a sample of an expense report form.)

BREAKING DOWN THE PAYCHECK

Employers should always pay employees by check, so both parties have a record of the payment. Checks need to be net—total wages after all taxes and benefit option payments are withheld. Even if an employer directly deposits paychecks per employees' request, a payment record or voucher should be supplied to the employee and kept on file for the employer to access if needed. (See p. 72, for a sample paycheck and payroll earnings statement.)

TAXES

Every employer is responsible for several federal, state and local taxes. A household employer is responsible for the timely payment or deposit of employment taxes withheld from an employee, his or her matching share of Social Security, Medicare (the Social Security and Medicare taxes are combined into what is known as FICA, the Federal Insurance Contribution Act) and all FUTA (Federal Unemployment Tax Act) taxes. (See payroll and taxes on p. 91.)

Table 5.2: Recommended Pay Stub information

Information an employer should include on an employee's pay stub include the following:

- employer name and address
- employee name
- pay period start and end dates
- check date
- check number
- current payroll information
  - gross earnings
  - total deductions
    - federal
    - old Age Survivors Disability Insurance (OASDI) (i.e., Social Security)
    - Medicare
    - state withholding
    - local tax withholding
  - net pay
- year-to-date payroll information
  - gross earnings
  - total deductions
    - federal
    - old Age Survivors Disability Insurance (OASDI) (i.e., Social Security)
    - Medicare
    - state withholding
    - local tax withholding
- sick/vacation time accruals
- withholding allowances (according to withholding status)
- health reimbursement account

Figure 5.3
Sample Paycheck and Payroll Earnings Statement

DO NOT ACCEPT THIS CHECK without confirming presence of Artificial Watermark on back. Other security features are listed on back.

Household Employer
123 Main Street
New York, NY 10028

Bank Name

Check Date 4/16/2004   Check Number 10006

Pay   *Nine Hundred Sixty Dollars and Twenty-Seven Cents* $******960.27

To the Order of: 0001 10006

Alice Nelson
123 Main Street
New York, NY 10028

Authorized Signature

⑈010006⑈ ⑆000000000⑆ 12345⑈

Alice Nelson   **Household Employer**

Company	Period Begin	Division
Household	4/3/2004	
Number	Period End	Branch
0001	4/16/2004	
Social Security #	Check Date	Department
123-45-6789	4/16/2004	
Hire Date	Check Number	Team
1/1/2004	10006	

Personal 24.00-2.00=22.00 HOURS
Sick 7.00-0.50=6.50 HOURS
Vacation 35.00-10.00=25.00 HOURS

Earnings						Deductions		
Description	Location / Job	Rate	Hours	Current	Year To Date	Description	Current	Year To Date
Salary					1100.00	Fed (S/1) (2392.00)	158.38	269.15
Hourly Rate 1		12.00	80.00	960.00	960.00	OASDI (2492.00)	86.30	154.50
Overtime Rate1		18.00	24.00	432.00	432.00	Medicare (2492.00)	20.18	36.13
Milege Reimb		12.00	0.00	13.44	26.88	NY (S /1) (2392.00)	55.65	91.54
MEMOS						New York City Res.(2418.88)	34.66	58.19
HRA			0.00	25.00	50.00	Life Insurance	10.00	20.00
						Health Insurance	30.00	60.00
						Simple IRA	50.00	100.00
Total Earnings			104.00	1405.44	2518.88	Total Deductions	445.17	789.51
NET PAY			960.27	Total Direct Deposits	0.00	Check Amount	960.27	1729.37

Case Study

Leann Brambach
Owner/Operator
Home Details, Inc.
Seattle, WA
GTM Partner Agency

Leann Brambach owns Home Details, Inc. (HDI), an agency that places household employees in positions throughout Seattle. Citing an example of one HDI nanny placement, Brambach said, "Both nannies and clients need to be educated from the get-go about their tax obligations and gross vs. net."

Brambach placed a woman in a position as a part-time nanny and household assistant for $13 per hour. The employee asked her employer to raise her salary to $15 per hour after learning that the job was more work than anticipated and after comparing salaries with other nannies. The employer agreed and asked Brambach to update the work agreement. In updating the work agreement, another issue became apparent—both the nanny and the employer thought that the other was paying income tax on the nanny's salary. In the end, the employment failed. The employer was willing to pay $15 per hour gross, which equaled approximately $12 per hour net. The nanny resigned, believing that she was misled.

"This was one big misunderstanding that left both parties feeling frustrated, and trust was broken," said Brambach.

Household employers can opt to not withhold federal and state income taxes from their employee's pay, placing the burden on the employee to make estimated tax payments throughout the year. The rule is that both parties must agree that the employer will withhold these taxes; otherwise, the employee is responsible. When an employee submits a completed W-4 form to the employer and the employer accepts it, the responsibility of withholding is then placed upon the employer. Withholding is commonly done through payroll deduction. Because this practice is so widespread, an employer who is unwilling to accept the responsibility must clearly spell out in the work agreement his or her stance, as well as notify the employee in person. If it is not, great friction can easily build to a breaking point in the employer-employee relationship—especially since employees frequently misunderstand the calculation and payment of their own income taxes.—*Guy*

Denise Shade, senior vice president of Key Bank's foreign exchange unit and mother of two, could easily be considered a financial whiz. Yet, despite her obvious executive-level financial affinity, Shade uses GTM's services for her nanny taxes and payroll.

"We first did our taxes and payroll on our own," said Shade, "because we really wanted to understand it. But, it is incredibly time consuming on a weekly basis."

Along with the standard time required to attend to payroll and taxes, Shade said that twice issues arose with the IRS causing payments to be tracked. While Shade was able to submit to the IRS proof of payments, she explained that the time required for this is particularly lengthy. Noting that such issues arise from time to time, she added that GTM's services were helpful in saving her from what could be stressful and painstaking record searches.

There are many considerations. For example, household employers need to only deduct the employee's share of Social Security and Medicare taxes and not the employer's portion. Doing so would be doubling Social Security and Medicare deductions.

Dependent Childcare Assistance Program (DCAP)—A Tax-saving Tip for Household Employers

A major concern for families today is how to provide dependent care for family members while family providers are at work. Companies may deduct expenses from an Employees salary to assist the employee with their dependent care obligations. The dependent care tax credit also helps families with lower household incomes.

Household employers can access DCAP information at their company's human resources department. DCAP may allow up to $5,000 in pre-taxed earnings per year to be set aside for childcare and/or eldercare. This is especially important if the family has undergone a "change of life experience" (i.e., the birth of a new baby) that might affect its eligibility for the program.

There are specific DCAP open enrollment periods during which to apply. A household employer can learn more through his or her company's HR department.

Table 5.3: Benefits of Paying an Employee Correctly

Employer benefits	Employee benefits
• It's the law. Federal and state law mandate that each time a taxpayer signs his or her Federal 1040 US Individual Income Tax Return, he or she is answering the household tax question. Anything reported that is less than actual amounts is tax evasion.	• It's the law.
	• Employees have a legal employment history to refer to when applying for future jobs, mortgages, loans, credit, etc.
• Peace of mind that employers are practicing good human resources and are legally operating a business.	• Employees are covered by Social Security, Medicare, unemployment and workers' compensation insurances (if applicable) benefits via payroll taxes.
• An employer saves money, as steep fines (and interest) and even jail time is paid by employers not paying above board.	• Employees may qualify for an Earned Income Credit, which enables them to, in some instances, claim more money from the government than their payroll taxes if their payroll taxes were calculated without the credit. An advantage is an even distribution of money in employees' paychecks throughout the year rather than having to wait for this payout amount until the end of the tax year.
• By paying payroll taxes, employers in most states are protecting themselves by paying into the workers' compensation insurance fund, which will help them cover expenses in the event that an employee is injured while working.	
• Employers may be eligible for federal assistance programs, such as the Earned Income Credit Program, Childcare Tax Credit and the Dependent Care Assistance Program (DCAP).	• Employees are eligible for Social Security credits for retirement, disability and death.
• Employees who know they are legally on the books feel more secure in their employment relationship, and the employer benefits by having a happy and secure employee.	

PLANNING AND SCHEDULING WAGES AND HOURS CHECKLIST

✓ Abide by all laws—local, state and federal.

✓ Check your state's minimum wage laws as some state and local minimum wage laws supersede the present federal minimum wage of $5.15 per hour (2004).

✓ Clearly communicate during pre-employment discussions whether wages are gross or net.

✓ Clearly identify whether the employer or employee will pay income tax from wages.

For up-to-date information, go to www.gtm.com/resourcecenter

Notes

Chapter 6

Employee Benefits to Help *Retain* the Best

While providing employee benefits is largely optional and seldom required by law, employee benefits greatly help the household employer *attract* and *retain* high-level employees. To get and keep the most talented employees, employers must treat employees like professionals. Therefore, offering employee benefits is an important consideration for all household employers. By providing an attractive employee benefits package, the employer is helping to maintain a satisfied workforce. Satisfied employees equal a happy workplace, which in turn equals a happy family and life for the employer.

Health insurance and other employee benefits covered in this chapter are instrumental in recruiting and retaining talented employees. It is prudent for an employer to take the time needed to secure a valuable employee benefits package by reviewing with his or her employee what benefits he or she requires.

MEDICAL INSURANCE COVERAGE

Health insurance is often the first benefit requested by any employee and one that is increasingly popular for household employers to provide. While health care is a benefit provided by most employers in the United States, the household employment industry has been slow to provide household help with medical benefits and health care insurance/coverage, although this is increasing. Health care insurance coverage is a priority for many workers, including those in household employment, because of the high cost of coverage and medical fees. The cost can be high for the employer as well—especially since most household employers have only one employee or just a few employees. However, various options are now on the market that make coverage more affordable than ever before.

Today, an employer's' choice to provide health care coverage as an employee benefit remains optional, except for employers in the state of Hawaii, which mandates that all employees achieving a specific monthly income must be covered. (Hawaii mandates that every employer paying a regular employee monthly wage amounting to at least 86.67 times the minimum hourly wage [see p. 63] must provide that employee with coverage by a pre-

Figure 6.1
Nannies: How do you learn about the benefits you should ask for?

Source: GTM Nanny Employment Survey, 2003

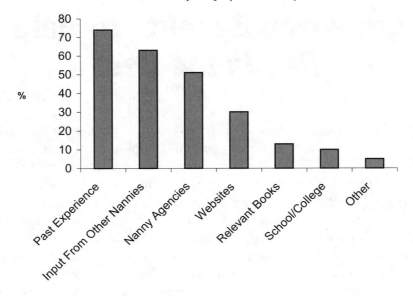

paid group health care plan. Since 2003, Hawaii has mandated that minimum wage be set at $6.25 per hour. Therefore, the employee earning a minimum of $541.69 [86.67 × $6.25] a month is eligible for health care coverage.)

Employers may offer employees certain types of health plans. The four most popular are described below:

1) Health Maintenance Organization (HMO)—a member-based organization that provides health care at affordable costs and, in general, emphasizes preventive care.

2) Closed Panel HMO—HMOs that own their own facilities or clinics and employ the medical staff who work in them.

3) Preferred Provider Organization (PPO)—much like HMOs in their operation, PPOs formed as a way to control managed care and health care costs. PPOs are groups of medical professionals and hospitals that may be controlled independently or by insurance companies. Unlike HMOs, in PPOs, doctors are not employed by the PPO, and facilities or clinics are not owned by the PPO. Another PPO advantage is that there are no referral requirements. A member can see any doctor he or she chooses at any time. A member may use doctors who are part of the PPO network, or not. However, using a PPO-member doctor, provider and/or facility usually offers financial incentives.

4) Major Medical—a health insurance policy with high deductibles to cover most serious health problems and conditions, up to a specific limit or reimbursement maximum. Although most major medical policies contain lifetime limits of $1 million or more, meeting the lifetime limit usually is not an issue. Major Medical policies are indemnity type policies in which the insurer covers most medical services with a significant cost-sharing element for the employee.

Figure 6.2
Benefits Offered to Nannies
Source: GTM 2003 Nanny Employer Survey

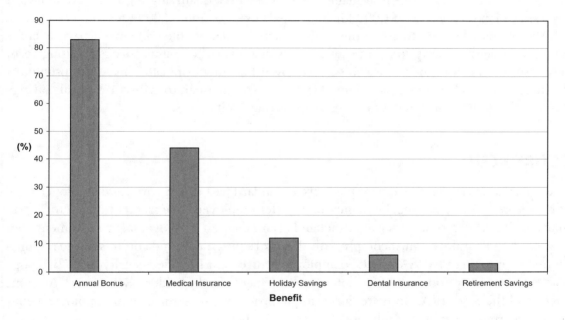

HRA

A Health Reimbursement Account (HRA) is a creative option available to the household employer regardless of budgets who wants to offer a contribution program for health-related expenses as an employee benefit. Growing in popularity, HRA is an employer-sponsored plan that reimburses an employee for eligible medical care expenses, as defined by the IRS. The employer funds a pre-determined amount of money for each eligible employee. Monies in the account are not subject to employment taxes. HRAs allow employees and employers to take advantage of the lower premiums offered by high-deductible major medical plans and help keep healthcare costs under control. The HRA advantage is that monies can roll over each year. Therefore, an employer does not lose a contribution if an employee does not use up the account in any given year. HRAs mandate an employee-employer relationship, so independent contractors paid by a Form 1099 are not eligible. For more information on setting up an HRA, go to www.gtm.com/health_options.

HSA

A Health Savings Account (HSA) is a tax-exempt trust or custodial account established exclusively to pay for qualified medical expenses, and it can be contributed to by an employer and/or an employee. A HSA is available to anyone with a qualifying high deductible health insurance plan (i.e., at least $1,000 for individual coverage and $2,000 for family coverage). HSA funds may be used to cover the health insurance deductible and any co-payments for medical services, prescriptions or products, as well as over-the-counter drugs and long-term care insurance. HSA funds may also be used toward payment of health insurance premiums during any period of unemployment. HSAs are very similar to MSAs (Medical Savings Accounts), but without many of the restrictions that limit MSAs.

RETIREMENT

Like medical coverage, retirement plans are a standard part of US corporate employee benefit packages. While not legally mandated to offer employees a retirement plan, employers may consider doing so in order to attract and retain the best employees. If a retirement plan is offered, the employer must comply with IRS tax requirements and administrative requirements as set forth in ERISA (the US Employee Retirement Income Security Act). Two popular retirement options for household employees are the Individual Retirement Account (IRA) and the Roth IRA. Both are fairly simple programs to establish as an employee benefit and, therefore, suitable as a household employee benefit.

An IRA is a special savings plan authorized by the federal government to help people accumulate funds for retirement. Traditional IRAs and Roth IRAs allow individual taxpayers to contribute 100 percent of their earnings up to the IRA's plan specified maximum dollar amount. Each year, the IRS sets maximum annual contributions for IRAs, with "catch up" contributions for people aged 50 and over. For 2004, maximum contributions are $3,000, with an additional "catch up" of $500 for those aged 50 or older. (See Table 6.1 for maximum contributions)

Traditional IRA contributions may be tax deductible, whereas Roth IRA contributions are not. Roth IRA principal and interest accumulate tax free. A Roth IRA usually is preferred by those ineligible for the tax deductions associated with the traditional IRA or those who want their qualified Roth IRA distributions to be tax and penalty free, which depends on all conditions being met. Some people prefer a Roth IRA as a means to simply build a retirement egg without the worry of paying taxes at a later date; Roth contributions have already been taxed.

Table 6.1: Maximum IRA contributions

Year	Maximum contribution	Additional catch up amount for those over age 50
2004	$3,000	$500
2005	$4,000	$500
2006	$4,000	$1,000
2007	$4,000	$1,000
2008	$5,000	$1,000

Pertains to both traditional and Roth IRAs.

Figure 6.3
Most Popular Employee Benefits
Source: GTM 2003 Nanny Survey

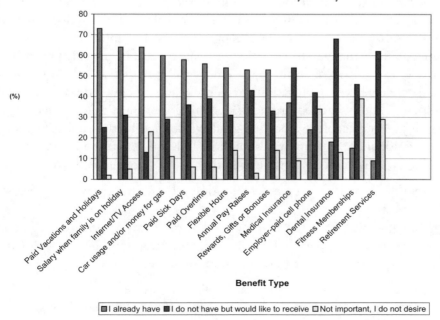

Benefit Type

■ I already have ■ I do not have but would like to receive □ Not important, I do not desire

LIFE INSURANCE

Some employers offer their employees life insurance coverage. The main purpose of life insurance is to provide a death benefit to the employee's dependents or beneficiaries to help replace lost income and protect against the financial losses that could occur from the insured's untimely death.

Generally, there are two types of life insurance: term and permanent (whole). Term insurance pays a death benefit to beneficiaries if the insured dies during the term the policy exists. Permanent life insurance generally is designed to provide long-term life insurance coverage for the insured's entire life—up to 100 years old. It has two components: 1. the death benefit, and 2. a cash accumulation benefit which differentiates it from term insurance.

The coverage may vary, but commonly it covers either: one full year of an employee's salary (up to a specified limit); or, double an employee's salary (up to a specified limit). A policy with a death benefit up to $50,000 is tax deductible to the employer. This helps protect the policy's designated beneficiary in the event of an employee's death. Life insurance coverage is not mandated by law, but it is a desirable employee benefit offered by an employer.

EDUCATIONAL ASSISTANCE

Another common employer benefit for employees is educational assistance for education or training pursued outside of working hours. Although optional for an employer to offer, educational assistance is beneficial in providing a satisfying workplace. The employer may tailor the assistance to best suit him or her. Guidelines provided in the employee handbook may include: educational pursuits that will be covered (i.e., classes must be provided by an accredited educational organization and/or relate to the employee's occupation); the limit available for educational assistance per year; educational expenses that are covered (i.e., tuition only, tuition and books, etc.); and, what requirements the employee must meet to receive assistance (i.e., the employee must achieve a passing grade as defined by the educational organization). With these guidelines, an employer should include information on the process the employee must follow for assistance. Consider whether the employee needs to:

- provide the employer with a course description and a written request for assistance prior to the class start
- obtain a signed approval from the employer prior to class start in order to be reimbursed for expenses, (see Appendix 19 for a sample tuition reimbursement form.)
- achieve a specific grade or higher to obtain reimbursement

Be precise to ensure that the employee understands what is required.

Also, employers may consider paying for professional membership fees, industry conferences or trade journal subscriptions.

Case Study

Mary Starkey
Founder, Owner
Starkey International Institute for Household Management
Denver, CO
A GTM Partner

Mary Starkey opened the first household service management educational institute in the United States and has mentored the household employment professionals for more than 24 years.

"Private service is experiencing an awakening and renaissance into the professional world," said Starkey. "With a new paradigm for private service in hand, certified household management graduates are bringing standards and professionalism to the American household employment industry."

Starkey noted that service management education for employers and staff is taking household service out of a crisis mode of operation into a defined process of identifying service expectations and performing accepted service etiquette practices. Household service management education guides employers to articulate overall household standards and to identify individual needs. She suggested that employers utilize Starkey's service management tool the *Day in the Life.* Employers plan and communicate with staff their expected daily activities, slotting them into a time-oriented weekly schedule. Then, the employers carry them out for a week or two. Next, the employers review their weekly plan to determine whether expectations were met and whether the tasks are functional and feasible for the family and the home.

"Private service has become a recognized and well-paid career path," she said. "Now, service professionals must focus on educating themselves and growing our industry in professional standards, state-of-the-art practices and industry ethics."

> Continuing education, training, seminars and conferences play an important role in corporate employment. This education, as well as Internet learning events that educate employees, are important in promoting professional growth and elevating employee performance-making the educational benefit a win-win proposition for both the employer and employee. It's important for a household employer to decide whether access to education is an important employee benefit and, if so, at what frequency.—*Guy*

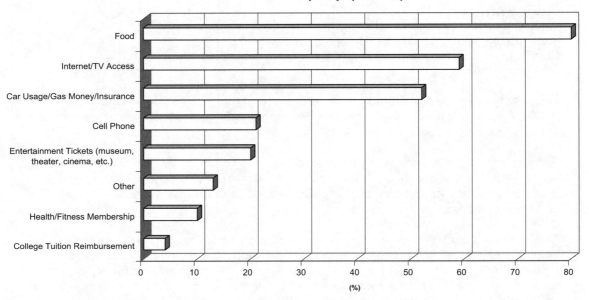

Figure 6.4
Job Perks Offered to Nannies
Source: GTM 2003 Nanny Employer Survey

FLEXIBLE WORK HOURS

Flexible work hours—an often overlooked employee benefit—enable an employee to work different (flexible) hours during the workweek. When an employee can determine elements of a flexible schedule, flexible work hours can be an important employee benefit for staff with significant personal obligations, such as the need to attend to regular medical treatment (i.e., physical therapy, chemotherapy, etc.) or family needs (i.e., children, parents or other dependents who need assistance at variable hours throughout the week).

Flexible work hours are not an alternative to personal or sick time. A flexible work schedule is most often a long-term arrangement with the employee working the full workweek but at "non-standard" hours. It is generally not to be used for the occasional doctor's appointment or parent-teacher meeting.

Although this may not suit all household schedules, employers willing to consider flexible working arrangements (when requested in advance) are likely to establish a more loyal, stable and happy household workforce. Recognizing and remembering that employees have a family, personal and social life outside of work is important to any employer-employee relationship. Many household employers allow for part-time work, time off during the week if the employee worked during the weekend, time off for the occasional personal commitment or infrequent sick day—with each potential circumstance being discussed in the work agreement, in the employee handbook and at the start of employment. Clear communication is essential for mutual understanding. Therefore, employers offering permanent flexible work arrangements should carefully plan schedules with the employee, particularly if the household help member is tasked with dependent care.

Figure 6.5
Benefits Household Employers Offer to Nannies
Source: GTM 2003 Nanny Employer Survey

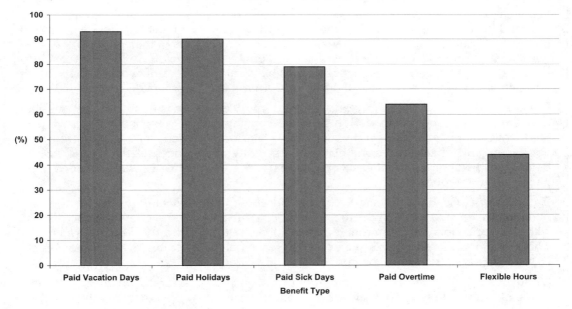

PRE-PAID LEGAL SERVICES

Some employers offer employees prepaid legal services as an employee benefit. Pre-paid legal services may involve citizenship, divorce, adoption, etc., and create a unique value to employees who require legal advice and representation. Pre-paid legal services may be available through a subscription plan. Employers need to clearly state in work agreements and the employee handbook the premium requirements for prepaid legal services, and if such services are provided at the employer's discretion.

Case Study

Arline Rubel
Owner and president
Town and Country Companion and Nursing Services, Inc.
New York City, NY

Arline Rubel, owner and president of the New York City-based Town and Country Companion and Nursing Services, Inc., relies on a lifetime of experience: from orchestrating home care for family members, to teaching mentally challenged adults independent living, to referring employees to work positions in the home. Growing up with a brother with cerebral palsy and then as an adult helping eight ailing family members obtain care in their homes enabled Rubel to hone her skills and expertise in this area.

Many caregivers believe that working in a private home or on a one-on-one basis offers tremendous benefits, noted Rubel. Many enjoy the close relationships that develop and derive pride and satisfaction from seeing first hand the results of their work. "Many frequently work closely with family and professionals and develop a team approach to ensure the client receives the best care possible," said Rubel. "The work is challenging and difficult. Those who do it well are to be admired and appreciated."

Rubel and her staff use lengthy and detailed interviews to learn as much as possible about applicants, including: work history, personality, level of responsibility previously held, communication skills, motivation ability, work preferences, etc. "An appropriate, consistent and checkable work history with written references is the best place to begin," said Rubel. "References communicate important and reassuring information particular to the position."

Employers, advised Rubel, should be candid about their expectations, job duties and difficulties that may arise on the job. In addition, Rubel said, employers need to discuss with job applicants how emergencies should be handled, who the decision maker is, who to call in differing situations, which professionals need to be involved, household expenses, meals, sick time, personal calls and visitors.

"A successful and long-term employment relationship is generally a two-way street," she said. Rubel offers a "friendly ear" to both her client and the caregiver she places—even years after the initial placement—because she believes that most jobs fall apart when issues are ignored or not dealt with constructively. According to Rubel, she encourages each party to find a workable solution. Most issues are solvable, she noted, when both parties use constructive communication.

> Professionalism includes open communication *throughout* employment to ensure employee and employer happiness. Some household employees look for no more employee benefits than just a few extra days off, extra pay on working holidays and professional treatment. Employee benefits are not necessarily all perks that an employer must purchase for the employer.—*Guy*

USE OF EMPLOYER PERSONAL PROPERTY AND FACILITIES

Use of personal property and facilities normally unavailable to the employee outside of work can be considered a great employee benefit. Many employers allow household employees to use certain household property and/or facilities not required to perform their jobs. This may include use of the home computer, television, exercise equipment/gym, swimming pool, etc. The employee handbook needs to clearly list which property and facilities are available for employee use and to whom this can extend in terms of friends and family of the employee. The employee handbook must also clearly state which property and facilities are off limits.

Employees should be reminded that the employer owns the property/facility, and that the employer has the right to inspect and monitor usage—including, for example, user history files on the Internet and sent email messages. The employee handbook should outline procedures for reporting needed repairs or any damage or misuse of property and facilities to the employer.

HOLIDAY CLUB SAVINGS ACCOUNT

An employer may choose to establish what is commonly known as a holiday club savings account, which works like other savings plans. Employees may authorize in writing that a specified amount be deducted from their pay-

---

Ask Guy

Q. I'd like to be as clear as possible when instructing my household help on what is available to them for use at my home while they are performing their duties. What is the best way to do this?

A. Employers will want to detail in the employee handbooks *all* relevant information. This includes not only wages, hours and job requirements but information on:

- auto insurance coverage when a staff member is required to drive in order to complete a work task (i.e., a nanny uses an employer's car to take a child to a play date or to school);
- use of an employer's facilities (TV, computer, exercise equipment) (i.e., a nanny may want to watch a TV program when a child is napping or in school, or a housekeeper may want to take a spin on an exercise bike while a load of laundry is drying); and,
- whether staffers may share in meals (i.e., a nanny may join in lunch with the children for whom she is preparing the meal or a cook may prepare a plate for her- or himself from a meal that she or he has prepared for the family).

Odds are, every question will not be answered, so be sure to meet with the employee to discuss any question or item that arises—particularly during the first week of employment. Once questions are answered, remember to update the employee handbook to clearly specify what has been agreed upon.

Figure 6.6
Gifts Household Empolyers Give to Nannies
Source: GTM 2003 Nanny Employer Survey

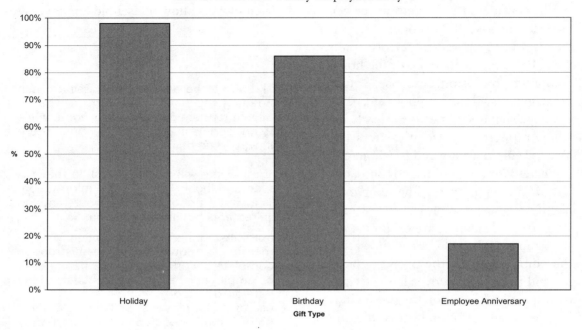

check and deposited into a holiday club savings account. This account usually runs just a few weeks short of a full year and enables the employee to collect his or her savings in the fall (generally mid-October) when he or she may require extra spending money for the holiday season.

20 OTHER IDEAS FOR BENEFITS OR PERKS

1. Sick/personal/vacation time

2. Cell phone use

3. Tuition waivers

4. Education/seminar/conference expense

5. Annual bonuses

6. Sponsorship of employee's family from other countries

7. Purchase of a home

8. Frequent flyer miles

9. Entertainment tickets: ball game/movies/shows

10. Time share/use of a vacation home

11. Gas card

12. Gift certificates

13. Purchase of a computer/PDA

14. Relaxation time

15. Housing allowance

16. Free medical care

17. Retirement funding

18. Education of dependent

19. Life insurance

20. Clothing allowance

BENEFITS CHECKLIST

✓ Investigate health and insurance coverage options thoroughly to see which one best fits an employee's needs and an employer's budget.

✓ For the benefit of the family and household help, calculate the amount of personal time to be offered to employees.

✓ Set regular review periods for salary changes and/or salary bonuses, and make sure employees know when these might occur.

✓ Be clear on the extra perks the employee receives while working within the household—including use of facilities and property.

For up-to-date information, go to www.gtm.com/resourcecenter

Notes

Chapter 7

Managing Payroll and Taxes

In the United States today, GTM Household Employment Experts™ estimates that there are at least 2 million household employees, whereas the United States Internal Revenue Service reports that there are only 250,622 employers of household employees who paid taxes using the IRS' Schedule H Form in 2001, leaving a massive 87.5 percent non-compliance rate.

Many people do not pay payroll taxes because they falsely believe that

- they won't be caught
- they know friends or neighbors who are noncompliant
- their employees do not necessarily want to be paid above board
- the employee will realize more income
- it costs the employer more
- it is not a "real" employment situation

Although household payroll taxes may be confusing to many, this chapter describes an easy-to-follow, step-by-step guide to manage household employment payroll and taxes. Thousands of household employers and their employees interact with GTM's payroll management services staff each week to simplify the payroll and tax process. The following information will help relieve the confusion. (For the latest information on payroll and taxes, visit www.gtm.com/resourcecenter.)

Household employers should be clear about the following responsibilities when hiring an employee:

- Be aware of the risks of not paying an employee "on the books".
- Understand federal and state employment laws.
- Obtain the necessary paperwork.
- Comply with employment tax laws.
- File the necessary forms.

Case Study

Hilary Lockhart
President
A+ Nannies, Inc.
Mesa, AZ
GTM Partner Agency

Hilary Lockhart, of A+ Nannies said a nanny she placed learned the importance of being paid above board. A nanny who was working in a position for nine months was told by her employer that her services were no longer needed. The employer and nanny agreed at the outset to payment under the table. So, when the nanny was let go, she was five months' pregnant and unable to collect unemployment insurance benefits. She looked for work for six or seven weeks unsuccessfully before her doctor ordered bed rest until she delivered her child.

"The nanny couldn't collect any (unemployment) money at all because there was no record of her ever working," said Lockhart. "So, the nanny—five months' pregnant—is unable to find work being a nanny. No one seems to want to hire a nanny for four months and then give six weeks off for maternity leave."

Now, Lockhart tells clients and nannies to follow the law and pay all taxes. "Number one, I tell them it's against the law to pay under the table," said Lockhart, whose business places an average of four to ten childcare workers a month. "I give all my clients a lot of information on taxes and the law. I used to ask clients if they were going to pay cash. I don't ask that any more. I tell (nannies) to get the taxes done right, especially in light of situations like this."

As a former nanny for seven years, Lockhart brings to her business a well-rounded perspective—a nanny, mother and referral agency. Constantly learning, she said she considers her clients' wishes and requirements against her own litmus test of placing herself as the nanny in that situation—which is why she now strongly advocates proper payroll and tax payments.

Paying household employment taxes involves a lot more than adherence to the law. Unemployment coverage also protects employees in instances when they become involuntarily unemployed. If a former employee files a claim for unemployment insurance coverage, then the state unemployment fund, which the employer had paid into through payroll taxes, pays the employee his or her unemployment insurance payment, which is a percentage of the employee's average weekly wage. The employer is not subject to additional or ongoing payments once the employee leaves the household. However, the household employer may incur higher payroll taxes (i.e., a higher unemployment insurance rate) with future employees.—*Guy*

Table 7.1: Household employer's tax guide

IF you	THEN you need to
A. pay cash wages of $1,400 or more in 2004 to any one household employee. do not count wages you pay to— • your spouse • your child under the age of 21 • your parent • any employee under the ages of 18 at any time in 2004	withhold and pay Social Security and Medicare taxes. • the taxes are 15.3 percent of cash wages • your employee's share is 7.65 percent. (You can choose to pay it yourself and not withhold it) • your share is a matching 7.65 percent
B. pay total cash wages of $1,000 or more in any calendar quarter of 2003 or 2004 to household employees. do not count wages you pay to your— • spouse, • child under the age of 21, or, • parent.	pay federal unemployment tax. • the tax is usually 0.8 percent of cash wages. • wages more than $7,000 a year per employee are not taxed. • you also may owe state unemployment tax.

Note: *If neither A nor B above applies, you do not need to pay any federal employment taxes, but you may still need to pay state employment taxes.*

Source: IRS Publication 926: Household Employer's Tax Guide for wages paid in 2004

PAYING OFF THE BOOKS—THE RISKS

Liability to household employer

- increased exposure to an IRS audit
- the penalty for "failing to file" (or attempting to evade or defeat tax payments) is $25,000–$100,000 and potential jail time
- a false or fraudulent statement or failure to furnish a tax statement could result in a $1,000 fine
- payment of all back employment taxes, interest and penalties
- no eligibility for tax breaks, Dependent Care Assistance Program (DCAP) or Child-care Tax Credit

Liability to household employee

- IRS penalties due to failure to file timely income taxes
- no unemployment insurance benefits
- no legal employment history or credit history
- no contributions to Social Security and Medicare and therefore no eligibility to these benefits
- no workers' compensation/disability coverage

Figure 7.1
Nannies Perceived Benefits when their Employer uses a Payroll and Tax Service
Source: GTM 2003 Nanny Survey

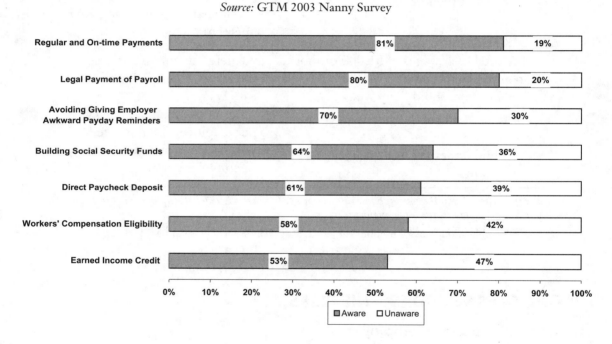

UNDERSTANDING THE LAWS

Employee vs. independent contractor

As detailed in Chapter 1, the determination of employee vs. independent contractor status is important in household employment. The majority of household employees are just that—employees—and, therefore they need to be accurately paid according to applicable labor and tax laws. More information on employee vs. independent contractor status is available in IRS

> "I cannot imagine trying to do my own tax payments. To me, doing payroll and tax payments yourself is pennywise and pound-foolish. I am a strong believer in having professionals do the work. These people are professionals, and this is what they're good at."
>
> Stephanie Oana
> Household employer
> Mother of two
> Lawyer
> Oakland, CA

Publication 926 (Household Employer's Tax Guide) and 15A (Employees Supplemental Tax Guide).

Researching tax laws

The IRS states that a household employer who pays an employee $1,400 or more (as of 2004) in gross wages during the calendar year must comply with all state and federal laws. (See Complying with Tax Law on p. 101.) For more information, see IRS Publication 926, Household Employer's Tax Guide, at www.irs.gov or www.gtm.com/resourcecenter.

Follow payroll regulations

According to the Fair Labor Standards Act (FLSA), all household employees must be paid at least the federal or state minimum wage, whichever is higher. The federal minimum wage is $5.15 per hour (in 2004), but state minimum wages may be higher. Under certain conditions, benefits such as room and board can account for a portion of the employee's wage. Overtime pay is required for most live-out employees (according to FLSA) and there may be additional requirements for household employees, including live-ins, depending on the state in which the household resides. (See p. 68 for more information on overtime). Paid vacations, holidays and sick days are not required by law, and are at an employer's discretion.

Employer responsibilities

Household employers are responsible for reporting and paying required payroll taxes (See Appendix 20 for a calendar on

---

Ask Guy

Q: Can we put our household employee on our company payroll?

A: Generally, no. Your company payroll should be reserved for those employees who work for your company. Equally important, you cannot deduct your household employee's wages from your company's expenses. Thus, in most cases, you must pay your federal household employment taxes on your own federal income tax return, either annually or quarterly. The only exception to reporting your federal household employment taxes on your personal federal income tax return is if you are a sole proprietor or your home is on a farm operated for profit. In either of these instances, you may opt to include your federal household employment taxes with your federal employment tax deposits or other payments for your business or farm employees. (See IRS Publication 926 for more information.)

employer tax responsibilities.) It is definitely not a fun part of household management, but it is a very necessary one. By complying with payroll tax requirements, such as Social Security, Medicare and Unemployment Insurance taxes, the employer ensures that the employee is eligible for benefits from these federal or state programs. Household employers are not obligated to withhold federal or state *income* taxes from the employee's gross wages unless the employer and employee mutually agree to it.

OBTAIN THE NECESSARY PAPERWORK

To properly pay an employee, an employer should obtain the following:

- **Federal forms** (necessary)
  - **Employer Identification Number (Form SS-4)** from the IRS
  - **Form W-4 (Employee's Withholding Allowance Certificate)** to provide to newly hired employees
  - **Form I-9 (Employment Eligibility Verification)** to provide to newly hired employees
  - **Form W-10 (Dependent Care Provider's Identification and Certification)** for DCA (Dependent Care Assistance)
  - **Form W-5 (Earned Income Credit Advance Payment Certificate),** if applicable
  - **Form 1040 Schedule H (Household Employment Taxes),** an annual form
  - **Form 1040ES (Estimated Tax for Individuals),** optional
- **State forms** (necessary)
  - registration form for a **state unemployment identification number;**
  - registration form for a **state withholding number** (if applicable)
  - **state's new hire report** (if necessary)

Federal Employer Identification Number (EIN)

All employers must have an Employer Identification Number (EIN), which is provided by the IRS. An EIN is provided by the IRS through Form SS-4 (Application for Employer Identification Number), which may be obtained by telephoning the IRS at 1.800.829.4933 or visiting www.irs.gov.

Employee's Social Security Number

Ensure that an employee has a Social Security Number, and verify the number with the Social Security Administration. Do not assume that the employee has one, especially if he or she is not a US citizen. If an employee does not have a Social Security Number and is a legal

US citizen, then he or she can apply for one with Form SS-5 (Application for a Social Security Card). If an employee is not a US citizen, an ITIN (Individual Tax Identification Number) can be obtained by using IRS Form W-7 (Application for IRS Individual Tax Payer Identification Number). An ITIN is only used for federal withholding tax purposes.

FEDERAL FORMS

Form W-4

If an employer and an employee have agreed to withhold income taxes, then employers should provide employees with a W-4 form (Employee's Withholding Allowance Certificate), and the employee must complete it. Form W-4 can be downloaded from www.irs.gov or www.gtm.com/resourcecen-

> ### ITINs
>
> Regardless of whether a person is legally employed, an IRS Individual Taxpayer Identification Number (ITIN) can be used by those ineligible to obtain a Social Security Number but who need to pay taxes on wages earned; these people include certain non-resident and resident aliens, and their spouses and dependents. The ITINs are nine-digit numbers beginning with the number nine formatted like a Social Security Number (9XX-XX-XXXX). They are not to be used for non-tax purposes (i.e., proof of identity for a driver's license, residency claim or employment, or to apply for welfare and health benefits). The IRS Form W-7 (Application for IRS Individual Taxpayer Identification Number) is used to obtain an ITIN and may be submitted to the IRS. According to the IRS, people using an ITIN cannot claim the earned income tax credit.

ter. The W-4 form documents how much income tax is withheld from an employee's salary. If the W-4 is not submitted, then the employer must withhold the employee's income tax at the highest rate—as a single person with no allowances.

Employers who have agreed to withhold income taxes for their employees are required to send a signed W-4 to the IRS when an employee:

- claims an exemption from withholding and the employee's wages are normally more than $200 per week; or,
- claims ten or more allowances.

Form I-9

Employers need to provide employees with an I-9 form (Employment Eligibility Verification). All employers in the United States must obtain a completed Form I-9 for every employee hired. Form I-9 attempts to ensure that only people legally authorized to work in the United States are hired. Therefore, employers use I-9 to verify the identity and employment eligibility of employees. (See Appendix 1 for a sample of an employment eligibility verification form.) The completed I-9 form should be kept in the employee's personnel file.

Form W-10

Form W-10 (Dependent Care Provider's Identification and Certification) is an optional informational form that any taxpayer can use to obtain information about the dependent care provider (household employees, or even day-care centers). This is the same information that the taxpayer reports on Form 2441 (Child and Dependent Care Expenses) with the 1040 Personal Tax Return. The IRS states that the taxpayer can use Form W-10 or any of the following other methods of "due diligence" to collect this information:

- a copy of the dependent care provider's social security card or driver's license that includes his or her social security number
- a recently printed letterhead or printed invoice that shows the provider's name, address and taxpayer identification number (TIN)
- if the provider is your employer's company's dependent care plan, a copy of the statement provided by your employer under the plan
- a copy of the household employee's W-4, if the provider is the household employee and he or she gave the employer a properly completed Form W-4, (Employee's Withholding Allowance Certificate).

Form W-5

Form W-5 (Earned Income Credit Advance Payment Certificate) allows employees to claim Earned Income Credit (EIC). Employees can receive this credit with their pay during the year. An employer is encouraged to notify each employee whose combinded or total wages for the year are less than $30,338 (2004 filing, single or $31,338, 2004, filing jointly) that she or he may be eligible for EIC. More information can be found in IRS Publication 596.

Schedule H

Starting in 1995, the Schedule H (Household Employment Taxes) form was added to federal Form 1040 US Individual Income Tax Return for employers who paid more than a total of $1,400 during the calendar year (as of tax year 2004) to household employees, or for employers who paid all employees more than $1,000 in any one quarter during the calendar year (see p. 93 for Table 7.1 of specific circumstances). Schedule H enables employers to report wages and taxes withheld for household help to the federal government with their own 1040 form (U.S. Individual Income Tax Return).

According to the IRS, for the tax year 2001, 130,255,237 individual income tax returns were filed. Of these, only 250,622 forms showed an entry for household employment taxes.

With the estimated number of households employing household help at about 2 million, this is a mere fraction of the taxes that should be filed for household employment each year.

Form 1040-ES

This option of transmitting taxes quarterly versus paying at the end of the year with form Schedule H (Household Employment Taxes) allows a household employer to make estimated tax payments to cover household employment taxes. These vouchers allow you to make payments and pay all of the employment taxes at once or in installments. This form is due on a quarterly basis. (Refer to 1040-ES filing instructions for due dates see p. 105, Table 7.2.)

STATE FORMS

State unemployment identification number

Household employers are required to obtain a state unemployment ID number with the state where the physical work will be performed. Refer to IRS Publication 926 for a list of State Unemployment Tax Agencies (also available online at www.irs.gov). The ID number is needed to pay state unemployment taxes on a quarterly basis and will appear on the W-2 (Wage and Tax Statement) form for each employee.

State withholding certificate

It is optional for an employer to withhold taxes from an the employee's paycheck. If an employer and employee decide to withhold state income taxes then the state's registration form should be completed by contacting the state's withholding agency. This provides an employer with an ID number, a coupon booklet and/or instructions on how to submit withholding taxes according to the state's laws. This number will also appear on Form W-2 for each employee.

State new hire report

New hire reporting is a process by which an employer has to register any newly hired employee with the state within a certain time of the hire date. This report usually gives contact and basic identification information for each new employee to the state's department of labor, which then transmits the report to the National Directory of New Hires (NDNH). (The most common use of this information is to help the child support collection unit track down debtors for child support payments.)

For a directory of state unemployment insurance, income tax withholding and new hire reporting, see Appendix 21.

Case Study

Zuzka Polishook
Household Employer
Pacific Palisades, CA (LA area)
GTM payroll and tax services client

Zuzka Polishook hired her first nanny in August 2003 after the birth of her second daughter. With a two-and-a-half daughter and a second daughter just a few months old, Polishook transitioned her babysitter into a full-time nanny and housekeeper to help care for the two girls, as well as for a large house and two dogs.

Although Polishook knew from experience that the employee was responsible and a hard worker, she still painstakingly drafted an employee contract signed by both the nanny/housekeeper and her. The contract will clear any potential problem areas and resolve any unspoken questions. "The nanny knows where she stands with it, and I know where I stand with it," said Polishook. "It's peace of mind for me. No matter how obvious, I wrote it down. It acts as a checklist for both parties."

The amount of paperwork involved in employing a domestic employee is what surprised her the most. "I am extremely busy," said Polishook. "Time is my most valued currency, and I was clueless where to start. I didn't even know what I needed to know."

Thus, Polishook took advice from a friend and contracted with a tax and payroll service, GTM, to manage the payroll and tax piece of the household employment equation.

"I'm in the know and in control," she said, "but I don't have to figure the details out. With GTM, I am buying peace of mind, which is a big thing for me. Now, I am able to dedicate the hours I would have spent figuring payroll and taxes to my children."

Polishook advises families considering a payroll and tax service to calculate the value of their time per hour with the number of hours per month spent addressing tax and wage requirements. "The equation will be very clear," she said. "It is a simple economic value: time plus costs . . . GTM is really a savior. I had a lot of questions during setup, and I felt I could call at any time. GTM is very professional and really fills my needs."

As a household employer going it alone, it can be difficult to devote the time and energy needed to stay abreast of the changing employment regulation and tax laws. GTM's EasyPay® service is an inexpensive way to save busy household employers valuable time and money.—*Guy*

Record retention

An employer should make sure that all hiring, tax and payroll documentation regarding an employee's hire, including all IRS and state forms, is kept in a safe place. It is recommended that these forms be kept on file for at least five years, in case the IRS or department of justice needs to check who is, or has been, employed by the employer.

Workers' compensation

Most states require household employers to carry a workers' compensation and/or disability policy if employing a full-time or part-time person. See worker's compensation on page 117. These policies provide compensation to an employee who is injured on the job. If the state requires this, an employer may contact the state's insurance fund or home owner's insurance carrier. It is recommended that even if the state does not require employers to have a policy, an employer should consider obtaining appropriate coverage for peace of mind. Some states also require insurance coverage for non-occupational injury or illness.

> **Ask Guy**
>
> **Q.** Must I carry workers' compensation insurance on full-time and part-time household employees?
>
> **A.** Most of the states require employers to carry a workers' compensation and/or disability policy for any person employed full-time or part-time. Workers' compensation policies protect the employer from lawsuits and liability in case an employee is injured in the home while performing her or his job duties. Workers' compensation also protects the employee who if hurt on the job can collect certain medical and wage-loss compensation.
>
> Even if your state does not require you to carry workers' compensation/disability insurance, it is a very good idea to do so.

COMPLYING WITH TAX LAWS

GTM Household Employment Experts™, which provides tax and payroll services to household employers through its EasyPay® Service, estimates that employers can expect to pay 9 percent-12 percent of the employee's gross pay for the following:

- federal unemployment insurance (0.8 percent)
- Social Security and Medicare (7.65 percent)
- state unemployment insurance (about 2 percent-4 percent in most states)
- other state and local taxes (i.e., employment training or workforce taxes)

GTM estimates that based on average salaries **employees** can expect to pay 10 percent–30 percent of their gross pay for:

- Social Security and Medicare at 7.65 percent
- other state and local taxes (i.e., disability), if applicable
- federal and state income taxes, if they choose (estimated at 15 percent–25 percent)

Although tempting to many, not paying taxes is illegal. By not paying an employee lawfully, the employer is liable for all unpaid taxes, interests and penalties, and may face a potential jail term.

FEDERAL TAXES

Social Security

Social Security tax, otherwise known as Old Age Survivor's Disability Insurance (OASDI), is required to be paid by both the employer and the employee. Each pays half of the Social Security taxes owed to the federal government. This calculates to 6.2 percent each (for both the employee and employer) of the employee's gross salary (6.2 percent for the employee is withholding, 6.2 percent from the employer is a matching contribution, totalling 12.4 percent. The tax is capped at a gross salary of $87,900 in a calendar (for both the employee and employer) year (as of 2004).

Medicare

Like Social Security, Medicare taxes require the employer and employee to contribute equally. This tax is 2.9 percent, both pay 1.45 percent of the employee's gross salary. There is no salary limit earned for this tax.

Federal income tax

Withholding FIT (Federal Income Tax) from an employee's paycheck is optional, but if agreed to by employer and employee, then the employer must withhold income taxes based on the employee's

---

Ask Guy

Q. Is there a difference between being covered by Social Security and being eligible for Social Security?

A. Yes, and it's significant. To be eligible for Social Security, an employee must work 40 calendar quarters to be fully insured and eligible for retirement, disability, death and survivor benefits. To be covered, you must work at least ten calendar quarters (as of 2004) to be insured and eligible for limited death benefits.

completion of Form W-4. This is an employee-only withholding, and the employer does not incur any additional expenses. The FIT amount owed by each employee varies according to his or her income and filing status.

FUTA

If an employer pays cash wages to a household employee, totaling $1,000 or more in any calendar quarter (in 2004), then he or she is responsible for paying FUTA (the Federal Unemployment Tax Act). This is an employer tax and is not withheld from an employee's pay. It is calculated on the first $7,000 of gross wages per employee at the tax rate of 0.8 percent, if an employer has paid his or her state unemployment taxes on time. An employer must report FUTA with the Schedule H form which is filed with his or her 1040 personal income tax return.

STATE AND LOCAL TAX LAWS

State unemployment insurance (SUI)

This is an employer tax and is normally due on a quarterly basis. Unemployment insurance contributions are accumulated in every state's unemployment insurance fund for workers who can claim eligibility. SUI is generally calculated as between 2 percent–4 percent on a certain amount of each employee's gross wages for the calendar year, which varies state by state. For

---

Ask Guy

Q. I am a housekeeper and my employer is paying my Social Security and Medicare but has asked me if I would like income taxes withheld. I am uncertain whether to have income tax withheld from my paycheck. What is the best scenario?

A. What is best depends on you. First, please know that choosing to withhold income tax from your paycheck is not the same as choosing whether to pay it. You must pay it. The option you ask about is whether you want your employer to withhold income tax from your paycheck or you want to pay the income tax yourself. So, this becomes a budgeting and convenience issue. GTM strongly discourages employees from trying to pay taxes on their own.

Ask Guy

Q. What state taxes am I required to pay as a household employer?

A. State employment laws are similar for a worker in the home or in the corporate office. All states have a state unemployment insurance tax, which employers must pay. This amount is a percentage (2 percent–4 percent) of the household employee's gross salary and is capped at an annual wage amount. For example, Illinois requires 3.3 percent on the first $9,000 of the gross wage per employee (in 2004). Some states, such as California and New Jersey, require the employee to contribute a small amount to disability or unemployment out of her or his own gross pay in addition to employer payments.

example, for new employers, Virginia's state unemployment insurance is set at 2.5 percent on the first $8,000 per employee, whereas Arizona requires 2.7 percent on the first $7,000 (in 2004).

State withholding taxes

This is an employee income tax based on filing status and wage level. This practice is not required, unless agreed upon by the employer and employee, but it generally helps employees distribute their owed income taxes throughout the year at regular intervals, rather than requiring a total payment at the end of the tax year. The employee may want the employer to withhold state income taxes from his or her paycheck.

Other taxes which can apply according to the state of employment

Disability insurance: some states may require the employer to withhold additional taxes or insurances from the employee's pay. For example, both New Jersey and California have a state disability tax. The California State Disability Insurance (SDI) is a partial wage-replacement insurance plan for California workers. The SDI program is state mandated and funded through employee payroll deductions. SDI provides affordable, short-term benefits to eligible workers who suffer a loss of wages when they are unable to work due to a non-work related illness or injury, or a medically disabling condition from pregnancy or childbirth.

Local tax: Some localities require an employer to withhold local income tax. Based on either the place of employment or residence of the employee. Such localities include those in Ohio and Pennsylvania, as well as New York City.

Ask Guy

Q. I am nervous about dealing with the IRS and all federal, state and local tax forms that I need to complete. What can I do to ensure that I'm doing all I need to be doing, particularly since two friends of mine do not file the same paperwork that I do?

A. Given the circumstance, you're right to be anxious. Following all tax requirements can be confusing and time consuming, but, it must be done. We suggest household employers refer to IRS Publication 926 and Publication 15, as well as, relevant state, and local labor and tax guides and keeping this book as a handy reference. Many household employers contract with GTM, to handle taxes and paperwork and to consult with experts regarding the precise, timely and lawful handling of wages. Many who choose not to adhere to the tax law unfortunately risk heavy penalties and jail.

Paying a household employee under the table puts the household employee in a very vulnerable spot, as he or she is without the protection of unemployment insurance, Social Security insurance, and so on. The important thing is to make sure you pay the correct taxes.

Paying an employee

Unless an employer already has a firm idea of when he or she wants an employee to be paid, it is probably best to talk to the employee to see what best suits his or her needs and to agree on a regular pay interval. Generally, workers must be paid at least twice a month, however, some states require a weekly pay frequency for household employment.

Wages should always be paid by check so both the employer and the employee have an earnings and deduction record for the current pay period and year-to-date accumulated totals (see Appendix 18 for a sample of a paycheck and payroll earnings statement.) The amount on the check should always be net (after all applicable taxes are withheld). An employer also can offer the option of direct deposit, which is a convenient payment method for both the employer and the employee.

REPORTING AND FILING PAYROLL TAXES

Filing federal taxes

There are two options for filing Federal payroll taxes: annually or quarterly. Household employers must report and file all federal taxes by using Schedule H, which is an annual reconciliation form that is used by the employer to report to the IRS wages paid to the household employee throughout the year.

Alternatively, employers may pay estimated taxes on a quarterly schedule to help alleviate the tax burden at the end of the year. In addition, Schedule H must be filed annually with the employer's personal tax return. To do this, an employer will need to file the 1040 Estimated Tax Form. This calculates an estimate of the following:

- employee federal income tax (FIT)
- employer and Employee Social Security and Medicare
- employer federal unemployment tax (FUTA)

This sum is an estimated amount for each quarter. The due dates for submitting this form are as follows:

Table 7.2: Filing federal taxes

Quarter	Due
First: January–March	April 15
Second: April–May	June 15
Third: June–August	September 15
Fourth: September–December	January 15

If the estimated tax payments are not made quarterly, then an employer may want to arrange to have additional federal income taxes withheld from his or her own salary. This will help to avoid owing a significant sum on his or her personal tax return and also to avoid a possible 10 percent "under payment" penalty.

Each year, an employer must provide employees with Form W-2 (Wage and Tax Statement) on or before January 31. This provides a breakdown of all withholding and income throughout the previous calendar year and helps the employee submit her or his individual income tax forms.

By February 28 (or March 31 if the W-2 is filed electronically), the employer must also file the employer copy of the employee's W-2 and W-3 (a Wage Transmission report) forms to the Social Security Administration. A W-3 is a reconciliation of all W-2s for each employee, even if only employing one employee.

Filing state taxes

Most states require the quarterly filing of state taxes (state unemployment and other taxes). Unfortunately, state tax quarters do not coincide with federal tax quarters. Instead, states require taxes to be submitted every three months, typically one month after the quarter ends. After an employer has registered with the state to file taxes, the state sends blank quarterly forms with instructions. If an employer uses a payroll service such as GTM, then he or she may avoid the hassle of signing checks and filing taxes accurately and timely.

If they so choose, the employer and the employee may file state income taxes (state withholding taxes) that are typically due each quarter. However, each state has specific filing frequencies based on how much income tax is withheld. The amount withheld from an employee's wages during a quarter generally determines the filing frequency in any given state (semi-weekly, monthly, quarterly, annually). When an employer registers with the state, state tax officials will inform her or him of the filing frequency. Another way to determine filing frequency is to refer to the welcome letter in the correspondence received with the state withholding income number.

Table 7.3: Filing state taxes

Quarter	Due
First: January–March	April 30
Second: April–June	July 31
Third: July–September	October 31
Fourth: October–December	January 31

PAYROLL TAX CHECKLIST

✓ Understand and abide by all laws.

✓ Be aware of state and local laws that may apply.

✓ Be clear about household tax needs and the importance of lawful tax payments for all household employees.

✓ Even if an employee asks to be paid under the table, do not do so. Explain that tax withholding is for the employee's benefit and will ensure unemployment and Social Security coverage.

When a household employee is hired

✓ Obtain an employer identification number (if not obtained previously).

✓ Have household employees complete Form W-4 if the employer is withholding income taxes.

✓ Obtain Form I-9 for employee egilibility verification.

✓ Apply for a state unemployment ID number.

✓ Apply for a state withholding number (if applicable).

✓ Apply for a state's new hire report (if necessary).

✓ Obtain form 1040-ES for estimated tax payments (if desired).

✓ Check workers' compensation policy requirements for the state.

✓ Establish a regular pay period schedule, and inform employee(s).

When household employee is paid

✓ Withhold Social Security and Medicare taxes.

✓ Pay on time federal, state and local taxes that may apply.

✓ Withhold federal and state income taxes, if agreed.

✓ Make advance payments of the Earned Income Credit (Form W-5), if applicable.

✓ Send copy A of Form W-2 with Form W-3 to the Social Security Administration by February 28 (or March 31 if filing electronically) each year.

✓ File Schedule H with the employer's federal income tax return (Form 1040) by April 15 each year.

✓ Keep records in a safe place for five years.

Source: IRS Publication 926 Household Employer's Tax Guide.

For an easy-to-follow step by step tax guide see Appendix 22.

For up-to-date information, go to www.gtm.com/resourcecenter

State tax form checklists can be found at http://www.taxadmin.org/fta/link

Notes

Chapter 8

Health and Safety Rules and Tips

It goes without saying that a satisfying workplace is only obtained in a healthy and safe environment. This chapter will discuss the Occupational Safety and Health Act (OSHA) and other safety issues within the household that will help make the workplace a better and safer one.

OSHA

The Occupational Safety and Health Act (OSHA) ensures that employers provide employees with a workplace that is free from recognized hazards that cause or could cause serious harm or death to employees. It is applicable to everyone except to sole proprietors and those employing family members in a business or on a farm. Under OSHA, employers must provide safety training to employees, inform employees about hazardous chemicals to which they may be exposed and notify regulators about workplace accidents.

Under OSHA of 1970, employers must follow requirements to ensure a healthy work environment, which includes providing training, medical examinations and record keeping. Some employer requirements follow:

- Provide a workplace free from serious hazards, and comply with OSHA rules and regulations.
- Ensure that employees have and use safe tools and equipment and properly maintain this equipment.
- Use color codes, posters, labels or signs to warn employees of potential hazards.
- Establish or update operating procedures, and communicate them to employees.
- Keep records of work-related injuries and illnesses. (OSHA exempts employers with ten or fewer employees and employers in certain low-hazard industries from this requirement.)

OSHA workplace concerns include the following:

- exposure to hazardous chemicals
- first aid and medical treatment required as a result of a workplace injury

- noise levels
- protective gear (i.e., goggles, work shoes and ear protectors)
- workplace temperatures and ventilation
- safety training

Because OSHA is so broadly written, household employers may want to contact a local OSHA office to determine specific requirements. Housekeepers might be instructed to wear protective gloves when in contact with cleaning solvents, or gardeners might be instructed to wear goggles and earplugs when performing landscaping work with certain equipment.

Employers also must follow OSHA record keeping rules, which include maintaining a log of workplace injuries requiring treatment beyond first aid.

A good practice is for employers to keep a written safety policy in the employee handbook, which could offer instructions on where the house's first aid kit is kept, a list of emergency service telephone numbers, protective gear required for specific tasks and an employee requirement to report all health and safety issues immediately to the employer. In addition, the safety policy could provide instructions that improper use of equipment (i.e., using equipment for purposes other than what it is intended or using equipment that is not properly connected) is prohibited within the household.

Along with federal OSHA requirements, an employer may need to meet state and local health and safety requirements.

HOME SAFETY

Aside from federal, state and local laws governing a healthy and safe workplace, household employers may take some basic steps to ensure household safety. These home safety measures apply to any home or household member, but can easily apply to household workers. This list is not exhaustive, but it does offer some general guidelines that employers may want to consider for their home.

HOME SAFETY CHECKS

Kitchen

- ✓ Are exhaust hood and duct on the kitchen stove cleaned frequently?
- ✓ Are cleaners, disinfectants, poisons, and so on stored away from food and out of children's reach?

> According to the US Department of Labor's Bureau of Labor Statistics, in 2001 (the latest year compiled data was available) 1.5 million reported injuries and illnesses in the private sector accounted for more than one day of lost work (other than the day the injury occurred).

✓ Are utensils and knives stored neatly and kept out of children's reach?

✓ Are pot and pan handles turned away from stove fronts?

✓ Are cupboard contents stored neatly to prevent falling?

✓ Are spills wiped up immediately?

✓ Are plastic grocery and shopping bags out of children's reach?

Entrances and stairways

✓ Are entrances, halls and stairways adequately lighted to prevent trips and falls?

✓ Are steps well maintained?

✓ Are steps cleared of objects and tripping hazards? Are there at least two exits that are designated fire exits and always kept clear?

✓ Is a child's gate used at the top and bottom of stairs if a toddler is living in the home? (Accordion-type gates are dangerous; children's heads can easily get trapped in them.)

✓ Are steps and railings sturdy and in good condition?

Living areas

✓ Are electrical cords kept away from carpets? Are cords in good condition (not frayed or overloaded)?

Ask Guy

Q. I recently argued with my full-time nanny about what I needed to provide her with to care for my five-year-old daughter with chicken pox. The nanny was concerned that she was exposed to the illness and was carrying it home to her husband, who had never had chicken pox. Am I liable for providing a nanny with medical protective gloves and masks for protection against a common childhood disease? Am I also responsible for providing protective gear for my housekeeper?

A. Every employer in the United States must ensure that a workplace—even one in the home—is a safe and healthy environment in which to work. Of course, anyone would work to ensure that his or her home is safe and healthy, which means, at times, providing protective measures for anyone in the home. This could mean that as a household employer you would provide your; housekeeper with gloves and a face mask when using a particularly potent chemical cleaner; gardener with eye goggles and ear plugs when using landscaping and yard care equipment; eldercare worker with medical gloves when injecting medication; or, your childcare worker with medical gloves and a face mask when caring for a child with the flu, measles, chicken pox and so on. Such universal precautions are standard in any work environment and are an ideal topic for employers to discuss with employees during the development of a work agreement and review of the employee handbook.

Also, household employers need to be aware of such safety concerns as ensuring that hallways, walkways and other pathways are free and clear to eliminate the risk of tripping and injury; that there is proper ventilation in areas where potent chemicals and materials are used (i.e., housecleaning, car maintenance); that proper measures are used by employees when lifting (i.e., a childcare worker lifting a child, a housekeeper lifting or moving furniture, a gardener lifting lawn care equipment); and, that proper measures are used by employees when a surface (i.e., kitchen floor) is wet.

✓ Are long electrical, blinds and drapery cords beyond a child's reach? (Excess cord can be bound with a twist-tie or a holder or spool specially designed to hide the extra cord.)

✓ Are all wires in the house properly insulated?

✓ Are there safety outlet covers in all of the unused electrical outlets?

✓ Are throw rugs secured to prevent tripping?

✓ Is furniture kept away from windows to prevent children from falling out? (Window screens will not prevent a child from falling out of the window.)

✓ Are furniture edges sharp?

✓ Are radiators and pipes covered to protect against burns?

✓ Are lamps located near beds to prevent tripping in the dark?

✓ Is there ample walking space between furniture and objects?

✓ Are all plants safe? (Some plants are toxic and need to be placed out of children's reach.)

Bathrooms

✓ Are medicines and vitamins stored out of children's reach?

✓ Is the home's hot water temperature set at the safe temperature of 120°F? (If the temperature cannot be altered [i.e., rented homes], then install an anti-scald device on the faucet.)

✓ Is there a toilet-lid locking device in households with small children?

Nursery

✓ Does the crib mattress snugly fit against the crib's sides? (No more than two fingers' distance should exist between the mattress and the crib railing.)

✓ Are crib bars 2⅜ inches or less apart? (Any more space and a child could be caught or strangled between the crib's bars.)

✓ Are crib side rails kept up?

Garage

✓ Are all tools, including those used for gardening, automotive and lawn care, stored in a locked container?

✓ Are recycling containers holding glass and metal far from children's reach?

Ask Guy

Q. I am a busy mother and working professional in New York, and I employ both a full-time childcare provider and occasional babysitters to tend to my two young children when I am out of the house. To what extent does my auto insurance coverage protect my employees and me while my full-time childcare provider and my babysitter(s) use my car during their work hours?

A. This is a very common question among all household employees. Of course, any household employer should first check with his or her insurance agent to be 100 percent positive about what his or her particular policy covers to ensure that he or she is adequately protected. Major liability could exist if your household employee is not properly covered and insured under the household's auto insurance policy.

While states' and carriers' requirements vary, the following is a general wrap-up on New York State auto insurance (requirements differ by state).

For occasional users, such as babysitters, driving the family's (employer's) car, protection is offered through the liability and medical insurance segments of the insured's (the family's) car insurance. An occasional user driving his or her own vehicle (the employee's) also is protected under the liability and medical insurance segments of the insured's (the employee's) car insurance. The employer should keep an annual copy of the employers insurance card to ensure that the employee has coverage and that it is sufficient.

A regular user, such as your full-time household employee, driving the employer's car should be listed as a driver with the insurance company. This protects the employer in the event that an accident occurs when the employee is driving the family's car. An employer who does not notify his or her insurance agent of the employee driver/regular user risks the insurer not renewing the insurance policy. (A regular user is a person who drives the vehicle three to four times a week for more than six to eight weeks.)

Typically, a household's auto insurance policy will protect other drivers, but, again, be sure to check with your insurance agent to confirm coverage and that limits are adequate for you, your family and your employee.

Note: According to the International Nanny Association, auto accidents are probably the most common type of claim involving a nanny and his or her employer. So, employers need to fully understand what is covered and who is covered by their insurance policies. To be safe, employers may want to consider adding the nanny or other household worker to his or her auto insurance policy.

Yard

✓ Is outdoor play equipment safe with no loose parts or rust?

✓ Are surfaces around swing sets and play equipment soft to absorb shock from falls? (Good surface equipment can be sand or wood chips. Concrete and packed dirt are not adequate to absorb shock from falls.)

✓ Is access to the swimming pool blocked for small children? Are dangerous cleaning chemicals kept locked away?

FIRE SAFETY CHECKS

✓ Are there smoke and carbon monoxide detectors on each level of the home and near the sleeping area? Are detectors checked monthly to ensure that they are operating? Are batteries replaced at least once a year?

✓ Are detectors cleaned monthly to clear away dust and cobwebs?

✓ Are detectors replaced every ten years? (Detectors become less sensitive over time.)

✓ Does the home have one or more fire extinguishers and do all household members know how to operate them? (The local fire department can provide training on how to properly use an extinguisher.)

✓ Does the home have an automatic sprinkler system? (Automatic sprinkler systems are a good consideration—even in the home.)

✓ Is there a clearly written fire escape plan for the home? Is the plan practiced at least twice a year?

HOME SECURITY

Nothing is more important than protecting loved ones. Keeping a household and the family safe and sound can be complicated, expensive and involved. Depending on the nature of the household and the location, an employer should make sure that the employee hired is aware of all necessary security systems, keys and locks, spotlights and video surveillance, etc. that may be required knowledge for the job. For example, if the employer is away during the day, the employee should know how to lock up the house, turn on the alarm system and so forth. It is advised that the employee have his or her own security code, if possible. It is a good idea, during the orientation of the employee in the first few days to go over all security procedures and what needs to be checked if the house is left unattended during the day (closing and locking windows, locking doors, turning lights on, setting the alarm system, etc.).

SECURITY PROFESSIONAL

If full-time personal security protection is warranted, then identifying the professional security for use in the household is not as difficult as it may seem. Some overall areas to consider include the following:

- Experience in: personal protection, business security, estate and asset protection.
- Background in: estate management practices, public relations and entertainment methodology, personnel management.
- Personal demeanor: personable countenance, flexibility, discretion.

A professional should have this experience and skill-set before being considered for a household security position. Without them, the individual is either lacking the security skills necessary to protect the household or missing the public relations skills needed to interact in a smooth, balanced and relaxed manner with both the client and the household staff.

> "Intelligence is recognizing possibilities; wisdom is preparing for those possibilities. The wise take steps before an unsavory event occurs. Well-planned security measures cause the nefarious to look elsewhere for their illicit gains. Thus, the wise protect their families and love ones."
>
> Barry Wilson
> President
> Certified Protection Specialist
> Anlance Protection, Ltd.

Table 8.1: Identifying Performance Behavior Issues

Performance	Behavior
Inconsistent work quality	Frequent financial problems
Poor concentration	Avoiding friends and colleagues
Lowered productivity	Blaming others for own problems
Increased absenteeism	Complaints about own home life
Unexplained disappearances from jobsite	Deterioration in personal appearance
Carelessness, mistakes, judgment errors Needless risk taking Disregard for safety	Complaints of vaguely-defined illness

Case Study

Ilo Milton
President
FamilyWise, Inc.
Bedford, NY
GTM Partner Agency

When clients and candidates ask Ilo Milton about the advantage of "above the table" pay, she readily describes a real-life incident that puts it all into perspective.

A family and its nanny mutually agreed that the nanny would be paid off the books. The nanny, playing with the two boys she was hired to care for, tripped, fell and severely injured her back—requiring at least three weeks of bed rest and subsequent physical therapy.

As an employee paid off the books, she was not covered by workers' compensation insurance. The nanny expected her employer to pay her full salary while she recovered—and even asked the employer to illegally submit a liability claim against the home owners' insurance.

"All were complicit in going outside of the law," said Milton. "The family was terrified the nanny would sue. The nanny thought the family should pay her while she was out of work. The solution would have been easy if the nanny was on the books." The family felt that the nanny was trying to take advantage of it without taking on any of the risks. They did not feel that they could trust the nanny any longer.

So the family paid the nanny, who no longer works through FamilyWise, four weeks severance pay, and then replaced her.

"Everyone took a risk here," noted Milton. "While I have my belief that all should pay on the books, people live at their own risk tolerance level. I'm certain [this story] has an impact. It makes household employers aware of the realities and possibilities."

As a household employer, you should ensure that you are adequately covered in the event that an accident occurs in the workplace. In this instance, New York State requires a workers' compensation insurance policy that covers accident-related medical expenses, as well as 66.66 percent of the employee's wages up to $400 per week until he or she is well enough to return to work. Many household employers fail to see that an attempt to save a few dollars in the short term could result in a huge liability later, putting stress on both the employer and the employee.—*Guy*

A DRUG-FREE WORKPLACE

A written drug-free workplace policy is the basis of the workplace's drug-free program. Included in the employee handbook, the policy needs to clearly state why the policy is being implemented to ensure a safe and healthy workplace. Prohibited behaviors should be clearly outlined within the policy. Use, at a minimum, language that states that the use, possession, transfer or sale of illegal drugs or controlled substances by employees is prohibited. Include consequences, such as immediate dismissal, but take care that these consequences are consistent with other existing personnel policies and, of course, any applicable laws. For instance, if a personnel policy states that any illegal act performed by an employee on workplace premises will result in immediate dismissal, then it follows that any illegal drugs or controlled substances found on the employee will result in immediate dismissal.

In the drug-free workplace policy, an employer may want to include information on drug testing. While in the United States most private employers have the right to test for a wide variety of substances, federal, state and local regulations may apply. However, according to the US Department of Labor, employers who drug test without a drug-testing policy are exposed to liability. Employers may request that employees take a drug test after a job is offered and that employment is contingent upon a successful outcome. Local drug stores sell drug testing kits for about $20.

According to the US Department of Labor, employers may be able to identify workers with substance abuse problems by noting aspects of their performance and behavior. While these symptoms may not mean that a worker has an alcohol or a drug abuse problem, employers should be alert to any of these aspects, outlined in Table 8.1 (see p. 115.)

Remember, it is not the employer's job to diagnose substance abuse, but it *is* the employer's job to ensure health and safety within the work environment. Clear and firm communication with the employee focused on her or his job performance is key, as is explaining the drug-free workplace policy, performance policies and what will occur when performance expectations are not met.

Some states have workplace-related substance abuse laws. To learn what states mandate, go to http://dol.gov/workingpartners

WORKERS' COMPENSATION

Many states require an employer to pay workers' compensation insurance. An employee can receive workers' compensation benefits to replace income and to cover medical expenses resulting from work-related illness or injury. Exercise caution, if state law requires workers' compensation insurance be aware that a household liability insurance policy will not cover any injuries, court awards or any other penalties.

The following states require workers' compensation insurance coverage for full-time and/or part-time household employees: Alabama, California, Colorado, Connecticut, Delaware, Florida, Georgia, Hawaii, Illinois, Iowa, Kansas, Maryland, Maine, Michigan, Minnesota, New Hampshire, New Jersey, New York, Ohio, Oklahoma, South Dakota, Montana and Washington. It is best to consult an insurance agent and state insurance department, as many states offer employers a state insurance fund option and laws requiring coverage may change.

HEALTH AND SAFETY RULES AND TIPS CHECKLIST

From time-to-time incidents will occur with employees, it is a good practice to document the incident and discuss the matter with the employee in hopes to correct the behavior. (See Appendix 23 for a sample of an incident report.)

✓ Establish a safety policy, and provide protective gear and equipment.

✓ Enforce universal precautions and use of safety equipment.

✓ Injuries happen. Consider workers' compensation insurance coverage even if it is not mandated by the state or locality.

✓ Conduct a home safety check to ensure a safe household and healthy work environment.

✓ Check with an auto insurance company if your employee is going to be driving your dependents.

✓ Call an insurance agent or the state insurance department for the contact information for your area's workers' compensation administration.

✓ Find out if your state requires workers' compensation insurance coverage and if it offers a state insurance fund option.

For up-to-date information, go to www.gtm.com/resourcecenter

Notes

Chapter 9

Illegal Discrimination in the Home

The US government enforces many laws and regulations that protect workers against discrimination. Many laws are implemented at both the federal and state levels, and employers need to be aware of all laws and regulations affecting them, including federal, state and local.

Often anti-discrimination laws are required for businesses with a specific number of workers. Although many federal laws require 5, 15 or even 20 employees for a law to apply, discrimination laws (especially state and local laws) could apply to household employers. A common best practice is to set fair hiring and employment procedures as if they do apply to the workplace. This creates a professional hiring attitude, while also designating the household as an equitable, unbiased work environment.

FEDERAL LAWS

General applications

The US Civil Rights Act of 1964 (Title VII) protects employees from being discriminated against based on their race, color, religion, sex or national origin. Federal law also prohibits discrimination based on age, pregnancy, disability and US citizenship status. While Title VII applies only to those who employ 15 or more people, all household employers should act fairly to avoid any workplace discrimination charge. Remember, federal, state and/or local laws may apply. For more

Federal law prohibits discrimination on the basis of:

- race, color, religion, sex, and national origin (Title VII of the Civil Rights Act)
- age (Age Discrimination in Employment Act)
- pregnancy (The Pregnancy Discrimination Act)
- citizenship (The Immigration Reform and Control Act)
- gender (The Equal Pay Act)
- disability (The Americans with Disabilities Act)
- union membership (The National Labor Relations Act)
- bankruptcy (The Bankruptcy Code)

In some circumstances, federal law may also be interpreted to prohibit discrimination against workers based on other factors, such as testing HIV positive, alcoholism, marital status and obesity.

information, go to the Equal Employment Opportunity Commission (EEOC) web site at www.eeoc.gov.

IRCA

This law requires employers to ensure that employees hired are legally authorized to work within the United States by mandating that all employers verify all new employees' employment eligibility. Under the US Immigration Reform and Control Act of 1986 (IRCA), a household with four or more employees is prohibited from committing document abuse or discrimination on the basis of citizenship status. Households with three or fewer employees are not subject to the IRCA's mandates.

DOCUMENT ABUSE

All US citizens and legal immigrants are protected from document abuse under IRCA. According to the US Department of Justice's Office of Special Counsel, document abuse

300+ illegal immigrant workers arrested at Wal-Mart stores throughout 21 states

The world's largest retailer, Wal-Mart, based in Bentonville, AR, made headlines throughout the country in late October 2003 when federal officials arrested more than 300 illegal immigrant workers in 60 Wal-Mart stores located throughout 21 states. Stemming from a US attorney investigation that dated back to 1998 as to whether Wal-Mart or its subcontractors knowingly hired illegal immigrants, the US immigration sweep involved the arrest of illegal workers, most of whom worked in cleaning crews for Wal-Mart's third-party contractors. Wal-Mart officials denied knowing the workers' immigration status or that its contractors failed to pay overtime or Social Security taxes, and a federal grand jury was convened to investigate. Additionally, just three weeks after the raids, nine of the illegal workers arrested filed a federal class-action suit against Wal-Mart and its janitorial contractors, alleging abuses of overtime, discriminatory pay and racketeering.

Arrests were made in 21 states. Since the raids, Wal-Mart has told all its contractors to review the legal status of their workforces, and Wal-Mart is also reviewing the legal status of all employees hired directly. Cooperating with the federal investigation, Wal-Mart officials stated in early 2004 that contractor cleaning crews were beginning to be replaced with in-house employees. According to a Wal-Mart spokesperson, Wal-Mart is doing background checks on all new workers to ensure they are legally eligible to work in the United States.

Source: The New York Times, November 9, 2003.

occurs when an employer (or potential employer) asks an employee (or an employee candidate) to produce a specific document other than what is required by US law to determine employment eligibility. (It can also occur, if a different document is requested other than what US law requires.) In addition, document abuse includes an employer's (or a potential employer's) rejection of valid documents that appear genuine and related to the individual. For instance, document abuse can occur when an employer requires an immigrant employee to produce upon hire proof of employment eligibility—but the employer refuses to accept the provided document, despite its reasonable appearance relating to the immigrant employee. The employee cannot be required to produce proof of employment eligibility until three business days after she or he begins work.

Proof of eligibility may be a green card or any US Citizen and Immigration Services (CIS)-issued document. According to IRCA, employers must accept any document or combination of documents listed on the CIS Form I-9 to establish identity and employment eligibility. Such documents can include:

- a US passport, an alien registration receipt card or a permanent resident card (Form I-551)
- an unexpired foreign passport containing an I-551 stamp
- an unexpired employment authorization document issued by the CIS that contains a photograph (forms I-766, I-688, I-688A or I-688B)

The list of documents to establish employment eligibility and/or identity is extensive. For a complete list of I-9 acceptable documents and for more information on Form I-9, go to www.uscis.gov or www.gtm.com/resourcecenter, or see Appendix 1 for a sample I-9 Form.

Employers will be sanctioned by the CIS if they hire aliens not authorized to work within the United States: fines may range from $250 to $10,000 per unauthorized alien. An employer demonstrating a persistent pattern of hiring unauthorized aliens may face a maximum six-month prison sentence.

CITIZENSHIP

Title VII of the Civil Rights Act of 1964, the Immigration Reform and Control Act of 1986 (IRCA) and the other anti-discrimination laws prohibit discrimination against individuals employed in the United States, regardless of citizenship. However, all workers must have legal authorization to work in the United States. Title VII applies to employers with 15 or more employees, and IRCA covers employers with four or more employees. Although many household employers with one or two household employees may not be required to follow the anti-discrimination rules put forth by these laws, it is best practice not to discriminate against any person lawfully admitted to the United States and authorized to work within the United States.

DIPLOMATIC OR OFFICIAL VISAS

There is a range of visas applicable for diplomatic personnel working in the United States from abroad. One such type that relates to household employment is the G-5 visa. According to the US Embassy, G-4 visas are issued to personnel of any rank who are going to the United States to take an appointment at a designated international organization, as well as their immediate family members. G-5 visas are issued to attendants and personal employees of people with G-1 through G-4 status. To qualify for a G visa, an individual must be entering the United States to pursue official duties. Domestic employees and personal servants may be issued G-5 visas, which can only be processed with an official request from the organization with which the employer is accredited. An employment contract must be submitted, showing the following:

- the hours of work
- a guarantee that the employee will be compensated at the state or federal minimum wage or the prevailing wage (whichever is greater)
- medical insurance coverage
- a statement that the employee will not accept any other employment while working for the employer
- a statement from the employer agreeing not to withhold the employee's passport

STATE AND LOCAL LAWS

Some states and localities protect employees with separate laws. For instance, the California Department of Fair Employment and Housing (DFEH) protects all workers from discrimination in all aspects of employment, including hiring, firing and terms and conditions. While Title VII (see p. 119) generally exempts employers with 14 or fewer employees, the California FEHA applies to employers with five or more employees.

Another example is the City of New York's Local Law No. 33, (see p. 17) which requires that licensed employment agencies provide to applicants for employment (as a household

> "All of us really do have two selves: our public selves and our home selves. It's the home self psyche that the household employee deals with. I remind my clientele that even though their home is their private domain, it is now also a work environment of another. As private employers, they have an obligation to provide a safe and healthy work environment, abiding by labor laws, at a minimum, but also establishing clear professional boundaries."
>
> Leann Brambach
> Owner/operator
> Home Details Inc.
> Seattle, WA

employee) a written statement of employee rights and employer obligations under local, state and federal law. Passed in 2003, the law is premised on the legislative finding that "the majority of domestic or household employees in New York City are immigrant women of color who, because of race and sex discrimination, language barriers and immigration status, are probably vulnerable to unfair labor practices."

All employers must comply with all laws pertaining to them—federal, state and local.

SEXUAL HARASSMENT

Sexual harassment policies stipulate that no employee should be subject to unwelcome verbal or physical conduct that is sexual in nature or that shows hostility to the employee because of his or her gender.

Sexual harassment can have devastating effects on the workplace. Therefore, an employer—including the household employer—needs to take any steps necessary to prohibit sexual harassment from occurring. Many workplaces have a zero tolerance policy, which means an employer will not tolerate any sexual harassment whatsoever.

It is best for an employer to include an anti-harassment/anti-discrimination policy in his or her employee handbook, which specifically addresses sexual harassment. According to the "Quick Reference to Sexual Harassment Prevention Training", such a policy needs to clearly state that:

- all employees and employers within the household are expected to treat one another with respect
- the employer will act immediately upon learning of a sexual harassment complaint. An employee should promptly file a complaint if the employee is made to feel uncomfortable or finds behavior unwelcome, offensive or inappropriate. A complaint may be made formally or informally. The law stipulates that the perception of misbehavior must be "reasonable". Employers need to assure employees that all complaints of sexual harassment will be handled as confidentially as possible
- the employer mandates a workplace free from all forms of discrimination
- everyone within the household is expected to act respectfully in order to enjoy a positive working environment

An employer must be prepared to respond to sexual harassment in the workplace—just as he or she is responsible for preventing any harassment or discrimination within the workplace. The employee handbook should cover the employer's sexual harassment policy and include: what is prohibited behavior in the workplace and what actions will be taken when a sexual harassment complaint is filed. In addition, the policy must state that no employee will experience retaliation for submitting a sexual harassment complaint.

THE EEOC

The federal Equal Employment Opportunity Commission (EEOC) enforces most federal laws prohibiting job discrimination. These laws include the following:

- Title VII of the Civil Rights Acts of 1964, outlawing job discrimination based on race, color, religion, sex or national origin
- Equal Pay Act of 1963, protecting against sex-based wage discrimination for men and women performing substantially the same work in the same establishment
- Age Discrimination in Employment Act of 1967, protecting people age 40 or older
- Titles I and V of the Americans with Disabilities Act of 1990, prohibiting discrimination against qualified individuals with disabilities in employment (see p. 125)

These laws offer a wide range of protection to employees. EEOC oversees and coordinates the large majority of federal equal employment opportunity regulations, practices and policies. Some anti-discrimination laws apply to employers with at least four employees, while some apply only to employers with 15 or more employees. (Household employment agencies may be subject to many of these laws therefore discrimination by such agencies is illegal.) Even employers not subject to anti-discrimination laws should use such laws as guidelines to ensure equal opportunity employment. In all, the federal anti-discrimination laws and the EEOC work to outlaw discrimination in employment, including: hiring, firing, compensation, promotions, layoffs, recruitment, testing, job advertisements, use of company facilities, fringe benefits, retirement plans, disability leaves and other terms and conditions of employment. Employers are required to post notices to all employees advising them of their rights under these laws.

It is important to note that Title VII of the Civil Rights Act of 1964 prohibits intentional discrimination *and* practices that have the effect of discrimination against individuals because of their race, color, national origin, religion or sex.

State and local agencies

The EEOC has cooperative relationships with the vast majority of the state and local Fair Employment Practices Agencies (FEPAs). The EEOC and FEPAs have workshare agreements that separate common workload to avoid duplication of charge processing.

Go to www.eeoc.gov or call 1.800.669.4000 for more information.

THE ADA

The ADA (Americans with Disabilities Act) prohibits discrimination against any qualified person with a disability. If an applicant is qualified to perform the job or can perform the work with reasonable accommodation, the ADA requires employers to consider that applicant equally with other non-disabled, qualified applicants. The ADA prohibits discrimination on the basis of disability in all employment practices—not only hiring and firing. Employment practices covered under the ADA include: recruitment, pay, hiring, firing, promotions, job assignments, training, leave, layoffs, benefits and all other employment-related activities.

> Under ADA, employers ensure people with disabilities:
>
> - have an equal opportunity to apply for jobs and to work in jobs for which they are qualified
> - have an equal opportunity to be promoted
> - have equal access to benefits and privileges offered to other employees
> - are not harassed because of their disability

The ADA covers employers with 15 or more employees, as well as applicable employment agencies. However, all employers should be aware of ADA regulations.
Under the ADA:

- a person with a disability is defined as someone who has a physical or mental impairment that substantially limits one or more of the major life activities of such individual (e.g., walking, seeing, hearing, speaking), has a record of such an impairment, or is regarded as having such an impairment
- a qualified employee or applicant with a disability is someone who satisfies skill, experience, education and other job-related requirements of the position held or sought and who can perform the position's essential functions with or without reasonable accommodation
- reasonable accommodation may include (but is not limited to) making existing facilities readily accessible to and usable by people with disabilities, such as a specially designed computer keyboard, or software, or perhaps just lowering a bulletin board to make it readable or lowering a paper cup dispenser in the employee break room for all to easily reach. Other accommodations could include allowing an employee to begin work at 10 a.m. instead of 9 a.m. in order for her or him to attend physical therapy appointments

- reasonable accommodation must be made if it would not impose "undue hardship" on an employer's business. Under the ADA, undue hardship is defined as an action requiring significant difficulty or expense when considered with an employer's size, financial resources and the nature and structure of the business' operation. According to the federal government, most accommodations are not expensive. The government estimates that the median cost of accommodation is about $240. In addition, to help businesses offset the cost of accommodations, tax credits may apply, such as the ADA Tax Incentives and the Small Business Tax Credit.

The ADA offers equal access and opportunities to people with disabilities. It does not offer people with disabilities an unfair advantage; an employer may hire a person without a disability who is more qualified than another applicant with a disability. While the ADA prohibits employers from asking about a disability, employers may ask whether an applicant will require a reasonable accommodation if it seems likely that he or she may need it. It is generally unlawful for an employer to ask an applicant whether she or he is disabled or to inquire about the nature or severity of her or his disability. Also it is unlawful for an employer to require an applicant to take a medical examination before a job offer is made. However, an employer *can* ask an applicant questions about his or her ability to perform job-related functions (as long as the questions are not phrased in terms of a disability). The ADA strictly limits questioning; employers may first check with an ADA specialist to determine what is allowable under the law.

Go to www.eeoc.gov or www.ada.gov for more information, or call the ADA Information Line at 1.800.514.0301 at which an ADA specialist may be reached. Information on ADA and its tax codes and incentives may be reached at www.irs.gov or 1.800.829.1040 or 1.202.622.3120.

Employers also should be aware of state and local laws pertaining to employment discrimination on the basis of disability. For instance, the Massachusetts Commission Against Discrimination (state law Chapter 151B) works with the federal ADA to protect people with disabilities against employment discrimination; yet, the Massachusetts law also extends to prohibit disability discrimination in housing, public accommodations and credit.

A household employer needs to be cautious about imposing certain requirements on the position. He or she may prefer to employ an older, unmarried, Christian woman, but implementing such preferences may violate federal, state and/or local law.

COMMON PRACTICE

Some common sense practices can help employers prevent illegal discrimination in the workplace, such as the following:

- Treat all employees equally. Hire, promote and fire without bias.
- Review employment policies for unfair and negative impact on a protected class (i.e., race, religion, ethnicity, gender, age, disability or pregnancy). Eliminate any unfair or negative policies or practices.
- Take immediate action to eliminate discriminatory conduct, including inappropriate comments or behavior.
- Encourage diversity.
- Never retaliate against an employee for filing a discrimination complaint, it's illegal.

Case Study

Denise Collins
CEO
In-House Staffing at Aunt Ann's
San Francisco, CA
GTM Partner

In-house Staffing at Aunt Ann's, a Californian agency, places eldercare workers, as well as nannies. According to Collins, some years ago, the agency placed an eldercare worker to join a fully staffed household. The employer needed 24-hour care for an elderly family member. The placed eldercare worker was a Hispanic woman, who was terminated with 30 days' notice and received a 30-day severance. Since the employer had more than five employees, the woman sued for discrimination stating that she was dismissed because she was Hispanic and that she was replaced by an English-speaking Irish woman. Because there were eight other household employees working as legal immigrants from Latin America, the court dismissed the case, saying the employer showed no discrimination.

> Household employers struggle with their home being a personal residence and, at the same time, a workplace for others. Be aware of any discrimination laws in your state or locality and how they apply to you, then implement employment practices to avoid the inconvenience of arguments or a lawsuit. The employment practices should be listed in the employee handbook.—*Guy*

DISCRIMINATION CHECKLIST

✓ Know all discrimination laws and regulations that apply to the household workplace, federal, state and local.

✓ Establish and enforce zero tolerance for unlawful activities and behaviors such as sexual harassment.

✓ Establish and implement procedures for dealing with illegal discrimination, and document them in the employee handbook.

✓ Keep in mind that many employment agencies are subject to equal employment opportunity (EEO) law and may not legally discriminate on the employers behalf.

For up-to-date information, go to www.gtm.com/resourcecenter

Notes

Chapter 10

Termination, Resignation and Saying Goodbye

All good things, and possibly some bad things, must come to an end. One of the most difficult aspects of being an employer is to face the end of an employee relationship, whether terminating an employee or dealing with a resignation. There are certain ways to handle the end of a relationship, which should be provided in the household's employee handbook, the work agreement and consistent with relevant laws. The best strategy that any employer can use when terminating an employee, accepting an employee's resignation or saying goodbye to an employee is to address the situation as soon as possible and to be honest.

Always end an employee relationship professionally. Deal with it head-on and without delay. Often, an employer's first instinct to terminate an employee should be acted upon, as seldom does an employer's perspective or situation change.

AT-WILL EMPLOYMENT

Typically, an employee works at the will of the employer, known as at-will employment, unless a contract has been signed for a fixed term of employment. At-will employment means that the employer can fire the employee at any time, and that the employee can quit at any time. Many employers ensure that they can apply at-will employment to their household by including as part of the job application an at-will employment statement, which the applicant usually initials or signs to acknowledge that he or she has read it and understands that he or she will be an at-will employee if hired. In addition, employers should include at-will employment language in job offer letters, employee handbooks and termination letters.

Without an at-will statement, the household employee's work agreement stipulates what was agreed upon regarding when employment ends.

In the United States, at-will employees can be terminated for good, bad or no cause. Three exceptions to the rule are:

1. violation of the state's public policy;

2. an implied contract for employment was established; and,
3. an implied covenant of good faith and fair dealing was established.

For information on how laws regarding termination apply to each state, go to http://csi. toolkit.cch.com/text/P05_8101.asp

TERMINATION

Firing an employee is an uncomfortable situation for many employers and their employees. Unless carefully done, firing an employee also can be downright dangerous for the employer. Be prepared to show support and documentation to prove legitimate cause for termination— and take care that all employees are treated equally.

First, carefully review the initial offer letter, any employment contract, handbook, appraisals and so on for oral and written agreements. Have the signed work agreement in

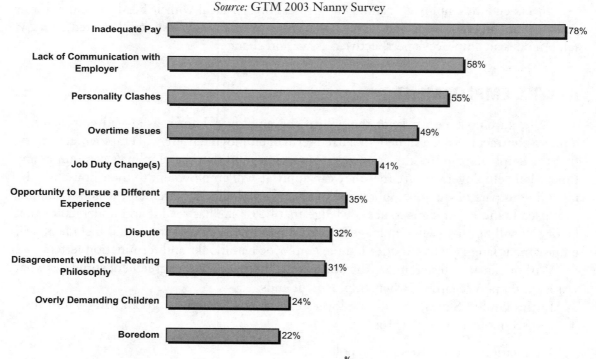

Figure 10.1
Reasons Nannies Leave Jobs
Source: GTM 2003 Nanny Survey

Reason	Percentage
Inadequate Pay	78%
Lack of Communication with Employer	58%
Personality Clashes	55%
Overtime Issues	49%
Job Duty Change(s)	41%
Opportunity to Pursue a Different Experience	35%
Dispute	32%
Disagreement with Child-Rearing Philosophy	31%
Overly Demanding Children	24%
Boredom	22%

hand. The work agreement should include described reasons for termination, as well as cause for mandated immediate termination clauses for any illegal or inappropriate behavior on the employee's part.

"It is best to terminate employees in a two-step process", said Wendy Sachs, president of the Philadelphia Nanny Network. "First, talk to the employee about the issue, and give him or her time to improve or change. Explain that non-compliance can result in termination. Document the conversation (see Appendix 17 for a sample performance evaluation form), providing a copy to the employee. If the situation changes in a positive way, the employer avoids turnover. If the situation remains unchanged, termination is justified." Second chances, though should never be considered if the employee has broken the law or put the family home or household members in danger.

Red flags when assessing termination

- Is it discriminatory?
- Is it on a whim?
- Is it to head off potential blackmail?
- Is it for financial hardship or difficulties?
- Is it because the employee is pregnant?
- Is it because the employee is involved with union activities?
- Is it because the employee is performing military service?
- Is it for any non-job related activity?

In addition, the employee handbook should have stipulated a progressive process for the employer to take to attempt to improve employee performance through the job performance evaluation. An employee who previously was made aware of unsatisfactory performance or incidents (see Appendix 23 for a sample incident report) and who knows his or her performance does not meet the employer's approval also knows that he or she risks termination. The progressive discipline method works well and provides the employer with a record of the employee's performance issues. The progress usually entails a verbal warning, then a written warning if the problem persists and lastly termination. Not only does this method help protect the employer from legal action, it also provides the employee with fair warning about unsatisfactory job performance and possible termination if performance is not improved.

When an employee leaves employment, stipulate in a termination letter the exact time and date of termination, what is included in the final paycheck and when that paycheck will be issued and other appropriate information. Also, some employers request that the employee return the employee handbook, which was stipulated in the statement release that was signed when the employee was issued the handbook. (See Appendix 24 for sample termination of employment letter.)

Termination Best Practice

Do

- Be prepared and be consistent.
- Have an adult witness present.
- Discuss/meet without children or dependents around.
- Be concise and to the point.
- Focus on measurable behavior (preferably written documentation.)
- Allow for an employee response to avoid oneway communication.
- State twice the decision to terminate.
- Inform the employee of the severance policy and unemployment compensation option.
- Avoid any lead time between firing and departing; the best time to set a termination meeting is at the end of the workday.
- Reiterate the confidentiality agreement that the employee signed at the beginning of employment; inform the employee that what he or she has learned about the family is very private, and that confidentiality was agreed upon for the term of employment, as well as after employment ended.
- Collect (from the employee) security codes, keys, car seats and other family items.
- Escort the employee from the premises.

Do not

- Delay—an employer's first hunch is usually the right one.
- Apologize, ramble or speak in generalities; speak directly and keep only to the facts.
- Make it a one-way conversation; allow the employee to provide feedback.
- Threaten an employee.
- Provide false hope; make the break clean.

Ask Guy

Q. How do I handle questions about a household employee no longer working for me?

A. The norm is that most employers talk freely about their previous employees to agencies and other employers. However, when providing references, always stick to the facts—and *only* the facts. Avoid stating your opinion or hearsay/gossip. Use the personnel file to help you answer reference questions, such as dates of employment and the employee's title or position. *Note:* that it is an accepted business practice to provide references with only a former employee's dates of employment and her or his title/position. However, this is not a common practice in household employment. Often families feel responsible to other families to provide references for the employee and insight into her or his job performance. When providing references, employers should remember that offering this information is generally at their discretion.

> **What to think about when considering terminating an employee**
>
> Is the reason to terminate an employee job related?
>
> - Does it relate to absenteeism?
> - Is it due to work quality?
> - Will it ensure the safety of the family and the household?
> - Is it the result of the employee's failure to perform tasks?
>
> Is the reason to terminate related to misconduct?
>
> - Is it the result of theft?
> - Is it because the employee is regularly tardy for work?
> - Is the employee neglecting her or his duties?
> - Has the employee misused family/household property?

- Withhold financial or insurance benefits.
- Hold a termination meeting in isolation or in public.
- Have children present.
- Provide prior notice of termination plans.
- Allow the employee to depart with employer/household belongings.

EXIT INTERVIEW/TERMINATION MEETING

The best practice is to hold a termination meeting, during which the employer states the reason for termination, reviews any severance package offerings and provides the employee with an opportunity to voice his or her views. Always have a concisely written letter prepared at the time of termination (see Appendix 24 for a sample termination of employment letter). Avoid lengthy explanations or apologies—be as straightforward as possible when explaining why the termination action is being taken. Keep your discussion short and to the point. Also, at the meeting have a prepared list of employer property and a deadline for its return. In some circumstances, unreturned property may be deducted from the final paycheck after the stated deadline has passed. Be sure to notify the employee that she or he may apply for unemployment insurance to determine whether if she or he is eligible.

Often it is suggested that a third party perform exit interviews, which may be a placement agency or a service such as GTM Household Employment Experts™ Household HR

Case Study

Pat Cascio
Owner/Operator
Morningside Nannies, LP
Houston, TX
(President, International Nanny Association)
GTM Partner Agency

Pat Cascio, of Morningside Nannies has a wealth of experience and a plethora of tales to tell regarding household employment. She lists one incident as "a classic case of the worst employer."

A live-out nanny, who had been employed for seven months, slipped on her employer's kitchen floor while caring for the family's one-year old child. Her injury, a broken ankle, was so significant that she called her employer, who arrived home in 15 minutes but refused to assist her. In fact, the nanny remained on the kitchen floor until her own son arrived to transport her to the hospital emergency room for treatment. (The nanny's ankle was set in a cast for three weeks, and then she required three weeks of physical therapy after the cast was removed.) The day after the injury, the employer, without workers' compensation insurance and concerned with liability, fired the nanny over the telephone, offering no reason for the termination. In addition, the employer withheld payment for work the nanny performed during that pay period.

Upon intervention by the nanny's son, the employer paid the nanny for the two days she worked but refused to pay for the workday on which the nanny was injured; paid one week's severance (not two weeks, as stipulated in the signed employment agreement); and agreed to write a recommendation letter only after the nanny signed a statement saying she would not sue the employer.

The nanny, who had no health insurance, paid for all medical expenses without any assistance from the employer. As a result of the injury and termination, the nanny was unemployed for two months.

According to Cascio, employers need to be educated about the possible occurrence of injury to employees in their household. "I recommend they be willing to help with medical bills or provide health insurance," she said. "They should also be educated in regard to wrongful termination issues, as the nanny could have sued on both accounts."

(continued)

> Household employers must have a sound termination policy, which is outlined in the employee handbook. As an employer isn't required to offer any explanation by law, it's helpful to provide closure to an employee, providing some items for her or him to improve upon for her or his next position and preventing any future problems or retaliation due to a feeling of mistreatment, and so on. Again, paying taxes, having the proper workers' compensation insurance, unemployment insurance and paying employee for all work hours helps eliminate the liability for the employer and employee.—*Guy*

Helpdesk, or that a disinterested person be present. (See Appendix 25 for a sample list of exit interview questions.) An effective exit interview can provide constructive feedback to allow an employer to improve the employment environment for future employees.

State laws vary on what constitutes legal practice when terminating an employee. (Go to www.dol.gov to determine which termination laws are enforced in specific states.) In addition, state laws vary in regard to when an employer is required to provide employees with their final paychecks, as well as whether the employer is mandated to pay an employee for unused vacation time and so on. Contact the state labor department's wage and hour division for more information.

Finally, consider offering the employee a severance package with a release of future claims contingency. Common severance is one week's pay for each year the employee has worked in the household, with a minimum of 2 weeks.

After the exit interview, the employer should write up what was discussed during the interview and file this with the termination letter in the employee's personnel file.

COBRA

Under Consolidated Omnibus Reconciliation Act (COBRA), employers with 20 or more employees who offer an employee health plan must offer employees and former employees the option of continuing their health care coverage if coverage is lost or reduced. COBRA coverage is only available when coverage is lost because of certain events. While COBRA seldom applies to household employment because of the "20 or more employees" stipulation, state and local laws may offer employees similar rights regardless of the number of employees. Under COBRA, coverage must be identical coverage provided to those beneficiaries not receiving COBRA. Employers need to be aware of their own state requirements and may contact their health plan administrator and/or their state insurance department to learn more.

The US Department of Labor offers an employer and employee hotline at 1.866.444.3272 or further information may be obtained at www.dol.gov/ebsa.

TERMINATION CHECKLIST

✓ Establish detailed information in the employee handbook regarding the employer's firing policy and practice. Also, detail termination procedures in the work agreement.

✓ When terminating an employee, have a prepared, concisely worded termination letter with information on final payment, and so on, at the termination meeting.

✓ Be prepared to support termination decision with backup materials kept in the employee's is file—signed work agreement, performance reviews, history of absences and so on.

✓ Provide the employee with a checklist and deadline to return employer property such as keys and the employee handbook.

✓ Termination can be an uneasy, tense procedure rife with damaging potential. Ensure that all explanations are legitimate and that employer actions can be documented.

✓ Follow COBRA by offering the employee the option to continue her or his health insurance coverage. Even if exempt from COBRA requirements, consider extending the employee an option for continued health insurance coverage.

RESIGNATION

Employees should be guided by an employer's preference when he or she resigns from his or her position. Common employment practice is for the employee to provide the employer with two weeks' notice. It would be advantageous for the employer to specify resignation expectations upon an employee's hire in the work agreement and the employee handbook. Be sure to include both employee and employer requirements to be followed when resigning.

In household employment, 30 days' notice is often preferred, due to the lengthy time involved in hiring and, or replacing household help and because there is not often a pool of staff (unless part of a bigger household estate) where someone else can pick up the resigned employee's duties while a replacement is found.

RESIGNATION CHECKLIST

✓ Establish and document a resignation procedure in the employee handbook and the employee work agreement. The handbook should detail requirements for both the employee and employer to meet when an employee resigns.

✓ Establish the length of time that will be required when giving notice.

✓ Note if the employee is required to train the replacement.

SAYING GOODBYE

Some households make an employee's goodbye an event, involving the entire family in a dinner celebration or a night of reminising. Some employers provide the employee with an album with stories and photos; others may provide a more "corporate" gift such as a watch or a plaque. The point is that some goodbyes are natural, and just because the employee is leaving, the household will not lose all contact with her or him. It is merely a change in the relationship; perhaps something that goes from full-time contact as an employee to occasional visits as a guest or a friend.

Of course, goodbyes affecting children have more of an impact. The household employer should be involved in communicating an employee's departure plans with the household. Household employers may want to work with a departing nanny or other household employee to explain to children why the employee is leaving employment, what his or her plans are and how the change may affect the children and the household.

Recognize that there can be a positive ending when one employee leaves, and take the necessary time to prepare the household for a new hire.

For up-to-date information, go to www.gtm.com/resourcecenter

Notes

APPENDIX 1

U.S. Department of Justice
Immigration and Naturalization Service

OMB No. 1115-0136

Employment Eligibility Verification

INSTRUCTIONS
PLEASE READ ALL INSTRUCTIONS CAREFULLY BEFORE COMPLETING THIS FORM.

Anti-Discrimination Notice It is illegal to discriminate against any individual (other than an alien not authorized to work in the U.S.) in hiring, discharging, or recruiting or referring for a fee because of that individual's national origin or citizenship status. It is illegal to discriminate against work eligible individuals. Employers **CANNOT** specify which document(s) they will accept from an employee. The refusal to hire an individual because of a future expiration date may also constitute illegal discrimination.

Section 1 - Employee. All employees, citizens and noncitizens, hired after November 6, 1986, must complete Section 1 of this form at the time of hire, which is the actual beginning of employment. **The employer is responsible for ensuring that Section 1 is timely and properly completed.**

Preparer/Translator Certification The Preparer/Translator Certification must be completed if Section 1 is prepared by a person other than the employee. A preparer/translator may be used only when the employee is unable to complete Section 1 on his/her own. However, the employee must still sign Section 1.

Section 2 - Employer. For the purpose of completing this form, the term "employer" includes those recruiters and referrers for a fee who are agricultural associations, agricultural employers or farm labor contractors.

Employers must complete Section 2 by examining evidence of identity and employment eligibility within three (3) business days of the date employment begins. If employees are authorized to work, but are unable to present the required document(s) within three business days, they must present a receipt for the application of the document(s) within three business days and the actual document(s) within ninety (90) days. However, if employers hire individuals for a duration of less than three business days, Section 2 must be completed at the time employment begins. **Employers must record: 1)** document title; **2)** issuing authority; **3)** document number, **4)** expiration date, if any; and **5)** the date employment begins. Employers must sign and date the certification. Employees must present original documents. Employers may, but are not required to, photocopy the document(s) presented. These photocopies may only be used for the verification process and must be retained with the I-9. **However, employers are still responsible for completing the I-9.**

Section 3 - Updating and Reverification. Employers must complete Section 3 when updating and/or reverifying the I-9. Employers must reverify employment eligibility of their employees on or before the expiration date recorded in Section 1. Employers **CANNOT** specify which document(s) they will accept from an employee.

- If an employee's name has changed at the time this form is being updated/ reverified, complete Block A.

- If an employee is rehired within three (3) years of the date this form was originally completed and the employee is still eligible to be employed on the same basis as previously indicated on this form (updating), complete Block B and the signature block.

- If an employee is rehired within three (3) years of the date this form was originally completed and the employee's work authorization has expired **or** if a current employee's work authorization is about to expire (reverification), complete Block B and:
  - examine any document that reflects that the employee is authorized to work in the U.S. (see List A **or** C),
  - record the document title, document number and expiration date (if any) in Block C, and complete the signature block.

Photocopying and Retaining Form I-9A blank I-9 may be reproduced, provided both sides are copied. The Instructions must be available to all employees completing this form. Employers must retain completed I-9s for three (3) years after the date of hire or one (1) year after the date employment ends, whichever is later.

For more detailed information, you may refer to the INS Handbook for Employers, (Form M-274). You may obtain the handbook at your local INS office.

Privacy Act Notice. The authority for collecting this information is the Immigration Reform and Control Act of 1986, Pub. L. 99-603 (8 USC 1324a).

This information is for employers to verify the eligibility of individuals for employment to preclude the unlawful hiring, or recruiting or referring for a fee, of aliens who are not authorized to work in the United States.

This information will be used by employers as a record of their basis for determining eligibility of an employee to work in the United States. The form will be kept by the employer and made available for inspection by officials of the U.S. Immigration and Naturalization Service, the Department of Labor and the Office of Special Counsel for Immigration Related Unfair Employment Practices.

Submission of the information required in this form is voluntary. However, an individual may not begin employment unless this form is completed, since employers are subject to civil or criminal penalties if they do not comply with the Immigration Reform and Control Act of 1986.

Reporting Burden. We try to create forms and instructions that are accurate, can be easily understood and which impose the least possible burden on you to provide us with information. Often this is difficult because some immigration laws are very complex. Accordingly, the reporting burden for this collection of information is computed as follows: **1)** learning about this form, 5 minutes; **2)** completing the form, 5 minutes; and **3)** assembling and filing (recordkeeping) the form, 5 minutes, for an average of 15 minutes per response. If you have comments regarding the accuracy of this burden estimate, or suggestions for making this form simpler, you can write to the Immigration and Naturalization Service, HQPDI, 425 I Street, N.W., Room 4034, Washington, DC 20536. OMB No. 1115-0136.

EMPLOYERS MUST RETAIN COMPLETED FORM I-9
PLEASE DO NOT MAIL COMPLETED FORM I-9 TO INS

Form I-9 (Rev. 11-21-91)N

How To Hire & Retain Your Household Help

U.S. Department of Justice
Immigration and Naturalization Service

OMB No. 1115-0136

Employment Eligibility Verification

Please read instructions carefully before completing this form. The instructions must be available during completion of this form. ANTI-DISCRIMINATION NOTICE: It is illegal to discriminate against work eligible individuals. Employers CANNOT specify which document(s) they will accept from an employee. The refusal to hire an individual because of a future expiration date may also constitute illegal discrimination.

Section 1. Employee Information and Verification. To be completed and signed by employee at the time employment begins.

Print Name: Last	First	Middle Initial	Maiden Name

Address (Street Name and Number)	Apt. #	Date of Birth (month/day/year)

City	State	Zip Code	Social Security #

I am aware that federal law provides for imprisonment and/or fines for false statements or use of false documents in connection with the completion of this form.

I attest, under penalty of perjury, that I am (check one of the following):
- ☐ A citizen or national of the United States
- ☐ A Lawful Permanent Resident (Alien # A_____)
- ☐ An alien authorized to work until ___/___/___
  (Alien # or Admission #) _____

Employee's Signature	Date (month/day/year)

Preparer and/or Translator Certification.   (To be completed and signed if Section 1 is prepared by a person other than the employee.) I attest, under penalty of perjury, that I have assisted in the completion of this form and that to the best of my knowledge the information is true and correct.

Preparer's/Translator's Signature	Print Name

Address (Street Name and Number, City, State, Zip Code)	Date (month/day/year)

Section 2. Employer Review and Verification. To be completed and signed by employer. Examine one document from List A OR examine one document from List B and one from List C, as listed on the reverse of this form, and record the title, number and expiration date, if any, of the document(s)

	List A	OR	List B	AND	List C
Document title:	_____		_____		_____
Issuing authority:	_____		_____		_____
Document #:	_____		_____		_____
Expiration Date (if any):	___/___/___		___/___/___		___/___/___
Document #:	_____				
Expiration Date (if any):	___/___/___				

CERTIFICATION - I attest, under penalty of perjury, that I have examined the document(s) presented by the above-named employee, that the above-listed document(s) appear to be genuine and to relate to the employee named, that the employee began employment on (month/day/year) ___/___/___ **and that to the best of my knowledge the employee is eligible to work in the United States. (State employment agencies may omit the date the employee began employment.)**

Signature of Employer or Authorized Representative	Print Name	Title

Business or Organization Name	Address (Street Name and Number, City, State, Zip Code)	Date (month/day/year)

Section 3. Updating and Reverification. To be completed and signed by employer.

A. New Name (if applicable)	B. Date of rehire (month/day/year) (if applicable)

C. If employee's previous grant of work authorization has expired, provide the information below for the document that establishes current employment eligibility.

Document Title:_____   Document #:_____   Expiration Date (if any): ___/___/___

I attest, under penalty of perjury, that to the best of my knowledge, this employee is eligible to work in the United States, and if the employee presented document(s), the document(s) I have examined appear to be genuine and to relate to the individual.

Signature of Employer or Authorized Representative	Date (month/day/year)

Form I-9 (Rev. 11-21-91)N Page 2

LISTS OF ACCEPTABLE DOCUMENTS

LIST A		LIST B		LIST C
Documents that Establish Both Identity and Employment Eligibility	**OR**	**Documents that Establish Identity**	**AND**	**Documents that Establish Employment Eligibility**

LIST A

Documents that Establish Both Identity and Employment Eligibility

1. U.S. Passport (unexpired or expired)

2. Certificate of U.S. Citizenship *(INS Form N-560 or N-561)*

3. Certificate of Naturalization *(INS Form N-550 or N-570)*

4. Unexpired foreign passport, with *I-551 stamp or* attached *INS Form I-94* indicating unexpired employment authorization

5. Permanent Resident Card or Alien Registration Receipt Card with photograph *(INS Form I-151 or I-551)*

6. Unexpired Temporary Resident Card *(INS Form I-688)*

7. Unexpired Employment Authorization Card *(INS Form I-688A)*

8. Unexpired Reentry Permit *(INS Form I-327)*

9. Unexpired Refugee Travel Document *(INS Form I-571)*

10. Unexpired Employment Authorization Document issued by the INS which contains a photograph *(INS Form I-688B)*

OR

LIST B

Documents that Establish Identity

1. Driver's license or ID card issued by a state or outlying possession of the United States provided it contains a photograph or information such as name, date of birth, gender, height, eye color and address

2. ID card issued by federal, state or local government agencies or entities, provided it contains a photograph or information such as name, date of birth, gender, height, eye color and address

3. School ID card with a photograph

4. Voter's registration card

5. U.S. Military card or draft record

6. Military dependent's ID card

7. U.S. Coast Guard Merchant Mariner Card

8. Native American tribal document

9. Driver's license issued by a Canadian government authority

For persons under age 18 who are unable to present a document listed above:

10. School record or report card

11. Clinic, doctor or hospital record

12. Day-care or nursery school record

AND

LIST C

Documents that Establish Employment Eligibility

1. U.S. social security card issued by the Social Security Administration *(other than a card stating it is not valid for employment)*

2. Certification of Birth Abroad issued by the Department of State *(Form FS-545 or Form DS-1350)*

3. Original or certified copy of a birth certificate issued by a state, county, municipal authority or outlying possession of the United States bearing an official seal

4. Native American tribal document

5. U.S. Citizen ID Card *(INS Form I-197)*

6. ID Card for use of Resident Citizen in the United States *(INS Form I-179)*

7. Unexpired employment authorization document issued by the INS *(other than those listed under List A)*

Illustrations of many of these documents appear in Part 8 of the Handbook for Employers (M-274)

APPENDIX 2

Form **SS-8** (Rev. June 2003) Department of the Treasury Internal Revenue Service	**Determination of Worker Status for Purposes of Federal Employment Taxes and Income Tax Withholding**	OMB No. 1545-0004

Name of firm (or person) for whom the worker performed services	Worker's name	
Firm's address (include street address, apt. or suite no., city, state, and ZIP code)	Worker's address (include street address, apt. or suite no., city, state, and ZIP code)	
Trade name	Telephone number (include area code) ( )	Worker's social security number
Telephone number (include area code) ( )	Firm's employer identification number	Worker's employer identification number (if any)

If the worker is paid by a firm other than the one listed on this form for these services, enter the name, address, and employer identification number of the payer.

Important Information Needed To Process Your Request

We must have your permission to disclose your name and the information on this form and any attachments to other parties involved with this request. **Do we have your permission to disclose this information?** . . . . ☐ Yes ☐ No
If you answered "No" or did not mark a box, we will not process your request and will not issue a determination.

You must answer ALL items OR mark them "Unknown" or "Does not apply." If you need more space, attach another sheet.

A This form is being completed by: ☐ Firm ☐ Worker; for services performed _____ to _____ .
   (beginning date)   (ending date)

B Explain your reason(s) for filing this form (e.g., you received a bill from the IRS, you believe you received a Form 1099 or Form W-2 erroneously, you are unable to get worker's compensation benefits, you were audited or are being audited by the IRS). ------------------------------
   ----

C Total number of workers who performed or are performing the same or similar services _____ .

D How did the worker obtain the job? ☐ Application ☐ Bid ☐ Employment Agency ☐ Other (specify) _____ .

E Attach copies of all supporting documentation (contracts, invoices, memos, Forms W-2, Forms 1099, IRS closing agreements, IRS rulings, etc.). In addition, please inform us of any current or past litigation concerning the worker's status. If no income reporting forms (Form 1099-MISC or W-2) were furnished to the worker, enter the amount of income earned for the year(s) at issue $ _____ .

F Describe the firm's business. --

G Describe the work done by the worker and provide the worker's job title. ------------------------------
   ----

H Explain why you believe the worker is an employee or an independent contractor. ------------------------
   ----

I Did the worker perform services for the firm before getting this position? . . . . ☐ Yes ☐ No ☐ N/A
   If "Yes," what were the dates of the prior service? --
   If "Yes," explain the differences, if any, between the current and prior service. ----------------------
   ----

J If the work is done under a written agreement between the firm and the worker, attach a copy (preferably signed by both parties). Describe the terms and conditions of the work arrangement. ------------------------------
   ----

For Privacy Act and Paperwork Reduction Act Notice, see page 5.   Cat. No. 16106T   Form **SS-8** (Rev. 6-2003)

How To Hire & Retain Your Household Help

Part I   Behavioral Control

1   What specific training and/or instruction is the worker given by the firm? ....
    ....
2   How does the worker receive work assignments? ....
    ....
3   Who determines the methods by which the assignments are performed? ....
4   Who is the worker required to contact if problems or complaints arise and who is responsible for their resolution? ....
    ....
5   What types of reports are required from the worker? Attach examples. ....
    ....
6   Describe the worker's daily routine (i.e., schedule, hours, etc.). ....
    ....
    ....
7   At what location(s) does the worker perform services (e.g., firm's premises, own shop or office, home, customer's location, etc.)? ....
    ....
8   Describe any meetings the worker is required to attend and any penalties for not attending (e.g., sales meetings, monthly meetings, staff
    meetings, etc.). ....
9   Is the worker required to provide the services personally? . . . . ☐ Yes ☐ No
10 If substitutes or helpers are needed, who hires them? ....
11 If the worker hires the substitutes or helpers, is approval required? . . . . ☐ Yes ☐ No
    If "Yes," by whom? ....
12 Who pays the substitutes or helpers? ....
13 Is the worker reimbursed if the worker pays the substitutes or helpers? . . . . ☐ Yes ☐ No
    If "Yes," by whom? ....

Part II   Financial Control

1   List the supplies, equipment, materials, and property provided by each party:
    The firm ....
    The worker ....
    Other party ....
2   Does the worker lease equipment? . . . . ☐ Yes ☐ No
    If "Yes," what are the terms of the lease? (Attach a copy or explanatory statement.) ....
    ....
3   What expenses are incurred by the worker in the performance of services for the firm? ....
    ....
4   Specify which, if any, expenses are reimbursed by:
    The firm ....
    Other party ....
5   Type of pay the worker receives: ☐ Salary   ☐ Commission   ☐ Hourly Wage   ☐ Piece Work
    ☐ Lump Sum   ☐ Other (specify)
    If type of pay is commission, and the firm guarantees a minimum amount of pay, specify amount $ _____ .
6   Is the worker allowed a drawing account for advances? . . . . ☐ Yes ☐ No
    If "Yes," how often? ....
    Specify any restrictions. ....
    ....
7   Whom does the customer pay? . . . . ☐ Firm   ☐ Worker
    If worker, does the worker pay the total amount to the firm?   ☐ Yes   ☐ No   If "No," explain. ....
    ....
8   Does the firm carry worker's compensation insurance on the worker? . . . . ☐ Yes ☐ No
9   What economic loss or financial risk, if any, can the worker incur beyond the normal loss of salary (e.g., loss or damage of equipment,
    material, etc.)? ....
    ....

How To Hire & Retain Your Household Help

Part III   Relationship of the Worker and Firm

1   List the benefits available to the worker (e.g., paid vacations, sick pay, pensions, bonuses). ------------------------------

2   Can the relationship be terminated by either party without incurring liability or penalty? . . . . ☐ **Yes**   ☐ **No**
       If "No," explain your answer. --

3   Does the worker perform similar services for others? . . . . ☐ **Yes**   ☐ **No**
       If "Yes," is the worker required to get approval from the firm? . . . . ☐ **Yes**   ☐ **No**

4   Describe any agreements prohibiting competition between the worker and the firm while the worker is performing services or during any later
       period. Attach any available documentation. --

5   Is the worker a member of a union? . . . . ☐ **Yes**   ☐ **No**

6   What type of advertising, if any, does the worker do (e.g., a business listing in a directory, business cards, etc.)? Provide copies, if applicable.
       ----

7   If the worker assembles or processes a product at home, who provides the materials and instructions or pattern? ----------------

8   What does the worker do with the finished product (e.g., return it to the firm, provide it to another party, or sell it)? ----------------

9   How does the firm represent the worker to its customers (e.g., employee, partner, representative, or contractor)? ----------------

10 If the worker no longer performs services for the firm, how did the relationship end? ------------------------------

Part IV   **For Service Providers or Salespersons**—Complete this part if the worker provided a service directly to
             customers or is a salesperson.

1   What are the worker's responsibilities in soliciting new customers? --

2   Who provides the worker with leads to prospective customers? --

3   Describe any reporting requirements pertaining to the leads. ---

4   What terms and conditions of sale, if any, are required by the firm? --

5   Are orders submitted to and subject to approval by the firm? . . . . ☐ **Yes**   ☐ **No**

6   Who determines the worker's territory? --

7   Did the worker pay for the privilege of serving customers on the route or in the territory? . . . . ☐ **Yes**   ☐ **No**
       If "Yes," whom did the worker pay? --
       If "Yes," how much did the worker pay? . . . . $ _____ .

8   Where does the worker sell the product (e.g., in a home, retail establishment, etc.)? --------------------------

9   List the product and/or services distributed by the worker (e.g., meat, vegetables, fruit, bakery products, beverages, or laundry or dry cleaning
       services). If more than one type of product and/or service is distributed, specify the principal one. -----------------

10 Does the worker sell life insurance full time? . . . . ☐ **Yes**   ☐ **No**

11 Does the worker sell other types of insurance for the firm? . . . . ☐ **Yes**   ☐ **No**
       If "Yes," enter the percentage of the worker's total working time spent in selling other types of insurance. . . . _____%

12 If the worker solicits orders from wholesalers, retailers, contractors, or operators of hotels, restaurants, or other similar
       establishments, enter the percentage of the worker's time spent in the solicitation. . . . . _____%

13 Is the merchandise purchased by the customers for resale or use in their business operations? . . . . ☐ **Yes**   ☐ **No**
       Describe the merchandise and state whether it is equipment installed on the customers' premises. ------------------

Part V   Signature (see page 4)

Under penalties of perjury, I declare that I have examined this request, including accompanying documents, and to the best of my knowledge and belief, the facts
presented are true, correct, and complete.

Signature ▶ _____   Title ▶ _____   Date ▶ _____
              (Type or print name below)

General Instructions

Section references are to the Internal Revenue Code unless otherwise noted.

Purpose

Firms and workers file Form SS-8 to request a determination of the status of a worker for purposes of Federal employment taxes and income tax withholding.

A Form SS-8 determination may be requested only in order to resolve Federal tax matters. If Form SS-8 is submitted for a tax year for which the statute of limitations on the tax return has expired, a determination letter will not be issued. The statute of limitations expires 3 years from the due date of the tax return or the date filed, whichever is later.

The IRS does not issue a determination letter for proposed transactions or on hypothetical situations. We may, however, issue an information letter when it is considered appropriate.

Definition

Firm. For the purposes of this form, the term "firm" means any individual, business enterprise, organization, state, or other entity for which a worker has performed services. The firm may or may not have paid the worker directly for these services. **If the firm was not responsible for payment for services, be sure to enter the name, address, and employer identification number of the payer on the first page of Form SS-8 below the identifying information for the firm and the worker.**

The SS-8 Determination Process

The IRS will acknowledge the receipt of your Form SS-8. Because there are usually two (or more) parties who could be affected by a determination of employment status, the IRS attempts to get information from all parties involved by sending those parties blank Forms SS-8 for completion. The case will be assigned to a technician who will review the facts, apply the law, and render a decision. The technician may ask for additional information from the requestor, from other involved parties, or from third parties that could help clarify the work relationship before rendering a decision. The IRS will generally issue a formal determination to the firm or payer (if that is a different entity), and will send a copy to the worker. A determination letter applies only to a worker (or a class of workers) requesting it, and the decision is binding on the IRS. In certain cases, a formal determination will not be issued. Instead, an information letter may be issued. Although an information letter is advisory only and is not binding on the IRS, it may be used to assist the worker to fulfill his or her Federal tax obligations.

Neither the SS-8 determination process nor the review of any records in connection with the determination constitutes an examination (audit) of any Federal tax return. If the periods under consideration have previously been examined, the SS-8 determination process will not constitute a reexamination under IRS reopening procedures. Because this is not an examination of any Federal tax return, the appeal rights available in connection with an examination do not apply to an SS-8 determination. However, if you disagree with a determination and you have additional information concerning the work relationship that you believe was not previously considered, you may request that the determining office reconsider the determination.

Completing Form SS-8

Answer all questions as completely as possible. Attach additional sheets if you need more space. Provide information for all years the worker provided services for the firm. Determinations are based on the entire relationship between the firm and the worker.

Additional copies of this form may be obtained by calling 1-800-829-4933 or from the IRS website at **www.irs.gov.**

Fee

There is no fee for requesting an SS-8 determination letter.

Signature

Form SS-8 must be signed and dated by the taxpayer. A stamped signature will not be accepted.

The person who signs for a corporation must be an officer of the corporation who has personal knowledge of the facts. If the corporation is a member of an affiliated group filing a consolidated return, it must be signed by an officer of the common parent of the group.

The person signing for a trust, partnership, or limited liability company must be, respectively, a trustee, general partner, or member-manager who has personal knowledge of the facts.

Where To File

Send the completed Form SS-8 to the address listed below for the firm's location. However, for cases involving Federal agencies, send Form SS-8 to the Internal Revenue Service, Attn: CC:CORP:T:C, Ben Franklin Station, P.O. Box 7604, Washington, DC 20044.

Firm's location:	Send to:
Alaska, Arizona, Arkansas, California, Colorado, Hawaii, Idaho, Illinois, Iowa, Kansas, Minnesota, Missouri, Montana, Nebraska, Nevada, New Mexico, North Dakota, Oklahoma, Oregon, South Dakota, Texas, Utah, Washington, Wisconsin, Wyoming, American Samoa, Guam, Puerto Rico, U.S. Virgin Islands	Internal Revenue Service SS-8 Determinations P.O. Box 630 Stop 631 Holtsville, NY 11742-0630
Alabama, Connecticut, Delaware, District of Columbia, Florida, Georgia, Indiana, Kentucky, Louisiana, Maine, Maryland, Massachusetts, Michigan, Mississippi, New Hampshire, New Jersey, New York, North Carolina, Ohio, Pennsylvania, Rhode Island, South Carolina, Tennessee, Vermont, Virginia, West Virginia, all other locations not listed	Internal Revenue Service SS-8 Determinations 40 Lakemont Road Newport, VT 05855-1555

Instructions for Workers

If you are requesting a determination for more than one firm, complete a separate Form SS-8 for each firm.

 Form SS-8 is not a claim for refund of social security and Medicare taxes or Federal income tax withholding.

If the IRS determines that you are an employee, you are responsible for filing an amended return for any corrections related to this decision. A determination that a worker is an employee does not necessarily reduce any current or prior tax liability. For more information, call 1-800-829-1040.

How To Hire & Retain Your Household Help

Time for filing a claim for refund. Generally, you must file your claim for a credit or refund within 3 years from the date your original return was filed or within 2 years from the date the tax was paid, whichever is later.

Filing Form SS-8 does not prevent the expiration of the time in which a claim for a refund must be filed. If you are concerned about a refund, and the statute of limitations for filing a claim for refund for the year(s) at issue has not yet expired, you should file **Form 1040X,** Amended U.S. Individual Income Tax Return, to protect your statute of limitations. File a separate Form 1040X for each year.

On the Form 1040X you file, do not complete lines 1 through 24 on the form. Write "Protective Claim" at the top of the form, sign and date it. In addition, you should enter the following statement in Part II, Explanation of Changes to Income, Deductions, and Credits: "Filed Form SS-8 with the Internal Revenue Service Office in (Holtsville, NY; Newport, VT; or Washington, DC; as appropriate). By filing this protective claim, I reserve the right to file a claim for any refund that may be due after a determination of my employment tax status has been completed."

Filing Form SS-8 does not alter the requirement to timely file an income tax return. Do not delay filing your tax return in anticipation of an answer to your SS-8 request. In addition, if applicable, do not delay in responding to a request for payment while waiting for a determination of your worker status.

Instructions for Firms

If a **worker** has requested a determination of his or her status while working for you, you will receive a request from the IRS to complete a Form SS-8. In cases of this type, the IRS usually gives each party an opportunity to present a statement of the facts because any decision will affect the employment tax status of the parties. Failure to respond to this request will not prevent the IRS from issuing a determination letter based on the information he or she has made available so that the worker may fulfill his or her Federal tax obligations. However, the information that you provide is extremely valuable in determining the status of the worker.

If **you** are requesting a determination for a particular class of worker, complete the form for **one** individual who is representative of the class of workers whose status is in question. If you want a written determination for more than one class of workers, complete a separate Form SS-8 for one worker from each class whose status is typical of that class. A written determination for any worker will apply to other workers of the same class if the facts are not materially different for these workers. Please provide a list of names and addresses of all workers potentially affected by this determination.

If you have a reasonable basis for not treating a worker as an employee, you may be relieved from having to pay employment taxes for that worker under section 530 of the 1978 Revenue Act. However, this relief provision cannot be considered in conjunction with a Form SS-8 determination because the determination does not constitute an examination of any tax return. For more information regarding section 530 of the 1978 Revenue Act and to determine if you qualify for relief under this section, you may visit the IRS website at **www.irs.gov**.

Privacy Act and Paperwork Reduction Act Notice. We ask for the information on this form to carry out the Internal Revenue laws of the United States. This information will be used to determine the employment status of the worker(s) described on the form. Subtitle C, Employment Taxes, of the Internal Revenue Code imposes employment taxes on wages. Sections 3121(d), 3306(a), and 3401(c) and (d) and the related regulations define employee and employer for purposes of employment taxes imposed under Subtitle C. Section 6001 authorizes the IRS to request information needed to determine if a worker(s) or firm is subject to these taxes. Section 6109 requires you to provide your taxpayer identification number. Neither workers nor firms are required to request a status determination, but if you choose to do so, you must provide the information requested on this form. Failure to provide the requested information may prevent us from making a status determination. If any worker or the firm has requested a status determination and you are being asked to provide information for use in that determination, you are not required to provide the requested information. However, failure to provide such information will prevent the IRS from considering it in making the status determination. Providing false or fraudulent information may subject you to penalties. Routine uses of this information include providing it to the Department of Justice for use in civil and criminal litigation, to the Social Security Administration for the administration of social security programs, and to cities, states, and the District of Columbia for the administration of their tax laws. We may also disclose this information to Federal and state agencies to enforce Federal nontax criminal laws and to combat terrorism. We may provide this information to the affected worker(s) or the firm as part of the status determination process.

You are not required to provide the information requested on a form that is subject to the Paperwork Reduction Act unless the form displays a valid OMB control number. Books or records relating to a form or its instructions must be retained as long as their contents may become material in the administration of any Internal Revenue law. Generally, tax returns and return information are confidential, as required by section 6103.

The time needed to complete and file this form will vary depending on individual circumstances. The estimated average time is: **Recordkeeping,** 22 hrs.; **Learning about the law or the form,** 47 min.; and **Preparing and sending the form to the IRS,** 1 hr., 11 min. If you have comments concerning the accuracy of these time estimates or suggestions for making this form simpler, we would be happy to hear from you. You can write to the Tax Products Coordinating Committee, Western Area Distribution Center, Rancho Cordova, CA 95743-0001. **Do not** send the tax form to this address. Instead, see **Where To File** on page 4.

APPENDIX 3
WORK AGREEMENT SAMPLE

This "Agreement" is made and entered into on_____(date), between _____ _____(employer) residing at _____ and _____(employee) residing at _____.

RECITALS

1. Employer is an individual and a "Household Employer", resident of _____(state), and over the age of 18.
2. Employee is an individual, resident of _____(state), and over the age of 18.
3. Employee is willing to be employed by Employer, and Employer is willing to employ Employee, on the terms and conditions set forth in this Agreement.

A. EMPLOYMENT

1. Employment under this agreement is to begin on _____ and continue unless sooner terminated as provided herein.
2. Subject to the supervision and control of Employer, Employee shall perform the usual and customary duties of _____, including but not limited to that of those described in the written job description.
3. Employee shall work at the convenience of Employer, arriving and leaving at times to be specified by Employer. Employee shall not be required to work more than ____hours per week, but may consent to do so.

B. COMPENSATION

1. Subject to the following provisions of this agreement, the Employer agrees to pay the Employee a gross compensation hourly rate of $_____.
2. Employer shall deduct and withhold appropriate amounts from Employee's gross pay as required by federal and state laws.
3. Employer shall pay Employee on a (weekly _____) basis on the Friday of each week.
4. Employee shall receive an overtime wage of 1.5 times the usual gross hourly rate for each hour worked exceeding 40 hours per week. At the Employer's option, the Employer may compensate Employee by either paying overtime or by giving Employee compensatory time off, during the same pay period.
5. Employer, at it's own discretion, may agree to increase Employee's hourly gross compensation from time to time in writing.

C. BENEFITS

1. Employee is entitled to _____ days of paid vacation annually. The vacation must be scheduled 30 days in advance and agreed to by employer. Vacation is based upon normal payment for a 40-hour workweek.

2. Employee will receive _____days per year as paid sick time. Sick time may not be accumulated from year to year. Sick time benefits cannot be taken in cash compensation and are forfeited on termination of employment.

D. TERMS AND CONDITIONS OF EMPLOYMENT

1. Employee may not drink alcohol, use illegal drugs or smoke while on duty for the employer.
2. Employer shall provide Employee with a petty cash fund for job related expenses. Employer shall reimburse Employee upon providing Employer with a complete expense report with related receipt(s). Reimbursements will be made weekly.
3. Employment with the Household employer lends itself to intimate and sensitive information. Therefore, Household employee agrees to treat household information as private and confidential both during and after his/her employment tenure. Household employee agrees that no information pertaining to the household, such as the home's security system code or a password for childcare drop offs, is to be repeated inside or outside of the worksite. This applies to any information that is discussed by parties within the household, as well. In addition, Household employee agrees not to discuss his/her salary and benefits with other household employees. Household employee acknowledges that a violation of this rule of conduct will be grounds for early dismissal.

E. TERMINATION OF AGREEMENT

1. Employer may terminate employment by Employee for violation of paragraph D 1.
2. Employer may terminate employment by Employee for failure to perform the duties set forth in the job description and employee handbook.
3. Termination means that benefits in paragraph C cease as of the date of termination.
4. Agreement may be ended by mutual agreement.
5. Employment is at the discretion of employer and employee. Either party may terminate this agreement with or without notice or cause.

F. MODIFICATION AND INTERPRETATION

1. The job description may change by mutual consent.
2. Each party expects that Employee will conform to the custom and practice of the _____ (household employment, i.e. Chef, nanny, butler).

G. APPLICABLE LAWS

1. The provisions of this agreement shall be construed in accordance with the laws of the state of _____.

_____   _____
Household employer   Date   Household employee   Date

(NOTICE)

The information in this sample is designed to provide an outline that you can follow when formulating personnel plans. Due to the variances of many local, city, county and state laws, we recommend that you seek professional legal counseling before entering into any agreement.

APPENDIX 4

INTERVIEW QUESTIONS

General:

- What made you choose this particular field of work?
- What motivates you at work? What is important to you about the household you work for? In the past, in what ways how have you demonstrated that you care about the work you do?
- What do you feel is the greatest strength that you bring to your job or your work? What is an area(s) in which you need or would like to improve? How do you plan to address this?
- How would you describe your ideal working conditions?
- What are your career plans for the future?

Educational Background:

- What is your educational background?
- How would you rate yourself academically?
- What are you doing now to develop your knowledge or talents? What have you done in the past to expand your knowledge in your field?
- What do you do to keep informed in your field?
- Tell me about a mistake you have made, in your current or previous positions, and what you did to resolve it.

Work History:

- Why are you leaving your current position (or why did you leave your most recent position?)?
- Of your previous positions, which did you like the best and why? Which did you like the least? Which motivated you the most?
- Describe your relationship with the last household. What do you think that your employer or manager would say about your job performance?
- At work, what have been your major work accomplishments? What are you most proud of in regards with past experience and why?
- Describe your working relationships with others.

Behavior:

- Name a specific problem you faced on the job. How did you resolve it?
- Describe a time when you had to go above and beyond the call of duty to get the job done.
- What frustrates you about your job? How did you handle it and what was the result?
- What was the toughest decision that you had to make recently in your job? What was it, why was it difficult, and how did you handle the situation?
- Describe how you solved a problem in a unique way.

Ethical:

- What process do you use to resolve an ethical dilemma? What, if anything, would you have done differently?
- Tell us when it was necessary to make an exception to the rules to get something accomplished.

Learning Orientation:

- What do you feel is a specific weakness of yours and how you overcame it? Be specific.

Results Focused:

- What is an accomplishment that you are especially proud of?

Change Orientation:

- Describe a time when you were faced with a change in your work environment. What was it and how did you handle it?
- Think of a situation in which when you were provided with very little instruction on how to perform a task. How did you proceed?

APPENDIX 5

APPLICATION FOR EMPLOYMENT

_____   _____
Name Last   First   Middle   Previous Name(s) if any

_____
Address   Number   Street   City   State   ZIP Code

_____   _____   _____   _____
Telephone   Email address   Driver's License #   State

EDUCATION

Name/Location of School	Degree Earned		Type	Year Graduated	Major
Grade School _____	Y	N	_____	_____	_____
High School _____	Y	N	_____	_____	_____
Vocational School _____	Y	N	_____	_____	_____
College _____	Y	N	_____	_____	_____
Graduate School _____	Y	N	_____	_____	_____

Courses in Child Development, Education
Extra-curricular Activities

EMPLOYMENT HISTORY (_Starting with current to most recent, list all previous positions. Explain any gap between employment in the space provided._)

DATES EMPLOYED	EMPLOYER	PHONE	POSITION HELD
1.			
2.			
3.			

Explanation of any gaps in employment

_____

BACKGROUND

A. Have you ever been convicted of a crime? [ ] No   [ ] Yes   If yes, explain the nature of the offense, date and court location.

B. Have you had any traffic citations, (including speeding tickets, DWI or DUI convictions) in the past five years? [ ] No   [ ] Yes

If yes, list all traffic citations for the past five years, including speeding tickets, DWI or DUI convictions.

Is your driver's license currently valid, not under a suspension or revoked?   [ ] Yes   [ ] No   Explain

_____

In what other states have you had a driver's licenses? _____
                                                        State   License numbers (if known)

C. List all addresses you have lived at for the past five years

	Address	County	State	Dates
1.				
2.				
3.				

AVAILABILITY/COMPENSATION

When can you start work? _____

Are you willing to make a one-year commitment?   [ ] Yes   [ ] No

What days and hours are you available to work? _____

Gross hourly rate requested $_____per _____

What benefits do you desire? _____

STATEMENT

I have not withheld any information a reasonable person would expect a prospective candidate to provide. I have been honest in revealing and explaining any undesirable background information. I do certify that all information noted here is true to the best of my knowledge.

I authorize full disclosure and release to any duly authorized agent of the Household employer of all information and records both public and private, including, but not limited to, criminal and financial history, as required to conduct a complete background investigation. I hereby release all persons and agencies from any liability associated with such disclosure. I understand such information may be duplicated and given to any prospective client seeking to hire me, and I hereby authorize this.

I also specifically request that all agencies and references fully cooperate with this investigation and provide the requested information.

_____

Applicant Signature   Date

APPENDIX 6
OFFER LETTER FOR HOUSEHOLD EMPLOYMENT

Confidential

(Date)

Mary Poppins
123 Main Street
Chicago, IL, 12345

Dear Mary,

To confirm our conversation of earlier today, _____ (date), I am pleased to offer you the fulltime position of nanny with our family. We would like you to start work on _____ (date).

Your hours will be Monday through Friday 8:15 a.m. until 5:30 p.m. Your compensation package is as follows.

- **Compensation:** $10 per hour
  Overtime $15 per hour
  $493.75 gross per week for 46.25 hours
  Paid weekly through GTM's EasyPay® service

- **Benefits:** (after 60 days of employment) Paid Health Insurance for a single individual of either major medical, HMO or PPO
  Health Reimbursement Account
  Guardian Dental Insurance coverage
  IRA retirement plan participation, 3% family contribution

- **Vacation:** two weeks after 60 days of Employment
  ○ one week—employer choice
  ○ one week—employee choice

- **Personal/Sick:** three personal days and two sick days per year after 60 days of employment

- **Holidays:** six holidays plus three floating (family choice) after 60 days of employment

We are happy you have accepted our offer, and we look forward to you joining our family! Please call me with any questions. Otherwise, we look forward to seeing you to finalize some customary paperwork, on _____ (date). Please return this letter to the address noted above to confirm your acceptance of this position.

Sincerely,

Household Employer

Accepted by,

_____   _____
Candidate Name   Date

All household employees are employed at-will. This employment is at the discretion of the employer and the employee. Employment may terminate with or without notice or cause. Employees are also free to end employment at any time, for any reason, with or without notice.

APPENDIX 7

REJECTION LETTER TO CANDIDATE

Date

Dear _____,

Thank you for your interest in employment with our household. We have reviewed your application and carefully considered your qualifications. At this time, we have selected another candidate for the position.

We will retain your application and if we need additional information concerning your qualifications, we will contact you.

Sincerely,

Household Employer

APPENDIX 8

JOB DESCRIPTION
(Nanny—Basic Sample)

1. Provide childcare in a loving, secure, positive and responsible manner following the parents ideologies of discipline and child rearing as described in the employee handbook.

2. Interact with the children keeping in mind developmental issues. Reading interesting and stimulating stories. Respond with thoughtful answers to questions. Help the children solve problems.

3. Maintain the children's' cleanliness. Hands and face. Soiled clothing.

4. Be able to handle emergency situations with swiftness, reassurance and promptness.

5. Provide daily communication with the parents regarding the children, such as good occurrences, or any problems.

6. Keep the children safe at all times inside and outside the house.

7. Manage the home, including light housework and picking up after the children and in their play area.

8. Provide nutritional meal planning, including snacks, for the children and on occasion also for the family.

9. Provide exhilarating, thought provoking learning recreation.

10. Provide teaching methods to children.

11. Be dependable and flexible with schedule; notify the family well in advance of any needed time off.

12. Take direction from the parents and maintain a patient, understanding, cheerful, and sense of humor.

13. Adhere to the Employer / Household Employee Work Agreement.

APPENDIX 9
CONFIDENTIALITY / NON-DISCLOSURE AGREEMENT

This Agreement (this "Agreement") is made effective as of _____ ____, 20__, by and between _____, ("Household employer"), of _____, _____, ____ _____ and _____, ("the Household employee"), of the _____Household.

    A. Household employer is a private household with an employment position.
    B. Household employer desires to have services of the Household employee.
    C. Household employee is willing to be employed by Household employer.

Therefore, the parties agree as follows:

1. CONFIDENTIALITY. Employment with the Household employer lends itself to intimate and sensitive information. Therefore, Household employee agrees to treat household information as private and confidential both during and after his/her employment tenure. Household employee agrees that no information pertaining to the household, such as the home's security system code or a password for childcare drop offs, is to be repeated inside or outside of the worksite. This applies to any information that is discussed by parties within the household, as well. In addition, Household employee agrees not to discuss his/her salary and benefits with other household employees. Household employee acknowledges that a violation of this rule of conduct will be grounds for early dismissal.

2. UNAUTHORIZED DISCLOSURE OF INFORMATION. If it appears that Household employee has disclosed (or has threatened to disclose) Information in violation of this Agreement, Household employer shall be entitled to a Court injunction to restrain Household employee from disclosing, in whole or in part, such Information, or from providing any services to any party to whom such Information has been disclosed or may be disclosed. Household employer shall not be prohibited by this provision from pursuing other remedies, including a claim for losses and damages.

3. CONFIDENTIALITY AFTER TERMINATION OF SERVICES. The confidentiality provisions of this Agreement shall remain in full force and effect for a one-year period after the termination of Household employee's services.

4. APPLICABLE LAW. The laws of the State of _____ shall govern this Agreement.

Household employer

By _____Date_____

AGREED TO AND ACCEPTED.
Household employee

By _____Date_____

APPENDIX 10

EMPLOYEE HANDBOOK ACKNOWLEDGEMENT RECEIPT

Date: _____

I acknowledge that I have received a copy of the household employee handbook, and that I am responsible for reading and understanding the information set forth within the handbook.

I understand that I am responsible for returning the employee handbook to my employer upon my resignation or termination of employment.

Employee Name (please print):

_____

Employee Signature:

_____

APPENDIX 11

EXPENSE REPORT OF HOUSEHOLD EMPLOYEE

Date	Day	Meals	Food & Grocery	Transport & Travel	Supplies	Equipment & Tool	Entertainment	Other
Totals								

MILEAGE REIMBURSEMENT WORKSHEET

	Sunday	Monday	Tuesday	Wednesday	Thursday	Friday	Saturday
Date							
# of Miles							
Reimbursement Rate (___¢/mile)							
Total							

SUBTOTAL	$
Less advance	$
Less pre-paid expenses	$
Total due employee	$

Approved by:

_____   _____
Household employee/date   Household employer/date

APPENDIX 12

MEDICAL CARE RELEASE FORM

I _____ (parent/guardian) authorize the following household employee

_____, to act on my behalf in the care of my dependent(s).

The above person has my authority to request emergency health and/or medical services for my

dependent in the case of a health emergency.

Primary Physician:_____

Dependent Name: _____ DOB _____ Known Allergies _____

Dependent Name: _____ DOB _____ Known Allergies _____

Dependent Name: _____ DOB _____ Known Allergies _____

_____

Parent/Guardian Signature   Telephone   Date

APPENDIX 13

MEDICATION PERMISSION

I give my permission that _____, who is caring for my dependent, give him/her the following medication.

Dependent's name_____

Medication _____

Condition for which medication is prescribed_____

Instructions for use

       Dosage _____

       Time(s) _____

              _____

              _____

Possible side effects to be aware of_____

_____
Parent/Guardian Signature   Date

APPENDIX 14

Form W-4 (2004)

Purpose. Complete Form W-4 so that your employer can withhold the correct Federal income tax from your pay. Because your tax situation may change, you may want to refigure your withholding each year.

Exemption from withholding. If you are exempt, complete only lines 1, 2, 3, 4, and 7 and sign the form to validate it. Your exemption for 2004 expires February 16, 2005. See **Pub. 505,** Tax Withholding and Estimated Tax.

Note: You cannot claim exemption from withholding if: **(a)** your income exceeds $800 and includes more than $250 of unearned income (e.g., interest and dividends) and **(b)** another person can claim you as a dependent on their tax return.

Basic instructions. If you are not exempt, complete the **Personal Allowances Worksheet** below. The worksheets on page 2 adjust your withholding allowances based on itemized deductions, certain credits, adjustments to income, or two-earner/two-job situations. Complete all worksheets that apply. **However, you may claim fewer (or zero) allowances.**

Head of household. Generally, you may claim head of household filing status on your tax return only if you are unmarried and pay more than 50% of the costs of keeping up a home for yourself and your dependent(s) or other qualifying individuals. See line **E** below.

Tax credits. You can take projected tax credits into account in figuring your allowable number of withholding allowances. Credits for child or dependent care expenses and the child tax credit may be claimed using the **Personal Allowances Worksheet** below. See **Pub. 919,** How Do I Adjust My Tax Withholding? for information on converting your other credits into withholding allowances.

Nonwage income. If you have a large amount of nonwage income, such as interest or dividends, consider making estimated tax payments using

Form 1040-ES, Estimated Tax for Individuals. Otherwise, you may owe additional tax.

Two earners/two jobs. If you have a working spouse or more than one job, figure the total number of allowances you are entitled to claim on all jobs using worksheets from only one Form W-4. Your withholding usually will be most accurate when all allowances are claimed on the Form W-4 for the highest paying job and zero allowances are claimed on the others.

Nonresident alien. If you are a nonresident alien, see the **Instructions for Form 8233** before completing this Form W-4.

Check your withholding. After your Form W-4 takes effect, use Pub. 919 to see how the dollar amount you are having withheld compares to your projected total tax for 2004, especially if your earnings exceed $125,000 (Single) or $175,000 (Married).

Recent name change? If your name on line 1 differs from that shown on your social security card, call 1-800-772-1213 to initiate a name change and obtain a social security card showing your correct name.

Personal Allowances Worksheet (Keep for your records.)

A Enter "1" for **yourself** if no one else can claim you as a dependent . . . . **A** _____

B Enter "1" if:
- You are single and have only one job; or
- You are married, have only one job, and your spouse does not work; or
- Your wages from a second job or your spouse's wages (or the total of both) are $1,000 or less.
. . **B** _____

C Enter "1" for your **spouse**. But, you may choose to enter "-0-" if you are married and have either a working spouse or more than one job. (Entering "-0-" may help you avoid having too little tax withheld.) . . . . **C** _____

D Enter number of **dependents** (other than your spouse or yourself) you will claim on your tax return . . . . **D** _____

E Enter "1" if you will file as **head of household** on your tax return (see conditions under **Head of household** above) . **E** _____

F Enter "1" if you have at least $1,500 of **child or dependent care expenses** for which you plan to claim a credit . . **F** _____
(**Note:** Do **not** include child support payments. See **Pub. 503,** Child and Dependent Care Expenses, for details.)

G **Child Tax Credit** (including additional child tax credit):
- If your total income will be less than $52,000 ($77,000 if married), enter "2" for each eligible child.
- If your total income will be between $52,000 and $84,000 ($77,000 and $119,000 if married), enter "1" for each eligible child plus "1" **additional** if you have four or more eligible children. **G** _____

H Add lines A through G and enter total here. Note: This may be different from the number of exemptions you claim on your tax return. ▶ **H** _____

For accuracy, complete all worksheets that apply.
- If you plan to **itemize or claim adjustments to income** and want to reduce your withholding, see the **Deductions and Adjustments Worksheet** on page 2.
- If you have **more than one job** or are **married and you and your spouse both work** and the combined earnings from all jobs exceed $35,000 ($25,000 if married) see the **Two-Earner/Two-Job Worksheet** on page 2 to avoid having too little tax withheld.
- If **neither** of the above situations applies, **stop here** and enter the number from line H on line 5 of Form W-4 below.

- - - - - - - - - - - - - - - - **Cut here and give Form W-4 to your employer. Keep the top part for your records.** - - - - - - - - - - - - - - - -

Form **W-4**	**Employee's Withholding Allowance Certificate**	OMB No. 1545-0010
Department of the Treasury Internal Revenue Service	▶ Your employer must send a copy of this form to the IRS if: (a) you claim more than 10 allowances or (b) you claim "Exempt" and your wages are normally more than $200 per week.	**2004**

1 Type or print your first name and middle initial	Last name	**2** Your social security number

Home address (number and street or rural route)	**3** ☐ Single ☐ Married ☐ Married, but withhold at higher Single rate.
	Note: If married, but legally separated, or spouse is a nonresident alien, check the "Single" box.
City or town, state, and ZIP code	**4** If your last name differs from that shown on your social security card, check here. You must call 1-800-772-1213 for a new card. ▶ ☐

5 Total number of allowances you are claiming (from line **H** above **or** from the applicable worksheet on page 2) **5** _____

6 Additional amount, if any, you want withheld from each paycheck . . . . **6** $ _____

7 I claim exemption from withholding for 2004, and I certify that I meet **both** of the following conditions for exemption:
- Last year I had a right to a refund of **all** Federal income tax withheld because I had **no** tax liability **and**
- This year I expect a refund of **all** Federal income tax withheld because I expect to have **no** tax liability.

If you meet both conditions, write "Exempt" here . . . . ▶ **7** _____

Under penalties of perjury, I certify that I am entitled to the number of withholding allowances claimed on this certificate, or I am entitled to claim exempt status.

Employee's signature
(Form is not valid unless you sign it.) ▶   Date ▶

8 Employer's name and address (Employer: Complete lines 8 and 10 only if sending to the IRS.)	**9** Office code (optional)	**10** Employer identification number (EIN)

For Privacy Act and Paperwork Reduction Act Notice, see page 2.   Cat. No. 10220Q   Form **W-4** (2004)

How To Hire & Retain Your Household Help

Deductions and Adjustments Worksheet

Note: Use this worksheet **only** if you plan to itemize deductions, claim certain credits, or claim adjustments to income on your 2004 tax return.

1	Enter an estimate of your 2004 itemized deductions. These include qualifying home mortgage interest, charitable contributions, state and local taxes, medical expenses in excess of 7.5% of your income, and miscellaneous deductions. (For 2004, you may have to reduce your itemized deductions if your income is over $142,700 ($71,350 if married filing separately). See **Worksheet 3** in Pub. 919 for details.) . . . **1** $ _____
2	Enter: { $9,700 if married filing jointly or qualifying widow(er) / $7,150 if head of household / $4,850 if single / $4,850 if married filing separately } . . . . **2** $ _____
3	**Subtract** line 2 from line 1. If line 2 is greater than line 1, enter "-0-" . . . . **3** $ _____
4	Enter an estimate of your 2004 adjustments to income, including alimony, deductible IRA contributions, and student loan interest **4** $ _____
5	**Add** lines 3 and 4 and enter the total. (Include any amount for credits from **Worksheet 7** in Pub. 919) . **5** $ _____
6	Enter an estimate of your 2004 nonwage income (such as dividends or interest) . . . . **6** $ _____
7	**Subtract** line 6 from line 5. Enter the result, but not less than "-0-" . . . . **7** $ _____
8	**Divide** the amount on line 7 by $3,000 and enter the result here. Drop any fraction . . . . . . **8** _____
9	Enter the number from the **Personal Allowances Worksheet,** line H, page 1 . . . . **9** _____
10	**Add** lines 8 and 9 and enter the total here. If you plan to use the **Two-Earner/Two-Job Worksheet,** also enter this total on line 1 below. Otherwise, **stop here** and enter this total on Form W-4, line 5, page 1 . **10** _____

Two-Earner/Two-Job Worksheet (See **Two earners/two jobs** on page 1.)

Note: Use this worksheet **only** if the instructions under line H on page 1 direct you here.

1	Enter the number from line H, page 1 (or from line 10 above if you used the **Deductions and Adjustments Worksheet**) **1** _____
2	Find the number in **Table 1** below that applies to the **LOWEST** paying job and enter it here . . . . **2** _____
3	If line 1 is **more than or equal to** line 2, subtract line 2 from line 1. Enter the result here (if zero, enter "-0-") and on Form W-4, line 5, page 1. **Do not** use the rest of this worksheet . . . . **3** _____

Note: If line 1 is **less than** line 2, enter "-0-" on Form W-4, line 5, page 1. Complete lines 4–9 below to calculate the additional withholding amount necessary to avoid a year-end tax bill.

4	Enter the number from line 2 of this worksheet . . . . **4** _____
5	Enter the number from line 1 of this worksheet . . . . **5** _____
6	**Subtract** line 5 from line 4 . . . . **6** _____
7	Find the amount in **Table 2** below that applies to the **HIGHEST** paying job and enter it here . . . . **7** $ _____
8	**Multiply** line 7 by line 6 and enter the result here. This is the additional annual withholding needed . . **8** $ _____
9	Divide line 8 by the number of pay periods remaining in 2004. For example, divide by 26 if you are paid every two weeks and you complete this form in December 2003. Enter the result here and on Form W-4, line 6, page 1. This is the additional amount to be withheld from each paycheck . . . . **9** $ _____

Table 1: Two-Earner/Two-Job Worksheet

Married Filing Jointly			Married Filing Jointly			All Others	
If wages from **HIGHEST** paying job are—	AND, wages from **LOWEST** paying job are—	Enter on line 2 above	If wages from **HIGHEST** paying job are—	AND, wages from **LOWEST** paying job are—	Enter on line 2 above	If wages from **LOWEST** paying job are—	Enter on line 2 above
$0 - $40,000	$0 - $4,000	0	$40,001 and over	31,001 - 38,000	6	$0 - $6,000	0
	4,001 - 8,000	1		38,001 - 44,000	7	6,001 - 11,000	1
	8,001 - 17,000	2		44,001 - 50,000	8	11,001 - 18,000	2
	17,001 and over	3		50,001 - 55,000	9	18,001 - 25,000	3
				55,001 - 65,000	10	25,001 - 31,000	4
$40,001 and over	$0 - $4,000	0		65,001 - 75,000	11	31,001 - 44,000	5
	4,001 - 8,000	1		75,001 - 85,000	12	44,001 - 55,000	6
	8,001 - 15,000	2		85,001 - 100,000	13	55,001 - 70,000	7
	15,001 - 22,000	3		100,001 - 115,000	14	70,001 - 80,000	8
	22,001 - 25,000	4		115,001 and over	15	80,001 - 100,000	9
	25,001 - 31,000	5				100,001 and over	10

Table 2: Two-Earner/Two-Job Worksheet

Married Filing Jointly		All Others	
If wages from **HIGHEST** paying job are—	Enter on line 7 above	If wages from **HIGHEST** paying job are—	Enter on line 7 above
$0 - $60,000	$470	$0 - $30,000	$470
60,001 - 110,000	780	30,001 - 70,000	780
110,001 - 150,000	870	70,001 - 140,000	870
150,001 - 270,000	1,020	140,001 - 320,000	1,020
270,001 and over	1,090	320,001 and over	1,090

APPENDIX 15
ATTENDANCE RECORD OF HOUSEHOLD EMPLOYEE

Employee: _____   Date hired: _____

Vacation due: _____

Sick/personal leave due: _____

For the month of: _____ 200__

Date	Day of the Week	Present (Hours)	Vacation (Hours)	Sick (Hours)	Comments
1					
2					
3					
4					
5					
6					
7					
8					
9					
10					
11					
12					
13					
14					
15					
16					
17					
18					
19					
20					
21					
22					
23					
24					
25					
26					
27					
28					
29					
30					
31					

APPENDIX 16

TIME OFF REQUEST FORM

Household Employee:_____

PERSONAL TIME OFF REQUESTS

<u>Paid Time Off:</u> Begins to accrue after 90 days of employment. Requests for PTO of two or more days must be submitted at least two weeks in advance.

<u>Bereavement Leave</u>: Up to three days of paid leave is available for a death in the immediate family.

	Start date	End date	Hours
Personal time off			
Bereavement			
Jury duty/witness			
Military service			
		Total paid time off	

VACATION REQUESTS

<u>Vacation Instructions:</u> Please submit your vacation request at least four weeks in advance of START DATE.

	Start date	End date	Hours	Employer approval
1st choice				
2nd choice				
3rd choice				
		Total paid time off		

Household Employee Name: _____   Date: _____

Household Employer Name: _____   Date: _____

APPENDIX 17

PERFORMANCE EVALUATION FORM

(To be used quarterly during a one-on-one performance review meeting)

Household Employee Name:_____ Date:_____

Projects, issues, etc.	Date Addressed	Estimated Date of Completion	Assistance Needed, Issues to Resolve, etc.
Current Items			
1			
2			
3			
Items Completed			
1			
2			
3			
Areas where employer can help you improve your skill set or improve your job performance:			
1			
2			
3			
Personal Job related growth items completed last month, and future plans for personal job related growth:			
1			
2			
3			

APPENDIX 18

PAYCHECK AND PAYROLL EARNINGS STATEMENT

DO NOT ACCEPT THIS CHECK without confirming presence of Artificial Watermark on back. Other security features are listed on back.

Household Employer
123 Main Street
New York, NY 10028

Bank Name

11
1000

Check Date 4/16/2004   Check Number 10006

Pay *Nine Hundred Sixty Dollars and Twenty-Seven Cents*

$******960.27

To the Order of:

PAY ONLY

0001   10006

Alice Nelson
123 Main Street
New York, NY 10028

Authorized Signature

⑈010006⑈ ⑆000000000⑆ 12345⑈

Alice Nelson

Company	Period Begin	Division
Household	4/3/2004	
Number	Period End	Branch
0001	4/16/2004	
Social Security #	Check Date	Department
123-45-6789	4/16/2004	
Hire Date	Check Number	Team
1/1/2004	10006	

Household Employer

Personal 24.00-2.00=22.00 HOURS
Sick 7.00-0.50=6.50 HOURS
Vacation 35.00-10.00=25.00 HOURS

Earnings

Description	Location / Job	Rate	Hours	Current	Year To Date
Salary					1100.00
Hourly Rate 1		12.00	80.00	960.00	960.00
Overtime Rate1		18.00	24.00	432.00	432.00
Milege Reimb		12.00	0.00	13.44	26.88
MEMOS					
HRA			0.00	25.00	50.00

Deductions

Description	Current	Year To Date
Fed (S/1) (2392.00)	158.38	269.15
OASDI (2492.00)	86.30	154.50
Medicare (2492.00)	20.18	36.13
NY (S /1) (2392.00)	55.65	91.54
New York City Res. (2418.88)	34.66	58.19
Life Insurance	10.00	20.00
Health Insurance	30.00	60.00
Simple IRA	50.00	100.00

		Hours	Current	Year To Date		Current	Year To Date
Total Earnings		104.00	1405.44	2518.88	Total Deductions	445.17	789.51
NET PAY	960.27	**Total Direct Deposits**		0.00	**Check Amount**	960.27	1729.37

APPENDIX 19

TUITION REIMBURSEMENT REQUEST FORM

Current position held: _____

Employee name: _____

Household employer: _____

Title of course #1: _____

Course description: _____

Dates of course: _____

Name of school/entity: _____

Reason for taking course: _____

Required Coursework: It is defined as necessary for degrees, certificates or an individual course that a household employer required an employee to complete in order to meet performance standards or to keep pace with new development in the current job. Tuition will be paid at ____% (tuition or tuition and books), upon receipt of fee statements and course transcript. For reimbursement, employees must achieve a passing grade as defined by the educational organization and as approved by the household employer.

Job Related Coursework: It is the responsibility of the employee to document the relationship of the reimbursed coursework to the household's employment needs and to obtain approval from the household employer. Tuition will be paid at ____% (tuition or tuition and books), upon receipt of fee statements and course transcript. For reimbursement, employees must achieve a passing grade as defined by the educational organization and as approved by the household employer.

Note: You are required to submit the course description, proof of successful course completion along with receipts for tuition, and grades to the household employer before reimbursement will be made.

Household employee_____ Date_____

Household employer_____ Date_____

APPENDIX 20

EMPLOYER TAX RESPONSIBILITY CALENDAR

Due Date	Item
January 15	Fourth federal estimated taxes (1040-ES)
January 31	Fourth quarter state income taxes Fourth quarter unemployment taxes
February 2	W-2 form(s) mailed to employee(s)
February 28	W-3 and W-2 forms for previous year to be filed with the Social Security administration
April 15	First federal estimated taxes (1040-ES) Schedule H with Form 1040 for wages paid during pervious year
April 30	First quarter state income taxes First quarter state unemployment taxes
June 15	Second federal estimated taxes (1040-ES)
July 31	Second quarter state income taxes Second quarter state unemployment taxes
September 15	Third federal estimated taxes (1040-ES)
October 31	Third quarter state income taxes Third quarter state unemployment taxes

APPENDIX 21

STATE CONTACT INFORMATION FOR TAX WITHHOLDING, UNEMPLOYMENT INSURANCE, AND NEW HIRE REPORTING

ALABAMA

Tax Withholding:
Department of Revenue
Income Tax Division, Withholding Tax Section
P.O. Box 327480
Montgomery, AL 36132-7480
Phone: (334) 242-1000; (334) 242-1300
Internet: http://www.ador.state.al.us

Unemployment Insurance:
Department of Industrial Relations
649 Monroe St.
Montgomery, AL 36131
Phone: (334) 242-8888
Internet: http://www.dir.state.al.us

New Hire:
Department of Industrial Relations
New Hire Unit
649 Monroe Street, Room 2683
Montgomery, AL 36131-0378.
Phone: (334) 353-8491
Internet: http://dir.alabama.gov/nh

APPENDIX 21 *(continued)*

STATE CONTACT INFORMATION FOR TAX WITHHOLDING, UNEMPLOYMENT INSURANCE, AND NEW HIRE REPORTING

ALASKA

Tax Withholding:
N/A

Unemployment Insurance:
Department of Labor and Workforce Development
Employment Security Division
P.O. Box 25509
Juneau, AK 99802-5509
Phone: (907) 465-2757
Internet: http://www.labor.state.ak.us

New Hire:
Alaska Child Support Enforcement Division
New Hire Reporting Section-Department of Revenue
550 West 7th Avenue, Suite 310
Anchorage, Alaska 99501-6699
Phone: (907) 269-6685
Internet: http://www.csed.state.ak.us/Employers/EmployerInformation.htm

APPENDIX 21 *(continued)*

STATE CONTACT INFORMATION FOR TAX WITHHOLDING, UNEMPLOYMENT INSURANCE, AND NEW HIRE REPORTING

ARIZONA

Tax Withholding:
Department of Revenue
1600 W. Monroe
P.O. Box 29009
Phoenix, AZ 85038-9009
Phone: (602) 255-2060 (Phoenix); 628-6421 (Tucson); (800) 843-7196 (within AZ)
Internet: http://www.revenue.state.az.us

Unemployment Insurance:
Department of Economic Security
P.O. Box 6028 SAT CODE 911B
Phoenix, AZ 85005
Phone: (602) 248-9354
Internet: http://www.de.state.az.us/esa

New Hire:
Arizona New Hire Reporting Center
PO Box 25638
Phoenix, AZ 85002
Phone: (602) 340-0555
Internet: http://www.AZ-NewHire.com

APPENDIX 21 *(continued)*

STATE CONTACT INFORMATION FOR TAX WITHHOLDING, UNEMPLOYMENT INSURANCE, AND NEW HIRE REPORTING

ARKANSAS

Tax Withholding:
Department of Finance and Administration
Revenue Division
Income Tax Withholding Section
P.O. Box 9941
7th and Wolfe Street
Little Rock, AR 72201
Phone: (501) 682-7290
Internet: http://www.state.ar.us/revenue

Unemployment Insurance:
Employment Security Division
P.O. Box 2981
Little Rock, AR 72203-2981
Phone: (501) 682-3274
Internet: http://www.state.ar.us/esd

New Hire:
Arkansas New Hire Reporting Center
P.O. Box 2540
Little Rock, AR 72203
Phone: (800) 259-2095
Internet: https://newhirereporting.com/ar-newhire/default.asp

APPENDIX 21 *(continued)*

STATE CONTACT INFORMATION FOR TAX WITHHOLDING, UNEMPLOYMENT INSURANCE, AND NEW HIRE REPORTING

CALIFORNIA

Tax Withholding:
Department of Employment Development
800 Capitol Mall
Sacramento, CA 95814
Phone: (916) 464-1056 (interstate office)
Internet: http://www.edd.cahwnet.gov

Unemployment Insurance:
Employment Development Department
P.O. Box 826880—MIC 94
Sacramento, CA 94280-0001
Phone: (916) 654-7401
Internet: http://www.edd.cahwnet.gov

New Hire:
EDD, MIC 23
P.O. Box 997016
West Sacramento, CA 95799-7016
Phone: (916) 657-0529
Internet: http://www.edd.ca.gov/taxrep/txner.htm

APPENDIX 21 *(continued)*

STATE CONTACT INFORMATION FOR TAX WITHHOLDING, UNEMPLOYMENT INSURANCE, AND NEW HIRE REPORTING

<u>COLORADO</u>

Tax Withholding:
Department of Revenue
1375 Sherman
Denver, CO 80261-0009
Phone: (303) 534-1208 or (800) 332-2085 (within CO)
Internet: http://www.revenue.state.co.us/main/home.asp

Unemployment Insurance:
Department of Labor and Employment
Division of Employment and Training
1515 Arapahoe St.
Tower 3, Suite 400
Denver, CO 80202
Phone: (303) 603-8234
Internet: http://www.coworkforce.com/UIT

New Hire:
Colorado State Directory of New Hires
P.O. Box 2920
Denver, CO 80201-2920
Phone: (303) 866-2894
Internet: http://www.newhire.state.co.us

APPENDIX 21 *(continued)*

STATE CONTACT INFORMATION FOR TAX WITHHOLDING, UNEMPLOYMENT INSURANCE, AND NEW HIRE REPORTING

CONNECTICUT

Tax Withholding:
Department of Revenue
25 Sigourney Street
Hartford, CT 06106
Phone: (860) 297-5962 or (800) 382-9463 (within CT)
Internet: http://www.ct.gov/drs

Unemployment Insurance:
Department of Labor
Employment Security Division
200 Folly Brook Blvd.
Wethersfield, CT 06109
Phone: (860) 263-6550
Internet: http://www.ctdol.state.ct.us

New Hire:
Department of Labor
Office of Research
200 Folly Brook Boulevard
Wethersfield, CT, 06109
Phone: (860) 566-5370
Internet: http://www.ctdol.state.ct.us/lmi/newhire.htm

APPENDIX 21 *(continued)*

STATE CONTACT INFORMATION FOR TAX WITHHOLDING, UNEMPLOYMENT INSURANCE, AND NEW HIRE REPORTING

<u>DELAWARE</u>

Tax Withholding:
Division of Revenue, Withholding Division
820 North French Street
Wilmington, DE 19801
Phone: (302) 577-3382
Internet: http://www.state.de.us/revenue

Unemployment Insurance:
Department of Labor
Division of Unemployment Insurance
P.O. Box 9953
Wilmington, DE 19809-0953
Phone: (302) 761-8482
Internet: http://www.delawareworks.com/unemployment/welcome.shtml

New Hire:
Division of Child Support Enforcement
PO Box 904
New Castle, DE 19720
Phone: (302) 326-6024 ext. 156
Internet: http://www.state.de.us/dhss/dcse/nhr.html

APPENDIX 21 *(continued)*

STATE CONTACT INFORMATION FOR TAX WITHHOLDING, UNEMPLOYMENT INSURANCE, AND NEW HIRE REPORTING

DISTRICT OF COLUMBIA

Tax Withholding:
Office of Tax and Revenue
941 North Capital St. N.E.
Washington, D.C. 20002
Phone: (202) 727-4829
Internet: http://cfo.dc.gov

Unemployment Insurance:
Department of Employment Services
Office of Unemployment Compensation
Tax Division
609 H St.
N.E., 3rd Floor
Washington, D.C. 20002
Phone: (202) 724-7000 or 698-7550
Internet: http://does.dc.gov/does/site/default.asp

New Hire:
The District of Columbia New Hire Registry
P.O. Box 97236
Washington, D.C. 20090-7236
Phone: (888) 689-6088
Internet: http://www.new-hires.com/dc

APPENDIX 21 *(continued)*

STATE CONTACT INFORMATION FOR TAX WITHHOLDING, UNEMPLOYMENT INSURANCE, AND NEW HIRE REPORTING

FLORIDA

Tax Withholding:
N/A

Unemployment Insurance:
Department of Revenue
Unemployment Compensation Tax Division
5050 W. Tennessee Street, Building K
Tallahassee, FL 32399-0100
Phone: (850) 488-6800 or 922-4825
Internet: http://sun6.dms.state.fl.us/dor/uc

New Hire:
Florida New Hire Reporting Office
P.O. Box 6500
Tallahassee, FL, 32314-6500
Phone: (888) 854-4791
Internet: https://newhirereporting.com/fl-newhire/default.asp

APPENDIX 21 *(continued)*

STATE CONTACT INFORMATION FOR TAX WITHHOLDING, UNEMPLOYMENT INSURANCE, AND NEW HIRE REPORTING

<u>GEORGIA</u>

Tax Withholding:
Department of Revenue Withholding Tax Unit
270 Washington St.
Room 504
Atlanta, GA 30334
Phone: (404) 656-4181
Internet: http://www2.state.ga.us/Departments/DOR

Unemployment Insurance:
Georgia Department of Labor
Unemployment Insurance Division
148 Andrew Young International Blvd., N.E.
Suite 744
Atlanta, GA 30303
Phone: (404) 232-3300 or 3220
Internet: http://www.dol.state.ga.us/em

New Hire:
The Georgia New Hire Reporting Program
P.O. Box 38480
Atlanta, GA 30334-0480
Phone: (888) 541-0469
Internet: http://www.ga-newhire.com

APPENDIX 21 *(continued)*

STATE CONTACT INFORMATION FOR TAX WITHHOLDING, UNEMPLOYMENT INSURANCE, AND NEW HIRE REPORTING

HAWAII

Tax Withholding:
Department of Taxation Taxpayer Services Branch
P.O. Box 259
Honolulu, HI 96809-0259
Phone: (808) 587-4242 or (800) 222-3229 (within HI)
Internet: http://www.hawaii.gov/tax/tax.html

Unemployment Insurance:
Department of Labor Unemployment Insurance Division
830 Punchbowl St.
Honolulu, HI 96813
Phone: (808) 586-8913
Internet: http://www.dlir.state.hi.us

New Hire:
CSEA New Hire Reporting
Kakuhihewa Building
601 Kamokila Blvd., Suite #251
Kapolei, HI 96707
Phone: (808) 587-3738
Internet: http://www.state.hi.us/csea/newhire.html

APPENDIX 21 *(continued)*

STATE CONTACT INFORMATION FOR TAX WITHHOLDING, UNEMPLOYMENT INSURANCE, AND NEW HIRE REPORTING

<u>IDAHO</u>

Tax Withholding:
State Tax Commission Income Tax Division
800 Park Plaza IV
Box 36
Boise, ID 83722
Phone: (208) 334-7797
Internet: http://www2.state.id.us/tax/index.html

Unemployment Insurance:
Department of Labor
317 Main Street
Boise, ID 83735
Phone: (800) 448-2977
Internet: http://www.labor.state.id.us

New Hire:
Idaho Department of Labor New Hire Reporting
317 Main Street
Boise, Idaho 83735-0610
Phone: (800) 627-3880
Internet: http://www.labor.state.id.us/newhire

APPENDIX 21 *(continued)*

STATE CONTACT INFORMATION FOR TAX WITHHOLDING, UNEMPLOYMENT INSURANCE, AND NEW HIRE REPORTING

<u>ILLINOIS</u>

Tax Withholding:
Department of Revenue
101 W. Jefferson Street
P.O. Box 19015
Springfield, IL 62794-9015
Phone: (217) 782-3336 or 800-732-8866 (within IL)
Internet: http://www.revenue.state.il.us

Unemployment Insurance:
Department of Employment Security
401 S. State Street
Chicago, IL 60605
Phone: (312) 793-4880
Internet: http://www.ides.state.il.us

New Hire:
Illinois New Hire Directory
P.O. Box 19473
Springfield, IL 62794-9473
Phone: (800) 327-HIRE
Internet: http://www.ides.state.il.us/employer/newhire/general.htm

APPENDIX 21 *(continued)*

STATE CONTACT INFORMATION FOR TAX WITHHOLDING, UNEMPLOYMENT INSURANCE, AND NEW HIRE REPORTING

<u>INDIANA</u>

Tax Withholding:
Department of Revenue, Compliance Division
Indiana Government Center North
Indianapolis, IN 46204-2253
Phone: (317) 233-4016
Internet: http://www.ai.org/dor/index.html

Unemployment Insurance:
Department of Workforce Development
10 N. Senate Ave.
Rm. 331
Indianapolis, IN 46204
Phone: (317) 232-7670
Internet: http://www.IN.gov/dwd

New Hire:
New Hire Directory Program Unit
Department of Workforce Development
10 N. Senate Ave.
Room SE003
Indianapolis, IN 46204-2277
(800) 437-9136
Internet: http://www.in-newhire.com

APPENDIX 21 *(continued)*

STATE CONTACT INFORMATION FOR TAX WITHHOLDING, UNEMPLOYMENT INSURANCE, AND NEW HIRE REPORTING

IOWA

Tax Withholding:
Department of Revenue and Finance
Hoover State Office Building
P.O. Box 10457
Des Moines, IA 50306-0457
Phone: (515) 281-3114 or 800-367-3388 (within IA)
Internet: http://www.state.ia.us/tax

Unemployment Insurance:
Department of Workforce Development
1000 E. Grand Ave.
Des Moines, IA 50319
Phone: (515) 281-6875
Internet: http://www.state.ia.us/iwd/index.html

New Hire:
Centralized Employee Registry
P.O. Box 10322
Des Moines, IA, 50306-0322
Phone: (515) 281-5331
Internet: https://secure.dhs.state.ia.us/epics/static/new_hire.htm

APPENDIX 21 *(continued)*

STATE CONTACT INFORMATION FOR TAX WITHHOLDING, UNEMPLOYMENT INSURANCE, AND NEW HIRE REPORTING

KANSAS

Tax Withholding:
Department of Revenue Withholding Tax Unit
Robert B. Docking State Office Building
Topeka, KS 66625-0001
Phone: (913) 296-0222
Internet: http://www.ink.org/public/kdor

Unemployment Insurance:
Department of Human Resources
Division of Employment
401 S.W. Topeka Blvd.
Topeka, KS 66603-3182
Phone: (785) 296-5000
Internet: http://www2.hr.state.ks.us/ui/html/EnUI.htm

New Hire:
New Hire Directory
KS Department of Human Resources
PO Box 3510
Topeka, KS 66601-3510
Phone: (888) 219-7801
Internet: http://www.hr.state.ks.us/ui/html/newhires.html

APPENDIX 21 *(continued)*

STATE CONTACT INFORMATION FOR TAX WITHHOLDING, UNEMPLOYMENT INSURANCE, AND NEW HIRE REPORTING

KENTUCKY

Tax Withholding:
Revenue Cabinet
200 Fair Oaks Ln
Frankfort, KY 40620
Phone: (502) 564-7270
Internet: http://www.revenue.ky.gov/revhome.htm

Unemployment Insurance:
Department of Employment Services
275 E. Main St., 2nd Floor East
Frankfort, KY 40621
Phone: (502) 564-2900
Internet: http://www.desky.org

New Hire:
Kentucky New Hire Reporting Center
P.O. Box 1130
Richmond, VA 23218-1130
Phone: (800) 817-2262
Internet: http://www.newhire-usa.com/ky

APPENDIX 21 *(continued)*

STATE CONTACT INFORMATION FOR TAX WITHHOLDING, UNEMPLOYMENT INSURANCE, AND NEW HIRE REPORTING

LOUISIANA

Tax Withholding:
Department of Revenue
P.O. Box 201
Baton Rouge, LA 70821-0201
Phone: (225) 925-4611
Internet: http://www.rev.state.la.us

Unemployment Insurance:
Department of Labor
Office of Regulatory Services
1001 N. 23rd Street
Baton Rouge, LA 70804
Phone: (225) 342-3017
Internet: http://www.ldol.state.la.us

New Hire:
Department of Social Services
Support Enforcement Service
PO Box 2151
Baton Rouge, LA, 70821-2151
Phone: (888) 223-1461
Internet: http://www.dss.state.la.us/departments/dss/New_Hire_Registry.html

APPENDIX 21 *(continued)*

STATE CONTACT INFORMATION FOR TAX WITHHOLDING, UNEMPLOYMENT INSURANCE, AND NEW HIRE REPORTING

<u>MAINE</u>

Tax Withholding:
Maine Revenue Services Income Tax Division
State Office Building
Augusta, ME 04333-0024
Phone: (207) 626-8475
Internet: http://www.state.me.us/revenue

Unemployment Insurance:
Bureau of Unemployment Compensation
P.O. Box 309
20 Union Street
Augusta, ME 04332-0309
Phone: (207) 287-2316
Internet: http://www.state.me.us/labor

New Hire:
Child Support Enforcement
Department of Human Services
11 State House Station
Augusta, ME 04333-011
Phone: (207) 624-7880
Internet: http://www.state.me.us/dhs/bfi/dser/New_Hire.htm

APPENDIX 21 *(continued)*

STATE CONTACT INFORMATION FOR TAX WITHHOLDING, UNEMPLOYMENT INSURANCE, AND NEW HIRE REPORTING

<u>MARYLAND</u>

Tax Withholding:
Comptroller of the Treasury
Revenue Administration Division
Income Tax Building
Annapolis, MD 21411-0001
Phone: (410) 260-7980
Internet: http://www.comp.state.md.us and http://www.marylandtaxes.com

Unemployment Insurance:
Department of Labor
Licensing and Regulation
1100 N. Eutaw St.
Baltimore, MD 21201
Phone: (410) 767-2414
Internet: http://www.dllr.state.md.us/employment

New Hire:
New Hire Registry
PO Box 1316
Baltimore, MD 21203-1316
Phone: (410) 347-9911
Internet: http://www.mdnewhire.com

. **APPENDIX 21** *(continued)*

STATE CONTACT INFORMATION FOR TAX WITHHOLDING, UNEMPLOYMENT INSURANCE, AND NEW HIRE REPORTING

<u>MASSACHUSETTS</u>

Tax Withholding:
Department of Revenue
100 Cambridge Street
P.O. Box 7022
Boston, MA 02204
Phone: (617) 727-4545 or (800) 392-6089 (within MA)
Internet: http://www.dor.state.ma.us

Unemployment Insurance:
Division of Unemployment Assistance
Charles F. Hurley Bldg.
19 Staniford St., 5TH Flr.
Boston, MA 02114
Phone: (617) 626-6895
Internet: http://www.detma.org

New Hire:
Department of Revenue
PO Box 7032
Boston, MA 02204
Phone: (888) 367-1334
Internet: http://www.cse.state.ma.us/programs/newhire/nh_temp.htm

APPENDIX 21 *(continued)*

STATE CONTACT INFORMATION FOR TAX WITHHOLDING, UNEMPLOYMENT INSURANCE, AND NEW HIRE REPORTING

MICHIGAN

Tax Withholding:
Department of the Treasury Sales, Use, and Withholding Taxes Division
430 W. Allegan Street
Lansing, MI 48922
Phone: (517) 373-3190
Internet: http://www.michigan.gov/treasury

Unemployment Insurance:
Department of Labor & Economic Growth
Bureau of Workers' and Unemployment Compensation Agency
3024 W. Grand Blvd.
Tax Office—11th Floor
Detroit, MI 48202
Phone: (313) 456-2010
Internet: http://www.michigan.gov/uia

New Hire:
Michigan New Hire Operations Center
P.O. Box 85010
Lansing, MI 48908-5010
Phone: (800) 524-9846
Internet: http://www.michigan.gov/emi/1,1303,7-102-112_216_229—-CI,00.html

APPENDIX 21 *(continued)*

STATE CONTACT INFORMATION FOR TAX WITHHOLDING, UNEMPLOYMENT INSURANCE, AND NEW HIRE REPORTING

<u>MINNESOTA</u>

Tax Withholding:
Department of Revenue
Withholding Tax Section
10 River Park Plaza
St. Paul, MN 55146.
Phone: (651) 282-9999
Internet: http://www.taxes.state.mn.us

Unemployment Insurance:
Department of Employment and Economic Development
390 N. Robert St.
St. Paul, MN 55101
Phone: (651) 296-6141
Internet: http://www.uimn.org/tax/index.htm

New Hire:
Minnesota New Hire Reporting Center
PO Box 64212
Saint Paul, MN 55164-0212
Phone: (612) 227-4661
Internet: http://www.mn-newhire.com

APPENDIX 21 *(continued)*

STATE CONTACT INFORMATION FOR TAX WITHHOLDING, UNEMPLOYMENT INSURANCE, AND NEW HIRE REPORTING

<u>MISSISSIPPI</u>

Tax Withholding:
State Tax Commission
P.O. Box 960
Jackson, MS 39205
Phone: (601) 359-1141
Internet: http://www.mstc.state.ms.us

Unemployment Insurance:
Employment Security Commission
P.O. Box 1699
Jackson, MS 39215-1699
Phone: (601) 961-7760
Internet: http://www.mesc.state.ms.us/tax/index.html

New Hire:
Mississippi State Directory of New Hires
P.O. Box 94673
Cleveland, OH, 44101-4673
Phone: (800) 241-1330
Internet: http://www.new-hires.com/Mississippi

APPENDIX 21 *(continued)*

STATE CONTACT INFORMATION FOR TAX WITHHOLDING, UNEMPLOYMENT INSURANCE, AND NEW HIRE REPORTING

MISSOURI

Tax Withholding:
Department of Revenue
Division of Taxation Withholding Tax Section
P.O. Box 3333
Jefferson City, MO 65105-3333
Phone: (573) 751-3683
Internet: http://www.dor.state.mo.us

Unemployment Insurance:
Division of Employment Security
Unemployment Insurance Department
421 E. Dunklin St.,
P.O. Box 59
Jefferson City, MO 65104-0059
Phone: (573) 751-3329
Internet: http://www.dolir.state.mo.us/es/index.htm

New Hire:
Missouri Department of Revenue
PO Box 3340
Jefferson City, MO 65105-3340
Phone: (800) 585-9234
Internet: http://www.dss.state.mo.us/cse/newhire.htm

APPENDIX 21 *(continued)*

STATE CONTACT INFORMATION FOR TAX WITHHOLDING, UNEMPLOYMENT INSURANCE, AND NEW HIRE REPORTING

MONTANA

Tax Withholding:
Department of Revenue
Withholding Tax Bureau
P.O. Box 5835
Helena, MT 59604-5835
Phone: (406) 444-3388
Internet: http://discoveringmontana.com/revenue/css/default.asp

Unemployment Insurance:
Department of Labor and Industry Unemployment Insurance Division
1327 Locky Rd
P.O. Box 1728
Helena, MT 59624-1728
Phone: (406) 444-2723
Internet: N/A

New Hire:
Montana New Hire Reporting Program
P.O. Box 8013
Helena, MT 59607-8013
Phone: (888) 866-0327
Internet: http://state.mt.us/revenue/css/3forbusinesses/08newhire.asp

APPENDIX 21 *(continued)*

STATE CONTACT INFORMATION FOR TAX WITHHOLDING, UNEMPLOYMENT INSURANCE, AND NEW HIRE REPORTING

NEBRASKA

Tax Withholding:
Department of Revenue
Nebraska State Office Building
301 Centennial Mall South
P.O. Box 94818
Lincoln, NE 68509-4818
Phone: (402) 471-5729 or 800-742-7474
Internet: http://www.revenue.state.ne.us/index.html

Unemployment Insurance:
Workforce Development-Department of Labor
Unemployment Insurance Division
P.O. Box 94600
Lincoln, NE 68509-4600
Phone: (402) 471-9000
Internet: http://www.dol.state.ne.us

New Hire:
Nebraska State Directory of New Hires
P.O. Box 540880
Omaha, NE 68154
Phone: (888) 256-0293
Internet: http://www.NEnewhire.com

APPENDIX 21 *(continued)*

STATE CONTACT INFORMATION FOR TAX WITHHOLDING, UNEMPLOYMENT INSURANCE, AND NEW HIRE REPORTING

NEVADA

Tax Withholding:
N/A

Unemployment Insurance:
Employment Security Department
500 E. Third St.
Carson City, NV 89713-0001
Phone: (775) 687-4545 or 4540
Internet: http://detr.state.nv.us

New Hire:
Department of Employment Training and Rehabilitation
Nevada Employment Security Division
500 East Third Street
Carson City, NV 89713-0030
Phone: (702) 684-8685
Internet: http://detr.state.nv.us/uicont/uicont_newhire.htm

APPENDIX 21 *(continued)*

STATE CONTACT INFORMATION FOR TAX WITHHOLDING, UNEMPLOYMENT INSURANCE, AND NEW HIRE REPORTING

NEW HAMPSHIRE

Tax Withholding:
N/A

Unemployment Insurance:
Department of Employment Security
32 S. Main St.
Concord, NH 03301-4857
Phone: (603) 224-3311
Internet: http://www.nhes.state.nh.us

New Hire:
New Hampshire Employment Security
P.O. Box 2092
Concord, NH, 03302-2092
Phone: (800) 803-4485
Internet: http://www.nhes.state.nh.us/newhire/newhire.htm

APPENDIX 21 *(continued)*

STATE CONTACT INFORMATION FOR TAX WITHHOLDING, UNEMPLOYMENT INSURANCE, AND NEW HIRE REPORTING

NEW JERSEY

Tax Withholding:
Division of Taxation
Gross Income Tax
CN 248
Trenton, NJ 08648-0248
Phone: (609) 588-2200 or (800) 323-4400 (within NJ)
Internet: http://www.state.nj.us/treasury/taxation

Unemployment Insurance:
Department of Labor
Division of Employer Accounts
P.O. Box 955, John Fitch Plaza
Trenton, NJ 08625-0955
Phone: (609) 292-2460
Internet: http://www.state.nj.us/labor

New Hire:
New Hire Operations Center
P.O. Box 4654
Trenton, NJ 08650-4654
Phone: (877) NJ-HIRES
Internet: http://www.nj-newhire.com

APPENDIX 21 *(continued)*

STATE CONTACT INFORMATION FOR TAX WITHHOLDING, UNEMPLOYMENT INSURANCE, AND NEW HIRE REPORTING

NEW MEXICO

Tax Withholding:
Taxation and Revenue Department
P.O. Box 630
Santa Fe, NM 87509-0630
Phone: (505) 827-0700
Internet: http://www.state.nm.us/tax

Unemployment Insurance:
Department of Labor
401 Broadway, N.E.
P.O. Box 2281
Albuquerque, NM 87103
Phone: (505) 841-8576
Internet: http://www.dol.state.nm.us

New Hire:
New Mexico New Hires Directory
P.O. Box 29480
Santa Fe, NM 87592-9480
Phone: (888) 878-1607
Internet: http://www.nm-newhire.com

APPENDIX 21 *(continued)*

STATE CONTACT INFORMATION FOR TAX WITHHOLDING, UNEMPLOYMENT INSURANCE, AND NEW HIRE REPORTING

NEW YORK

Tax Withholding:
Department of Taxation and Finance
Income Tax Bureau
W.A. Harriman Campus
Albany, NY 12227-0125
Phone: (518) 438-8581 or (800) 225-5829 (within NY)
Internet: http://www.tax.state.ny.us

Unemployment Insurance:
Division of Unemployment Insurance
State Campus, Bldg. 12
Albany, NY 12240
Phone: (518) 457-2177
Internet: http://www.labor.state.ny.us

New Hire:
New York State Department of Taxation and Finance
New Hire Notification
P.O. Box 15119
Albany, NY 12212-5119
Phone: (800) 972-1233
Internet: http://www.labor.state.ny.us

APPENDIX 21 *(continued)*

STATE CONTACT INFORMATION FOR TAX WITHHOLDING, UNEMPLOYMENT INSURANCE, AND NEW HIRE REPORTING

NORTH CAROLINA

Tax Withholding:
Department of Revenue
P.O. Box 25000
Raleigh, NC 27640
Phone: (919) 733-4626
Internet: http://www.dor.state.nc.us

Unemployment Insurance:
Employment Security Commission
P.O. Box 26504
Raleigh, NC 27611
Phone: (919) 733-7156
Internet: http://www.ncesc.com

New Hire:
New Hire Operations Center
P.O. Box 900004
Raleigh, NC 27675-9004
Phone: (888) 514-4568
Internet: http://www.ncnewhires.com

APPENDIX 21 *(continued)*

STATE CONTACT INFORMATION FOR TAX WITHHOLDING, UNEMPLOYMENT INSURANCE, AND NEW HIRE REPORTING

NORTH DAKOTA

Tax Withholding:
State Tax Commissioner
State Capitol
600 E. Boulevard Avenue
Bismarck, ND 58505-0599
Phone: (800) 638-2901, Ext. 3124 or (701) 328-3124
Internet: http://www.state.nd.us/taxdpt

Unemployment Insurance:
Job Service of North Dakota
Job Insurance Administration
P.O. Box 1537
Bismarck, ND 58502
Phone: (701) 328-5000
Internet: http://www.state.nd.us/jsnd

New Hire:
Department of Human Services
Division of Child Support Enforcement
PO Box 7369
Bismarck, ND 58507-7369
Phone: (701) 328-3582
Internet: http://www.state.nd.us/humanservices/redirect.html?OpenDocument

APPENDIX 21 *(continued)*

STATE CONTACT INFORMATION FOR TAX WITHHOLDING, UNEMPLOYMENT INSURANCE, AND NEW HIRE REPORTING

<u>OHIO</u>

Tax Withholding:
Department of Taxation
P.O. Box 2476
Columbus, OH 43266-0076
Phone: (614) 846-6712 or (800) 282-1780 (within OH)
Internet: www.ohio.gov/tax

Unemployment Insurance:
Unemployment Compensation Tax Division
Department of Job and Family Services
P.O. Box 182404
Columbus, OH 43218-2404
Phone: (614) 466-2319
Internet: http://jfs.ohio.gov/ouc

New Hire:
Ohio New Hire Reporting Center
PO Box 15309
Columbus, OH 43215-0309
Phone: (888) 872-1490
Internet: http://www.oh-newhire.com

APPENDIX 21 *(continued)*

STATE CONTACT INFORMATION FOR TAX WITHHOLDING, UNEMPLOYMENT INSURANCE, AND NEW HIRE REPORTING

OKLAHOMA

Tax Withholding:
Withholding Tax Division
Oklahoma Tax Commission
2501 Lincoln Boulevard
Oklahoma City, OK 73194
Phone: (405) 521-3155
Internet: http://www.oktax.state.ok.us

Unemployment Insurance:
Employment Security Commission
Unemployment Insurance Division
2401 N. Lincoln Blvd.
Oklahoma City, OK 73105-4495
Phone: (405) 557-7141
Internet: http://www.oesc.state.ok.us

New Hire:
Child Support Enforcement Division
New Hire Reporting
PO Box 53552
Oklahoma City, OK 73152
Phone: (800) 317-3785
Internet: http://www.oesc.state.ok.us/newhire

APPENDIX 21 *(continued)*

STATE CONTACT INFORMATION FOR TAX WITHHOLDING, UNEMPLOYMENT INSURANCE, AND NEW HIRE REPORTING

OREGON

Tax Withholding:
Department of Revenue
Revenue Building
955 Center Street, N.E.
Salem, OR 97310
Phone: (503) 378-4988 or (503) 945-8091
Internet: http://www.dor.state.or.us

Unemployment Insurance:
Employment Division
Unemployment Insurance Tax
875 Union St., N.E.
Salem, OR 97311
Phone: (503) 947-1488
Internet: http://www.emp.state.or.us

New Hire:
Department of Justice Employer Reporting Program
3200 Lancaster Dr. NE
Salem, OR 97305
Phone: (503) 373-7300
Internet: N/A

APPENDIX 21 *(continued)*

STATE CONTACT INFORMATION FOR TAX WITHHOLDING, UNEMPLOYMENT INSURANCE, AND NEW HIRE REPORTING

PENNSYLVANIA

Tax Withholding:
Department of Revenue-Bureau of Business Trust Fund Taxes
Employer Tax Division
Department 280903
Harrisburg, PA 17128-0903
Phone: (717) 787-8201
Internet: http://www.revenue.state.pa.us

Unemployment Insurance:
Department of Labor and Industry
Seventh & Forster Streets
Labor & Industry Bldg.
Harrisburg, PA 17121
Phone: (717) 787-2097
Internet: http://www.dli.state.pa.us

New Hire:
Commonwealth of Pennsylvania
New Hire Reporting Program
P.O. Box 69400
Harrisburg, PA 17106-9400
Phone: (888)-PAHIRES
Internet: http://www.panewhires.com

APPENDIX 21 *(continued)*

STATE CONTACT INFORMATION FOR TAX WITHHOLDING, UNEMPLOYMENT INSURANCE, AND NEW HIRE REPORTING

PUERTO RICO

Tax Withholding:
Department of the Treasury Bureau of Income Tax
Intendente Alejandro Ramirez Building
Paseo Covadonga, Stop 1
P.O. Box S-4515
San Juan, PR 00903
Phone: (787) 725-8835
Internet: http://www.hacienda.gobierno.pr

Unemployment Insurance:
Bureau of Employment Security
505 Munoz Rivera Ave.
Hato Rey, PR 00918
Phone: (787) 754-5375

New Hire:
Administration for Child Support Enforcement
State New Hire Registry
P.O. Box 70376
San Juan, PR 00936-8376
Phone: (787) 767-1851
Internet: N/A

APPENDIX 21 *(continued)*

STATE CONTACT INFORMATION FOR TAX WITHHOLDING, UNEMPLOYMENT INSURANCE, AND NEW HIRE REPORTING

RHODE ISLAND

Tax Withholding:
Division of Taxation
One Capitol Hill
Providence, RI 02908-5800
Phone: (401) 277-6400
Internet: http://www.tax.state.ri.us

Unemployment Insurance:
Department of Administration
Division of Taxation
Employer Tax Section
One Capitol Hill
Providence, RI 02908
Phone: (401) 222-3684
Internet: http://www.dlt.state.ri.us

New Hire:
Rhode Island State Directory of New Hires
P.O. 540220
Omaha, NE 68154-0220
Phone: (888) 870-6461
Internet: http://RInewhire.com

APPENDIX 21 *(continued)*

STATE CONTACT INFORMATION FOR TAX WITHHOLDING, UNEMPLOYMENT INSURANCE, AND NEW HIRE REPORTING

SOUTH CAROLINA

Tax Withholding:
Department of Revenue and Taxation
Box 125
Columbia, SC 29214
Phone: (803) 737-4752
Internet: http://www.dor.state.sc.us

Unemployment Insurance:
Employment Security Commission
P.O. Box 995
Columbia, SC 29202
(803) 737-3075
Internet: http://www.sces.org

New Hire:
South Carolina Department of Social Services
Child Support Enforcement Division
PO Box 1469
Columbia, SC 29202-1469
Phone: (888) 454-5294
Internet: http://www.state.sc.us/dss/csed/newhire.htm

APPENDIX 21 *(continued)*

STATE CONTACT INFORMATION FOR TAX WITHHOLDING, UNEMPLOYMENT INSURANCE, AND NEW HIRE REPORTING

SOUTH DAKOTA

Tax Withholding:
N/A

Unemployment Insurance:
Department of Labor
Unemployment Insurance Division
Box 4730
420 S. Roosevelt St.
Aberdeen, SD 57402-4730
Phone: (605) 626-2452
Internet: http://www.state.sd.us/dol/dolui/tax/TX_home.htm

New Hire:
New Hire Reporting Center
P.O. Box 4700
Aberdeen, SD 57402-4700
Phone: (888) 827-6078
Internet: http://www.state.sd.us/dol/dolui/new_hire/NH_home.htm

APPENDIX 21 *(continued)*

STATE CONTACT INFORMATION FOR TAX WITHHOLDING, UNEMPLOYMENT INSURANCE, AND NEW HIRE REPORTING

TENNESSEE

Tax Withholding:
N/A

Unemployment Insurance:
Labor and Workforce Development
Employment Security Division
Davy Crockett Tower, 11th Floor
500 James Robertson Pkwy.
Nashville, TN 37245-1200
Phone: (615) 741-2486
Internet: http://www.state.tn.us/labor-wfd/esdiv.html

New Hire:
Tennessee New Hire Operation Center
P.O. Box 140700
Nashville, TN 37214
Phone: (888) 715-2280
Internet: http://www.tnnewhire.com

APPENDIX 21 *(continued)*

STATE CONTACT INFORMATION FOR TAX WITHHOLDING, UNEMPLOYMENT INSURANCE, AND NEW HIRE REPORTING

TEXAS

Tax Withholding:
N/A

Unemployment Insurance:
Texas Workforce Commission
T.E.C. Bldg.
101 E. 15th Street
Austin, TX 78778-0001
Phone: (512) 463-2731
Internet: http://www.twc.state.tx.us

New Hire:
Texas Employer New Hire Reporting
P.O. Box 149224
Austin, Texas, 78714-9224
Phone: (888) TEXHIRE
Internet: http://www.newhire.org/tx

APPENDIX 21 *(continued)*

STATE CONTACT INFORMATION FOR TAX WITHHOLDING, UNEMPLOYMENT INSURANCE, AND NEW HIRE REPORTING

<u>UTAH</u>

Tax Withholding:
State Tax Commission
210 North 1950 West
Salt Lake City, UT 84134
Phone: (801) 297-2200 or (800) 662-4335 (within UT)
Internet: http://tax.utah.gov/index.html

Unemployment Insurance:
Department of Workforce Services
Unemployment Insurance Division
140 East 300 South
Salt Lake City, UT 84111
Phone: (801) 526-9340
Internet: http://dws.state.ut.us/ui

New Hire:
Utah New Hire Registry
P.O. Box 45247
Salt Lake City, UT 84145-0247
Phone: (801) 526-4361
Internet: http://jobs.utah.gov/newhire

APPENDIX 21 *(continued)*

STATE CONTACT INFORMATION FOR TAX WITHHOLDING, UNEMPLOYMENT INSURANCE, AND NEW HIRE REPORTING

VERMONT

Tax Withholding:
Department of Taxes
P.O. Box 547
Montpelier, VT 05601-0547
Phone: (802) 828-2551
Internet: http://www.state.vt.us/tax

Unemployment Insurance:
Department of Employment & Training
P.O. Box 488
Montpelier, VT 05601-0488
Phone: (802) 828-4258
Internet: http://www.det.state.vt.us

New Hire:
Department of Employment and Training
PO Box 488
Montpelier, VT 05601-0488
Phone: (802) 241-2194
Internet: https://www.ssl.det.state.vt.us/empservices/c-63.htm

APPENDIX 21 *(continued)*

STATE CONTACT INFORMATION FOR TAX WITHHOLDING, UNEMPLOYMENT INSURANCE, AND NEW HIRE REPORTING

VIRGINIA

Tax Withholding:
Department of Taxation
Division of Income Tax Withholding
P.O. Box 1880
Richmond, VA 23282-1880
Phone: (804) 367-8037
Internet: http://www.tax.state.va.us

Unemployment Insurance:
Virginia Employment Commission
Unemployment Insurance Division
703 E. Main Street
Richmond, VA 23218
Phone: (804) 786-2173
Internet: http://www.vec.state.va.us

New Hire:
Virginia New Hire Reporting Center
P.O. Box 25309
Richmond, VA 23260-5309
Phone: (800) 979-9014
Internet: http://www.va-newhire.com

APPENDIX 21 *(continued)*

STATE CONTACT INFORMATION FOR TAX WITHHOLDING, UNEMPLOYMENT INSURANCE, AND NEW HIRE REPORTING

VIRGIN ISLANDS

Tax Withholding:
N/A

Unemployment Insurance:
Department of Labor
P.O. Box 789, Christiansted
St. Croix, VI 00821
Phone: (340) 773-1440
Internet: N/A

New Hire:
N/A

APPENDIX 21 *(continued)*

STATE CONTACT INFORMATION FOR TAX WITHHOLDING, UNEMPLOYMENT INSURANCE, AND NEW HIRE REPORTING

<u>WASHINGTON</u>

Tax Withholding:
N/A

Unemployment Insurance:
Employment Security Department
212 Maple Park, Mail Stop KG-11
Olympia, WA 98504-5311
Phone: (360) 902-9670
Internet: http://www.wa.gov/esd

New Hire:
SD Data Control
Employer Reporting Program
PO Box 9023
Olympia, WA 98507-9023
Phone: (800) 562-0479
Internet: http://www.wa.gov/dshs/newhire

APPENDIX 21 *(continued)*

STATE CONTACT INFORMATION FOR TAX WITHHOLDING, UNEMPLOYMENT INSURANCE, AND NEW HIRE REPORTING

WEST VIRGINIA

Tax Withholding:
State Tax Commissioner
Capitol Complex, Building 1, W417
Charleston, W.Va. 25305
(304) 558-3333 or 800-982-8297 (within W.Va.)
Internet address: http://www.state.wv.us/taxdiv

Unemployment Insurance:
Bureau of Employment Programs
112 California Ave.
Charleston, WV 23505-0112
(304) 558-2624
Internet: http://www.state.wv.us/bep/uc/default.htm

New Hire:
Child Support Enforcement Division
Employment Reporting Program
1900 Kanawha Blvd. East, Building 6, Room 817
Charleston, WV 25305.
(304) 558-1134
Internet: None

APPENDIX 21 *(continued)*

STATE CONTACT INFORMATION FOR TAX WITHHOLDING, UNEMPLOYMENT INSURANCE, AND NEW HIRE REPORTING

WISCONSIN

Tax Withholding:
Depart of Revenue Income, Sales, Inheritance and Excise Tax Division
Compliance Bureau
P.O. Box 8910
Madison, Wis. 53708
(608) 266-2776
Internet address: http://www.dor.state.wi.us

Unemployment Insurance:
Department of Workforce Development
Division of Unemployment Insurance
201 E. Washington Ave., P.O. Box 7905
Madison, WI 53707
(608) 266-7074
Internet: http://www.dwd.state.wi.us/ui

New Hire:
Wisconsin New Hire Reporting
P.O. Box 14431
Madison, WI 53714-0431
(888) 300-HIRE
Internet: http://www.dwd.state.wi.us./uinh

APPENDIX 21 *(continued)*

STATE CONTACT INFORMATION FOR TAX WITHHOLDING, UNEMPLOYMENT INSURANCE, AND NEW HIRE REPORTING

<u>WYOMING</u>

Tax Withholding:
N/A

Unemployment Insurance:
Department of Employment
Employment Tax Division
P.O. Box 2760
Casper, WY 82602
(307) 235-3217
Internet: http://wydoe.state.wy.us

New Hire:
Wyoming New Hire Reporting Center
P.O. Box 1408
Cheyenne, WY, 82003-1408
(307) 638-1675
Internet: https://newhirereporting.com/wy-newhire/default.asp

APPENDIX 22

Tax & Payroll Guide
for Household Employers

Whether you employ a nanny, housekeeper, eldercare worker or other household professional, here is a step-by-step guide for you to use when setting up and administering your employee's payroll and taxes.

Understanding the Laws

Step 1 – Determine if you have an employee or independent contractor

Household professionals include nannies, home health aides, private nurses, cooks, gardeners, caretakers, and other similar domestic workers. The main difference between an employee and a contractor is that an employee operates under the control and supervision of his/her employer (you), and a contractor retains all control over himself and his services. For example, a nurse who has her own company and comes by once a week to provide medical services to an aging parent is a contractor; a nanny who cares for your children in your home is an employee. For more information contact the IRS at (800) 829-1040 and order publication 926.

Step 2 – Research Tax Laws

The IRS states that anyone who pays an individual $1,400 or more in gross wages during the calendar year legally employs a household employee and must comply with all state and federal tax laws.

Household Employer Taxes
Employers can expect to pay 9-11% of their employee's gross pay, including:
- Federal and state unemployment insurance (about 2-4% for most states)
- 50% of Social Security and Medicare (7.65%)
- Other state taxes where required, such as employment training or work force taxes

Household Employee Taxes
Employees can expect to pay 15-20% of their gross wages, including:
- Federal and state income taxes (not required, but advised)
- 50% of Social Security and Medicare (7.65%)
- Other state taxes where required, such as Disability Insurance

For more information contact the IRS at (800) 829-1040 and order publication 926.

Step 3 – Follow Payroll Regulations

According to the Federal Labor Standards Act, all household employees must be paid at least minimum wage ($5.15/hour — higher in some states), however, benefits such as room and board can account for a portion of that wage. There is no limit to the number of hours an employee can work – provided there is mutual agreement. However, overtime may be required in your state. Paid vacations, holidays and sick days are not required by law.

Filing the Paperwork

Step 4 – Submit Federal and State Forms

- Complete SS4 Form for an Employer ID # (download at www.GTM.com/resourcecenter)

- Register for State Unemployment ID # (contact state for form)

- Register for State Withholding Tax ID # (contact state for form)

- Complete your State New Hire Report (contact state for form)

- Have employee complete W-4 Form (download at www.GTM.com/resourcecenter and keep on file)

- Have employee complete I-9 Form (download at www.GTM.com/resourcecenter and keep on file)

Step 5 – Add Workers' Compensation to Your Insurance Policy

Most states require household employers to carry a workers' compensation and/or disability policy if you employ someone on a full or part-time basis. These policies will cover you from lawsuits and liability in the event that your employee is injured on the job. If your state requires this, you can either contact your state's insurance fund or your homeowner's insurance company. GTM strongly recommends that even if you're not required to have a policy, you obtain one anyway.

For more information, visit www.GTM.com or call 1-888-4-EASYPAY today

Step 6 – Set Up Dependent Care Assistance

You can pay your household employee with pre-taxed funds through an employer-sponsored Dependent Care Assistance Program (DCAP), if your employer offers this plan. This plan allows you to set aside up to $5,000 per year "tax free" money that you can use to pay for your childcare or eldercare. Contact your employer's Human Resources department for more details.

Complying with Payroll and Tax Laws

Step 7 – Calculate Withholding Taxes

Weekly Gross Pay   = _____

Social Security
& Medicare Taxes   **Less:** _____
(7.65% of Gross Salary)

Federal, State & Local
Income Taxes   **Less:** _____
(Estimated 10-20%)*

Net (take-home) Pay   = _____

Varies based on state, gross pay and withholding allowance.

Example: *$400 gross salary per week x 22.65% (7.65%+15%) = $309.40 weekly NET (take-home) salary*

In addition to paying your employee a weekly gross salary, household employers have their own payroll taxes that need to be calculated weekly and paid on a quarterly basis to the IRS and your state.

Weekly Gross Pay   = _____

Social Security
& Medicare Taxes   + _____
(7.65% of Gross Salary)

Federal Unemployment
Insurance (0.80%)   + _____

State Unemployment
Insurance (2-4%)*   + _____

Total Weekly Costs   = _____

Varies from state to state.

Example: *$400 gross salary per week x 11.45 (7.65%+.8%+ 3%) = $445.80 weekly total costs*

* *Also found online at www.GTM.com/resourcecenter*

Step 8 – Distribute Paychecks Regularly

You have the option of paying your employee weekly, bi-weekly, monthly or at any other agreed upon interval. Wages should always be paid via check so both parties have a record, and the amount should always be net (after all applicable taxes are withheld). You can also offer the option for direct deposit (check with your bank for details).

Step 9 – File Payroll Taxes Every Quarter

January
15th   4th quarter estimated taxes due
31st   4th quarter Income and State Unemployment Taxes Due
31st   W-2 forms mailed to employees

February
28th   W-3 and/or W-2 forms to be filed with the Social Security Administration

April
15th   1st quarter estimated Taxes Due
15th   Schedule H of Form 1040 for wages paid from January-December of previous year due
31st   1st quarter Income and State Unemployment Taxes due

June
15th   2nd federal estimated payment due

July
31st   2nd quarter Income and State Unemployment Taxes due

September
15th   3rd estimated tax payment due

October
31st   3rd quarter Income and State Unemployment Taxes due

GTM is the most established household payroll and tax service in the U.S., serving families who employ household professionals since 1985. With EasyPay®, we'll help you eliminate penalties, interest or costs of unnecessary accounting and legal fees. We'll show you how to qualify for significant tax breaks and credits and, because our associates stay informed on new and changing tax laws, we'll keep you up to date on all state and federal regulations.

APPENDIX 23

INCIDENT REPORT

Household employee name _____   Incident time _____
Employee position/title _____   Incident date _____
Today's date _____   Incident location _____

Description of the incident that occurred
_____
_____
_____

Witnesses to the incident (if applicable)
_____
_____
_____

Corrective or disciplinary action to be taken
❏ Verbal   ❏ Written   ❏ Probation   ❏ Suspension   ❏ Other (explain below)
_____
_____

(If on probation, period begins _____ and ends _____.)

Corrective action(s)/improvement(s) to be achieved
_____
_____
_____

Consequences for failure to improve future performance or correct behavior
_____
_____

Household employee statement
_____
_____

I acknowledge that I have read and understand the above information and consequences.

Household employee _____ Date_____
Household employer _____ Date_____

Witness _____ Date_____

APPENDIX 24

TERMINATION OF EMPLOYMENT TO HOUSEHOLD EMPLOYEE LETTER

Date _____

Dear _____,

As we have discussed, your employment with our household will terminate at the close of business on _____. You are entitled to the following benefits, per our household's policy:

1. Your salary will be continued through _____.
2. Your health insurance benefits will continue through _____. Beyond that date, your rights to continue coverage under COBRA will be provided to you under separate cover.
3. You will be paid for your unused, accrued vacation and personal time.
4. You may be entitled to unemployment insurance. It's your responsibility to contact the local office of unemployment to understand your entitled benefits, if any.

Should you have further questions, you may contact _____ at _____.

Sincerely,

Household Employer

All household employees are employed at-will. This employment is at the discretion of the employer and the employee. Employment may terminate with or without notice or cause. Employees are also free to end employment at any time, for any reason, with or without notice.

*(Certain states require "service letters" which must also include a reason for the termination. If this is the case in your state, or if you wish to document the reason(s), make sure to include only verifiable facts).

NOTE:

APPENDIX 25
EXIT INTERVIEW QUESTIONS

Today's date_____
Date employment began_____   Work days/schedule_____
Date employment ended_____   Name of household employer_____

1. Why are you leaving your household position?

   _____

2. What will you be doing when you leave your position?

   _____

3. If you are to be employed in another household position, please explain why.

   _____

4. How would you rate the job?   Excellent   Good   Average   Fair   Poor
   If average or less, why?

5. How would you rate the family?   Excellent   Good   Average   Fair   Poor
   If average or less, why?

6. Did you have written job description?   Yes   No
7. Did you have a written work agreement?   Yes   No
8. What were your duties?

   _____

9. What problem(s) did you encounter in the job/household?

   _____

10. If you were in the same situation again, would you accept a position with this family?
    Yes   No

11. Would you recommend that other household employees work for this family? Yes   No
    If no, why not?

    _____

12. Would you consider working as a household employee again in the future if applicable?
    Yes   No

13. What would you suggest the household improve upon?

    _____

14. Other Comments:_____

    _____

_____   _____
Household Employee Signature   Date

Resources and References

WEBSITES

WEBSITES	NAME
www.gtmhouseholdemploymentexperts.com	GTM Household Employment Experts
www.gtmassociates.com	GTM Household Employment Experts
www.gtm.com	GTM Household Employment Experts
www.gtm.com/resourcecenter	GTM Household Employment Experts
www.householdhelp.com	GTM Household Employment Experts
www.usda.gov/oce/oce/labor-affairs/ircasumm.htm	United States Dept. of Agriculture (imigration reform and control act)
www.usda.gov/oce/oce/labor-affairs/i9rule.htm	United States Dept. of Agriculture (employment eligibility)
www.wagehour.dol.gov	Dept. of Labor (wage and hour division)
www.uscis.gov	U.S. Citizenship and Immigration Service
www.dol.gov	Dept. of Labor
www.eeoc.gov	U.S. Equal Employment Opportunity Commission
www.ada.gov	Americans with Disabilities Act
www.ssa.gov	Social Security Administration
www.irs.gov	Internal Revenue Service
www.nanny.org	International Nanny Association
www.theapna.org	Alliance of Profesional Nanny Agencies
www.nannyassociation.com	National Association of Nannies
www.butlersguild.com	International Guild of Professional Butlers

TELEPHONE NUMBERS

GTM Household Employment Experts 1.888.432.7972
US Dept. of Justice National Customer Service Center 1.800.375.5283

US Dept. of Labor Wage-Hour Toll-free Information and Helpline 1.866.4USWAGE
  (1.866.487.9243)
Immigration and Naturalization Service Office of Business Liaison 1.800.357.2099
US Equal Employment Opportunity Commission 1.800.669.4000 (call will be automati-
  cally directed to the nearest EEOC field office)
American with Disabilities Act Specialist 1.800.514.0301
Social Security Number Verification 1.800.772.1213
IRS Taxpayer Advocate 1.877.777.4778
IRS Tax Questions 1.800.829.1040
IRS Small Business 1.800.829.3676
Employer-related Immigration Matters (USCIS Office of Business Liaison) 1.800.357.2099

Household Employment Glossary

The following definitions are used by the household employment industry to describe various in-home jobs or aspects of household employment.

At-will Employment
At-will employment allows an employer to fire an employee any time, and the employee can quit at any time.

Au Pair (Foreign)
An au pair is a foreign national living in the United States as part of the host family and receives a small stipend in exchange for babysitting and help with housework. Legally authorized to live and work in the United States for up to one year in order to experience American life, an au pair may or may not have previous childcare experience.

Babysitter
A babysitter provides supervisory, custodial care of children on an irregular basis. No special training or background is expected.

Butler
According to the International Guild of Professional Butlers Household Employee Definitions, a butler uses his or her skills and attitude to provide service to his employer. Attitude is defined as energy, commitment and attention to detail while striving for perfection. The butler role fills myriad services, including: overseeing and scheduling all household help and contracted vendors; keeping household budgets; managing inventories; greeting callers; managing household, family and estate security; organizing and overseeing events and parties held in the household; serving meals and drinks; and, many other supervisory and hands-on tasks to operate the household professionally and efficiently.

Cook
In contrast to the chef, a cook is home schooled, typically very talented in the local cuisine, and not responsible for creating the menu. Prepared meals are often house favorites. A cook cleans and serves like a chef.

Couples

Couples work together to provide a service package and offer a great variety of skills and talents. Two broad categories of couples are domestic couples and house manager couples. The major difference between the two types of couples is educational and private service experience along with the sophistication of their employment situations and salary history.

Domestic Couples

Domestic Couple teams are generally inside/outside teams: one partner may cook and clean while the other handles all outside work. The tasks involved incorporate aspects of the maid, housekeeper, houseman, house manager and gardener roles.

Doula

Doula, a word from ancient Greek, today refers to a person experienced in childbirth who provides continuous support to the mother before, during and for several weeks after childbirth.

Driver

A licensed professional who drives the employer to and from all specified destinations. A driver may also be responsible for maintenance of the employer's vehicles.

Earned Income Credit (EIC)

EIC, which is claimed on an employee's federal income tax return, reduces his or her tax or allows him or her to receive a payment from the IRS.

Eldercare Provider

A generic term referring to someone who helps an elderly person with daily care, health care, financial matters, companionship and social activity. An eldercare provider may offer this assistance for payment or voluntarily.

Estate Manager or Executive Estate Manager

A true estate manager is typically responsible for a substantial property(ies) and aircraft, yachts and other employer personal interests. Management authority over inside and outside staffs and operations is held at varying degrees, depending on the employer. The executive estate manager refers to the highest level in this category, and, in complex situations, is similar to the chief executive officer in the corporate world. Some key tasks include: developing personnel and financial management plans, as well as written position descriptions, standards of quality and operating manuals; providing overall leadership to household service staff; organizing, planning and evaluating all estate job activities; providing primary human resources for estate employees; coordinating and monitoring all property(ies) building, development and maintenance; coordinating and monitoring all contracted services such as security, outside cleaning services, etc.; and, effectively communicating with employer.

Gardener
A gardener tends to the landscaping, lawn and outside environment of the employer's property.

Gentleman's Gentleman
The gentleman's gentleman provides similar services as the butler, but with service focused on the gentleman employer.

Governess
Traditionally an educated person (minimum of a bachelor's degree), the governess is employed by families for the full- or part-time at-home education of school-age children. A governess functions as a teacher and is not usually concerned with domestic work or the physical care of younger children.

Health Maintenance Organization (HMO)
A health maintenance organization (HMO) is a plan that provides medical services to its members for a fixed, pre-paid premium and requires members to use only the plan's participating (or networked) providers.

Home Health Care
Home health care is professional health care, provided under the direction of a physician and in the patient's home, is a viable and often preferable alternative for those people who do not need 24-hour supervision or an extended hospitalization to recover.

Homemaker Service
For people who are unable to perform daily household duties and who have no available help, a homemaker service includes light housekeeping, laundry, limited personal care, grocery shopping, meal preparation and other shopping assistance.

House Manager Couples
House manager couples are less hands-on than domestic couples and more managerial. While they may handle cooking and/or service, house manager couples manage service delivery per house standards. Often, one partner performs personal assistant duties while the other handles butler or house manager tasks.

Household Employer
Per the IRS, a household employer is an individual who employs housekeepers, maids, gardeners and others who work around that individual's private residence.

Household Manager
The household manager is another term for a butler with few subtle differences, such as a butler is knowledgeable and sophisticated in the finer details of privilege and wealth, particularly in the area of wines and food. A household manager usually oversees staff in one residence, greets callers, assists in staff training, schedules and coordinates staff, plans and organizes parties and events in the home, serves meals and drinks, and may be involved in many more functions akin to a butler's responsibilities.

Hours Worked
According to the US Fair Labor Standards Act, in general, hours worked include all time an employee must be on duty, on the employer's premises, or at any other prescribed workplace.

Housekeeper
The housekeeper handles general cleaning, laundry, ironing, mending and other basic household functions.

Individual Health Plan
An individual health plan is for people not connected to an employer, such as self-employed people who have no other employees.

Immigrant
Per the US Justice Department, an immigrant is a foreign national who is authorized to live and work permanently in the United States.

In-home child care
A situation in which a caregiver cares for children in the child's home.

Maids
Parlor maids, scullery maids, kitchen maids, laundry maids, house maids, and ladies maids refer to various positions in a staffed home. A maid performs specialized tasks, primarily care and cleaning duties and is often associated with a particular area of the home.

Migrant Worker
A worker who travels from one area to another in search of work.

Nanny
Lives-in or lives-out, a nanny works in the household to undertake all tasks related to the care of children. Duties are generally restricted to childcare and the domestic tasks related to childcare. May or may not have had any formal training, though often has a good deal of actual experience. Nanny's work week ranges from 40-60 hours per week, and a nanny usually works unsupervised.

Nursery Nurse
The nursery nurse is a title used in Great Britain for a person who has received special training and preparation in caring for young children, in or out of the home. The nursery nurse may live-in or live-out, works independently and is responsible for everything related to childcare. Duties are generally restricted to childcare and the domestic tasks related to childcare, and the work week is usually 50-60 hours per week. In addition to specialized training, the nursery nurse successfully passed Great Britain's certification examination of the National Nursery Examination Board.

Parent/Mother's Helper
Lives-in or lives-out and works to provide full-time childcare and domestic help for families in which one parent is home most of the time. The parent/mother's helper may be left in charge of the children for brief periods of time and may or may not have previous childcare experience.

Personal Assistant
The personal assistant is a key position in the private life of household employer and performs a broad category of services. Generally, the personal assistant focuses on handling: the employer's correspondence and communications; staff coordination; travel planning; errands; and, odd jobs.

Personal Time Off
Personal time off (PTO) refers to all the time offered to the employee for time off or work benefits.

Preferred Provider Plan (PPO)

A preferred provider plan (PPO) is a managed care health plan that contracts with providers. Plan members are offered a financial incentive to use providers on the plan's network but are able to see non-network providers as well.

Private/Personal Chef

A private/personal chef is professionally trained and seasoned in the various cuisines, and caters to the preferences, tastes and diets of their employers. The private/personal chef: performs or cooks in the home, as well as on a family-owned yacht and aircraft; may serve meals and refreshments; and, cleans the kitchen and related facilities such as coolers and freezers.

Security Professional

An individual who is responsible for household security, including household property and personal security.

US Citizen

Per the US Justice Department, citizens include people who are born in the United States, Puerto Rico, Guam, the Northern Mariana Islands and the US Virgin Islands, as well as others who obtain US citizenship.

US National

Per the US Justice Department, US nationals include people born in America Samoa, including Swains Island.

Workweek

According to the US Fair Labor Standards Act, a workweek is a period of 168 hours during seven consecutive 24-hour periods.

Index

About Guy Maddalone

Guy Maddalone is founder and CEO of GTM Household Employment Experts™, which offers household payroll services, human resources and employee benefits. Recognized in the United States household employment industry as the national expert, Maddalone has been operating businesses that attend to household employment for nearly 20 years.

Maddalone founded GTM in 1991 to specialize in household employment—beginning with eldercare providers, nannies and private service professionals. He evolved the business to include all household employment professions and more than 300 referral partners throughout the United States. A New England Nanny, a faction of GTM, is a nanny agency that Maddalone has operated for 13 years, placing thousands of childcare providers and nannies throughout upstate New York. GTM is also the nation's premier household payroll and tax service, managing more than $250 million in payroll each year.

Maddalone conducts educational seminars throughout the country on the household employment industry, household human resources, household payroll taxes, IRS audits, tax compliance and dependent care services for corporate employers. He is also a work/life dependent care consultant to the General Electric Company, a licensed health and life insurance agent in New York and a member of the Society of Human Resource Management (SHRM).

Involved with several prominent business organizations, including the Massachusetts Institute of Technology's (MIT) and *Inc. Magazine's* executive training program, Birthing of Giants, and as president of the Albany Chapter of the Young Entrepreneur's Organization, Maddalone also contributes greatly to the community in which he lives—from coaching youth sports teams, mentoring local college entrepreneurs and giving to the Make-A-Wish Foundation. Maddalone is also heavily involved with industry associations, such as Alliance of Professional Nanny Agencies, International Nanny Association, and serves on many committees. The eldest son of 13, the importance of family is integral to Maddalone. He and his wife, Diane, reside in upstate New York with their three children.

GTM Products/Services Overview

GTM is the most established household payroll and tax service provider in the U.S., serving thousands of clients and processing over **$250** million a year in payroll processing. Since 1991, our EasyPay® service has saved clients a tremendous amount of time and money in payroll processing, from not having to spend more than **60** hours a year handling tax and payroll issues, including researching tax and labor laws, registering for state and federal tax accounts, calculating and paying wages, and filing tax returns.

We offer a variety of other products and services to help you retain your household employee and make your relationship enjoyable and that much stronger between you and your employee.

- **EasyPay Payroll and Tax Service** - This service provides an easy way to pay household employees as well as filing appropriate federal, state and local taxes. With EasyPay you elect to pay your employee with either a live check or direct deposit. GTM's Tax service allows you the flexibility for GTM to file and pay your taxes on your behalf, or you can have GTM prepare your signature ready tax reports.

- **Health Options -** from our health reimbursement account which offers household employers' a way to provide healthcare assistance through a defined savings plan — to our state-by-state network of health insurance partners we can help you chose an insurance plan that is right for your employee.

- **Household HR™ Library Online** - help for all your human resource needs and is sues from hiring to firing, including useful links to labor laws, resources and helpful tools and forms to better manage your employee.

- **Household Employee Handbook** - a customized employee handbook written specifically for the household employment industry. Our online service allows you the ability to customize each section to your household 's specific circumstance.

- **Household HR Helpdesk** - With a subscription to this service, any household human resource questions can be telephoned or emailed to our helpdesk or for more detailed issues, our consultants will help you find answers to problems and advise you on best practice and employment regulations as it applies to your situation.

- **Employer Continuing Education** - With a variety of household employer seminars available ranging from industry trends and tips, best practice, HR issues, plus educational materials that support each seminar.

- **Business Payroll Service -** GTM also offers a business-to-business payroll service. Our payroll service can easily accommodate 1 to 1,000 employees. Enjoy competitive pricing, online access and reporting and the flexibility to design your payroll service around your needs.

- **Pinch Hitter®**— once your corporation enrolls for this program, your company can offer this service to all eligible employees. Pinch Hitter provides subscribers with last minute dependent care in the event of sick ness, an unexpected business trip or emergency meeting. With one phone call, Pinch Hitter arranges to have a sitter at your house to cover the unexpected ,enabling you to meet your obligations.